Advance Praise for

This Treasure Within is a rema̶ upbringing to an amazing non-stu̶ ̶ ̶y̶ ̶t̶o̶ ̶o̶n̶e̶ ̶w̶h̶o̶ ̶n̶o̶w̶ ̶r̶e̶f̶l̶e̶c̶t̶s̶ on the significance of a life lived. It is the inspiring story of one person who lives the vocation of Pastor, and yet it has a profound impact on the reader! Here is a clear and rousing account of a life of one who was in the room when so many things happened in the life of Baptists in the southern United States in recent decades. Daniel Vestal is my nominee for what the power of education does for clarifying a life's vocation, and I am grateful for the opportunity to read his memoir.

—*W. H. Bellinger, Jr.*
Professor of Religion Emeritus, Baylor University

I have known and admired Daniel Vestal my entire life. He baptized me at First Baptist Church, Midland and embodied the role of pastor in such a noble and pure way that I chose to serve God as a pastor myself. Daniel has been a consummate leader in the Baptist movement, and, to me, he has been an invaluable colleague and good friend. After reading his memoir, he has become even more ensconced in my heart and mind as an exemplar worthy of immolation. Daniel has recounted the details of his extraordinary and influential life with tremendous humility, insight, honesty, and faithfulness. The work he has done here is truly unique and beautiful. I feel certain all who read these words will find them as meaningful, edifying, and inspiring as I have.

—*Kelly K. Burkhart*
Pastor, Baptist Temple
Houston (2004–2021)

Daniel Vestal set out to write an autobiography and ends up providing an illustrated primer on leadership in the ecclesial community. He provides a paradigm of what authentic leadership looks like. Among the principal values he affirms are these: a Christ-centered faith that is ever open to the promptings of the Holy Spirit; a thirst for knowledge that leads to encounters with the other through reading and friendship making; a Spirit-empowered trust that knows no insecurity in asking and seeking answers to difficult questions; and a humility that permits the possibility of a change of opinion on controversial issues and opens a window to joyful living marked by a lively hope. To read *This Treasure Within: A Memoir* is to share in the Christian pilgrimage of one who is rightly regarded as a vibrant Christian and an exemplary leader."

—*Neville Callam*
General Secretary Emeritus
Baptist World Alliance

If you have ever spent much time with Daniel Vestal, it will make sense when I say that while reading his memoir, I had to occasionally remind myself that he wasn't right next to me. This is an honest self-portrait of a student, husband, father, pastor, and leader but it is also a graceful offer of historical mentorship from someone who deeply loves the church.

—*Paul Capps*
Pastor, Peachtree Baptist
Atlanta, Georgia

This book is the autobiography of a gifted and experienced pastor who loves the local church. Gratefully nurtured in the cradle of Southern Baptist life in Texas, it is a refreshingly honest odyssey of a theological awakening. But the unique factor is the eyewitness account of the fragmentation of the Southern Baptist Convention and the testimony of a prayerful peacemaker attempting to do the best of things in the worst of times. It has acute observations on how a community of faith should handle discords and disagreements. As one of the pioneering leaders who eventually departed the SBC, Daniel Vestal speaks with personal authority on the forming of the Cooperative Baptist Fellowship. It is a profoundly significant work offering a unique interpretation of three turbulent decades of Baptist life in North America.

—*David Coffey OBE*
President of the Baptist World Alliance (2005–2010)
Free Churches Moderator and Co-President of
Churches Together in England (2003–2007)

Daniel Vestal defines himself as a pastor, and this memoir tells the story of the best sermon he could preach: a life lived in service to the God of love, justice, and compassion. From stories of a childhood spent shaping a calling as a preacher to his time as coordinator of the Cooperative Baptist Fellowship, *This Treasure Within* contains thoughtful remembrances and life lessons that are at once moving and edifying. This book is a gift to all who find a home under the Baptist umbrella and to any who claim Jesus is Lord.

—*Rev. Emily Holladay*
First recipient of the Daniel and Earlene Vestal Scholarship
Pastor, Village Baptist Church, Bowie, Maryland

In this deeply reflective and forthright spiritual autobiography, Daniel Vestal has demonstrated both his deep grounding in the biblical teaching and his outward spiral of learning. With humility he writes about how his mind was expanded as he engaged critical issues of the epoch: the resurgence of fundamentalism in Southern Baptist life, the role of women in ministry, interfaith relations, human sexuality, and lay ministry in the church. His piety is palpable; his prayer is centering and there are hints of mysticism in his writing. He continues to open himself to the mystery of the gracious God in whom Daniel desires to dwell, through the power of the Holy Spirit. From the pen of a wise spiritual guide comes this cartography of grace. I commend it highly, for I have found it profitable to read.

—*Molly Marshall*
Professor of Theology and Spiritual Formation
Interim President of United Theological Seminary

Daniel Vestal has lived a remarkable life. Reading the story of his spiritual journey as a man, husband, father, pastor, denominational leader, and teacher will inspire and motivate. I witnessed his denominational leadership up close when I held leadership positions in the Cooperative Baptist Fellowship from 1997 to 2000. I soon was in awe of both Daniel the man and Daniel the servant-leader, and I am even more in awe of him now that I know his full story. He has made a giant impact for the gospel everywhere he has set his feet.

—*John R. Tyler*
Eighth Moderator of the Cooperative Baptist Fellowship

Daniel Vestal is not only a transformational figure in Baptist life but also a transitional figure, someone who has stood in the gap and brought people together as the tides of religion pulled us ever more apart. The stories of this memoir illustrate his own journey from the kind of warm evangelicalism Southern Baptists once were known for to the broader community of faith that also values social justice. If you want to understand who Southern Baptists and Cooperative Baptists are today, you need to know where we've come from and how we've grown apart. That is Daniel's story.

—*Mark Wingfield*
Executive Director and Publisher, Baptist News Global

Daniel Vestal is a voice of leadership, conviction, and wisdom in God's kingdom. Reading this memoir is like sitting down with a friend who's journeyed just a little bit ahead of you and has gathered much to share. This memoir is the voice of his heart as he opens up his life's journey with God, and offers us words to consider in our own lives. Daniel's honesty and transparency with his life experiences are a gift, and this book is a treasure.

—*Joy Yee*
Pastor, 19th Ave. Baptist Church
San Francisco, California

THIS TREASURE WITHIN

Smyth & Helwys Publishing, Inc.
6316 Peake Road
Macon, Georgia 31210-3960
1-800-747-3016

Library of Congress Cataloging-in-Publication Data

Names: Vestal, Daniel, 1944- author.
Title: This treasure within : a memoir / by Daniel Vestal.
Description: Macon, GA : Smyth & Helwys Publishing, Inc., 2021. | Includes
bibliographical references.
Identifiers: LCCN 2021048031 | ISBN 9781641733441 (paperback)
Subjects: LCSH: Vestal, Daniel, 1944- | Baptists--United
States--Clergy--Biography. | Southern Baptist
Convention--Clergy--Biography.
Classification: LCC BX6495.V45 A3 2021 | DDC 286/.1092
[B]--dc23/eng/20211109
LC record available at https://lccn.loc.gov/2021048031

THIS
TREASURE
WITHIN

A MEMOIR

DANIEL VESTAL

Dedicated to the seven grandchildren
Earlene and I love and enjoy—
Brice Daniel Vestal, Hallie Caroline Vestal, Paul Chandler Vestal,
Zayd Albert Vestal, Daya Teresa Vestal, Sophia Elizabeth England, and
Charlotte Miriam England

Acknowledgments

Many have contributed to this project. Brenda Watkins, a cousin to my wife, made her rural home in Madison County, Georgia, available as a place for research and writing. Lauren Hooie Lamb, a McAfee student worker at the Baugh Center, was very helpful in preparing the manuscript. Jeff Huett, a colleague in ministry, graciously offered himself as a conversation partner and adviser. Libby Allen is a trusted colleague and coworker at Mercer. She has provided invaluable research and editorial assistance as well as her friendship and prayers. William Underwood, president of Mercer University, has graciously given me a place and position at Mercer as distinguished university professor of Baptist leadership and director of the Eula Mae and John Baugh Center for Baptist Leadership. I wish to express appreciation to him as well as Scott Davis, the provost at Mercer, for their encouragement. I also express appreciation to the leadership at Smyth & Helwys Publishing who worked with me in preparing the manuscript for publication: Keith Gammons, Leslie Andres, and Dave Jones. Finally, my wife since 1966, Earlene, is my greatest support and my constant companion. I am eternally thankful for her.

Contents

Preface

I decided to write this memoir during the height of the COVID-19 pandemic of 2020. The excuse of not having enough time was taken from me, and I could not find a good reason for not doing what friends and family had been encouraging me to do for some time. So I plunged into the project with abandon. The excuse about time, however, was not the primary reason for my reluctance. The deeper reason was that I viewed myself as rather pedestrian and unworthy of a book-length memoir to be read by anyone.

The biographies and autobiographies on my library shelves are written by and about people of significant renown and accomplishment. I am neither a famous person nor a world changer, but I have been given much and been blessed with much. This autobiography is a way to celebrate these gifts and offer an account of what I have done, and not done, with them.

No one can be objective about their life because motives are mixed and memory is clouded. But I have tried to offer as honest an account as possible of what happened in my past and why it happened. I have also sought to offer some lessons learned and some present-day convictions that are intertwined with the past.

These pages contain part historical record, part remembrance of what I have experienced, part reflection on what I still value. They are also an attempt to pay tribute to the many people who have influenced me. The process of research and writing has made me even more aware of the primacy of relationships and reinforced the conviction that we are all intertwined together with one another.

However, in the following pages I also recount dissonance and discord in relationships, primarily my sharp disagreements with fellow Baptists. I have not hesitated to give specific names and details about conversations and events because I think it is important to speak truthfully. I hope I have spoken the truth in love without judging the motives of those with whom I disagreed. I know all too well that I am a finite and flawed person who will give an account to God for my sins, which as I grow older is both a sobering and comforting thought because of what I have come to believe about the reality and nature of God.

Now more than ever, I am conscious of God's grace in the past and God's love in the present and future. As I age, I become less certain about many things but more certain about a few things. In the words of the King James Version of the Bible, which I memorized as a child, I offer the underlying thesis of this memoir: "But we have this treasure in earthen vessels, that the excellency of the power may be of God and not of us. We are troubled on every side, yet not distressed; we are perplexed, but not in despair; persecuted, but not forsaken; cast down, but not destroyed" (2 Cor 4:7-8).

These biblical words ring true for me and contain the essential message I wish to convey. I am very much "an earthen vessel" conditioned by my family of origin, my time and place in history, and many circumstances over which I had no control. I am also a result of the choices I have made, some good and some bad. I am a strange mixture of noble aspiration and abysmal failure, one with great capacity to soar and to fall. More than anything else, I am inhabited and indwelt by the living presence of Christ "who loved me and gave himself for me" (Gal 2:20). I am a person in whom a treasure dwells—a priceless, beautiful treasure.

I have not found life to be easy or simple. Rather I found it to be complex and complicated but also glorious. Not long after I became a pastor, I met another pastor, John Claypool, whose wise words I have never forgotten. He said, "Every day with Jesus is sweeter than the day before, but every day with Jesus is harder than the day before." This has proven true for my life journey. The battles become more intense as one loses the naivete and idealism of youth and confronts entrenched evil. Struggles for holiness, righteousness, and goodness continue and increase both for me as an individual and for the world in which I live.

But again, in the words of the apostle Paul, I can say, "For God, who commanded the light to shine out of darkness, has shined in our hearts, to give the light of the knowledge of the glory of God in the face of Jesus Christ" (2 Cor 4:6). The witness I wish to give in this memoir is that I have glimpsed that light and experienced a bit of that glory, even if only in a minuscule fraction and often in times of trouble and weakness. The treasure is within the earthen vessel.

I also wish to give witness that the treasure within is not limited to me alone. I have found my greatest and most satisfying joys in the context of community with others. I have participated in realities larger than me and far beyond me. I have been a part, often a small part, of divine agency working through both personal and communal human agency. As in a concert or symphony, I have played an instrument along with many others under the direction of a Maestro, both performing the music and being enraptured by the music. At times it has felt like an "out-of-body" experience, both watching myself and others while at the same time participating.

This Treasure Within is an apologia and witness to the abiding truths that have sustained me for more than sixty years in Christian ministry. I have tried to write as if I were telling a story to my grandchildren. In fact, as I have composed the following pages I have kept my seven grandchildren before me in my mind's eye. I dedicate this book to them with the prayer that they will experience and enjoy the treasure within even more than I have.

Chapter 1

Beginnings

A Longing After

I cannot remember a time in my life when I didn't love God. From childhood I have had a longing, sometimes an ache, for the transcendent, the spiritual. Stirrings in my soul came early, and like the boy Samuel, I didn't know how to interpret them except that they were real. These longings and stirrings have been like a subterranean stream flowing beneath my conscious decisions and even deeper than my insecurities. I understand now that the source of that stream wasn't just from deep within me but rather was from outside me and beyond me. But while growing up, I couldn't discern that. All I knew—and I did *know*—was that I felt a deep desire for God and the things of God.

I didn't know the language of vocation or identity, but I was aware of an identifiable feeling, a quiet confidence and consciousness that I would seek and serve God with my life. That inner consciousness has resulted in a recurring pattern through the years—hopes realized, then denied or displaced, then realized again. The pattern has repeated itself often. It also created a lifelong curiosity, even a compulsion, to explore the religious, the mystical, the theological. My heroes have been ministers and missionaries, preachers and prophets, theologians and sometimes fanciful storytellers. My companions have been authors who either chronicled their own spiritual journeys or explained the Scripture.

The first time I read *Pilgrim's Progress*, with vivid pictures illustrating the various characters, I knew I was Pilgrim. The first novels I read were by Lloyd Douglas, *The Robe* and *The Big Fisherman*. The books on prayer that my sainted mother had at her bedside were my primers in Christian devotion, especially the ones by Andrew

Murray, a South African mystic, and F. B. Meyer, a British Baptist pastor. In early adolescence, I read Charles Finney's *Revivals of Religion: The Biography of D. L. Moody* as well as Richard Day's *Bush Aglow: The Life Story of Dwight Lymon Moody* and his biography of Charles Spurgeon, *The Shadow of the Broad Brim*.

The writings of Watchman Nee, a Chinese preacher, captivated me. Even if I was too young to understand his *Normal Christian Life*, it fed my spiritual hunger. Nee was influential in beginning the house church movement in China before the Communist revolution. Many years later when I traveled to China and met leaders in the "Three Self Movement" and China Christian Council, I mentioned my early love for Nee. Much to my surprise, I discovered that some of the leadership had also grown up in the "little flock" movement that Nee had so powerfully influenced.

The biography of Dawson Trotman, founder of "The Navigators," a parachurch organization, inspired me to memorize Scripture. I completed their "Topical Memory System" and learned to recite scores of Bible verses as well as extended passages. This practice was important in equipping me early for my vocation, but even more than that, it formed me intellectually and spiritually. I was learning words, phrases, and ideas without fully knowing their meaning, but the words, phrases, and ideas influenced both the framework of my thought and the thought process itself. I began to think, imagine, and speak in "biblical" terms early in life. The Bible's words also brought inspiration and comfort. Many years later when I discovered meditation and contemplation, I realized how Bible memorization had influenced me.

My father prayed often, out loud, on his knees. I didn't understand Dad's theology, but I was impacted by the fervor of his prayers. My mother's disposition was quiet but pious, and she often cried when she prayed. In our household the talk was not about religion but about a relationship with God. And for both of my parents, that relationship was as real and as integral to life as eating and drinking. It was everywhere, every day, and in every corner of our modest home. I wanted that relationship. I wanted that reality. I wanted other things as well, but I wanted, more than anything else, what I saw and felt in Dan and Marie Vestal and in the individuals who inspired them. My mother kept journals of her daily activities, and my father kept scrapbooks of his ministry. I remember reading them and imagining, pondering, wondering, hoping. I had "a longing after."

The culture of my childhood was saturated with a spirituality and morality that some would call strict. I experienced it, however, as nourishing because it was translated to me through loving parents. Both Dan and Marie Vestal were demonstrative in their love for one another and in their love for each of their four children: Daniel, James, Ruth, and Martha. I am the eldest of the four siblings, and we each shared a common experience of profound parental love. We received that love from parents who also lived with integrity and humility.

We prayed before every meal. We were in church at least three times a week. Our social lives centered on church activities, and our friends were made in those activities. We were nurtured in a family that emphasized personal conversion and personal holiness, and for us that was interpreted to mean a distinct separation from "worldliness" and anything that would compromise our influence on others. We were not allowed to go to movies or school dances. We didn't play card games or any other games that required dice, because it looked like gambling. When we finally purchased a television, we were prohibited from watching commercials that advertised alcohol or tobacco.

There were moral warnings about impure thoughts, profanity, and friendship with non-Christians. There were moral affirmations about honesty, responsibility, and kindness. There was moral instruction about being a good neighbor, a good friend, and a good witness. This came from parents who themselves set an impeccable moral example. All of this contributed to my having an active conscience, perhaps an overactive conscience, with a childhood desire to please my parents and please God.

Our faith tradition was Baptist. More specifically it was Southern Baptist. Even more specifically it was Texas Baptist. We didn't use the word "evangelical" to describe ourselves; rather we used the word "evangelistic." We believed the Bible was the inspired word of God, and we believed that it taught the sinfulness of all humanity, God's plan of salvation through Jesus Christ, and the certainty of heaven and hell. The gospel I heard preached by my dad and others like him was primarily about not going to hell after death. The only way to escape hell and go to heaven was by accepting Jesus Christ as Lord and Savior. I easily made that decision early in childhood because I didn't want to go to hell.

My worldview was that of my parents, and it centered on "the plan of salvation," the importance of prayer, and the Great Commission. As Christians we were "called" out from the world but then "sent" into the world to preach the gospel to everyone. The worldview I learned in my home was similar to the one I learned in my home church but narrower in its focus. My parents joined the Gambrell Street Baptist Church in Fort Worth, Texas, in 1947, and remained as members until their deaths. When Mom died in 2018, she was the matriarch of the congregation, having been a member for seventy-one years.

The earliest influence of the church came through "Royal Ambassadors," a missions organization of Southern Baptists for boys. It was similar to the Boy Scouts, except the advancement and ranks were awarded on the basis of Bible study and mission study. I relished the challenge of learning and completed all the ranks: Page, Squire, Knight, Ambassador, Ambassador Extraordinary, Ambassador Plenipotentiary. I was rewarded and recognized for achieving these ranks, and I was even asked to offer a brief "testimony" at a large men's rally when I was only nine years old. These experiences were preparatory for my vocational calling, and they enhanced my ego.

Gambrell Street Baptist Church was located across the street from Southwestern Baptist Theological Seminary, which at the time was the largest of all Southern Baptist seminaries. Several professors were church members and leaders: T. B. Maston, William Hendricks, Ray Summers, Jack Gray, J. W. MacGorman, W. R. Estep, and C. W. Scudder. These men were acclaimed Baptist scholars, and they brought their influence into the church and into my life. I wouldn't realize it until later, but GSBC was not a typical Southern Baptist church. It was a unique place with unique people who instilled in me a deep respect for the institutional church.

Named after J. B. Gambrell, a former president of the Southern Baptist Convention and a prominent professor at the seminary, the church called W. T. Connor as its first pastor. Connor was a distinguished Baptist theologian and one of the founding professors of the seminary. The church was conservative in theology, cooperative in spirit, and fiercely Baptist in polity and practice. It offered a stable and mature Christian community that was like an extended family.

I owe an unpayable debt to GSBC and the pastors who led it. The church licensed me to the gospel ministry at age sixteen and ordained me at age twenty-two. The pastor who influenced me most in childhood was Arthur Travis, a thoughtful and humble leader, but every pastor was beloved by my parents and provided spiritual shepherding to our family. In turn, our family, especially my mother, was integral to the life of the church and supportive of every pastor. In our household we never spoke bad words either about the church or its pastor.

Evangelists

The towering figure in my childhood and adolescence was my father. The shadow of his influence was cast over me, and it was one I gladly accepted. I wanted to be like Dad. For a while I wanted to *be* Dad. He was a preacher. I would be a preacher. He was an evangelist. I would be an evangelist. He held a Bible in his hands when he preached. I would hold a Bible in my hands when I preached. He was not just a model or mentor; he was a father who shaped my early understanding of God as father.

But Dad was also something of what one might call a "character," colorful and a bit eccentric. He was strong willed, determined, and could be both tough and tender in his demeanor. He had jet-black hair, a booming voice, and piercing eyes. And then there was the scar. On the left side of his face was a permanent reminder, visible to all, of a severe burn. As a six-month-old baby, Dad fell into an open fireplace and suffered third-degree burns. His face was severely disfigured.

His family was poor and unable to pay for the medical attention he needed, but when he was eighteen, members of a rural community in Northeast Texas collected money, and he began treatments for his burn. Over a three-year period, he had fourteen plastic surgery operations with skin grafts from his arms and a lowering of his eyelid on one side of his face. The surgeries didn't erase the scar, but they made it less severe. Medical science worked wonders through these operations, but divine providence also worked wonders through these operations. Dan Vestal became a Christian.

The lengthy surgeries were performed under local anesthetics, and recovery was slow. Dad had ample time to think and reflect. A chaplain at Baylor University Hospital in Dallas read Scripture and tended to this young renegade who had no religious background. My father had mental images of a crucified Savior and would make promises to God that if his life were spared, he would live in a different way. Soon he was converted and called to preach. Without education and against his family's wishes, he became something of a firebrand. He attended college and seminary, though he never graduated from either, married Lindle Marie Savage, and became a pastor.

When I was six months old, he resigned his church, and for the next forty years he conducted 1,162 revivals in small- to medium-sized Southern Baptist churches. He kept meticulous diaries of his ministry, and he recorded the place, date, and text of 18,149 sermons. He and Mother lived by faith and never had a regular income, health insurance, or annuity benefits from a supportive congregation. Dad was the same age as a much better-known evangelist, Billy Graham, and while his fame would increase, the recognition of my father's integrity as a lesser-known evangelist would also increase.

Our home became something of a shrine to be visited by other evangelists and an assortment of itinerant ministers within the Southern Baptist culture. I watched them come and go with amazement and awe. I read their correspondences with my father and was fascinated by the accounts Dad kept in his scrapbooks of their crusades and campaigns as well as his own. Each of them had an abundance of charisma with an overabundance of self-confidence. Some were brilliant and brash. Some were just brash. They came from a variety of backgrounds, but when they were in our home they were charming with winsome personalities. All of them were fierce apologists for the faith, as they understood it, and they exhibited a passion I didn't see in most ministers.

Some of these evangelists became somewhat well known within the Baptist culture of the 1940s, '50s, '60s, and '70s. Others had a lower profile, but they all traveled the country preaching in stadiums, arenas, tents, and local churches. I remember Mordecai Hamm (preaching when Billy Graham was converted), Hyman Appleman (a Messianic Jew), Angel Martinez (converted off the streets of San Antonio), Freddie Gage (an ex-convict from Houston whom Dad led to Christ), Paul Carlin, Larry Taylor, James Robison, Manley Beasley, Jack Taylor, Ron Dunn, Lockett Adair (a Presbyterian evangelist), Michael Gott, Eddie Martin, Fred Lowery, Dick and Bo Baker, William Jester (a physician and lay evangelist), Bob Harrington (the chaplain of Bourbon Street), Dick Pratt (a lawyer and lay evangelist), and Joe Atkinson (a special friend of our family).

These troubadours were never part of the ecclesiastical system or the pastors' guild. They were surely never a part of an academic community or a denominational structure. They were outsiders to religious systems, but their influence on me, and the Christian culture where I came from, was enormous. I still speak their names with emotion.

Youth Evangelist

From early childhood, I wanted to be a preacher and never desired any other vocation. That desire has been a constant and consistent ingredient in my self-understanding and vocational identity. I was aware of having some oratorical talent and an ability to memorize Scripture. The powerful presence of my father was certainly a factor in my feelings, but deep down I also felt an intuitive awareness that preaching was to be my life's work. I became a youth evangelist at age twelve. Traveling most weekends during the school year and all during the summer months, I conducted youth revivals in Baptist churches that would invite me, host me, and give me money. I reveled in the travel, the notoriety, and the results. It was a heady time, especially in the 1960s.

The decade of the sixties was a turbulent time in American culture, a time of societal deconstruction. But for me it was a time of incredible busyness with satisfying experiences and experiments of ministry. I was now able to do what my dad, and others like him, did week after week. I was preaching in churches, primarily in Texas, and people listened to me even though I had no theological education and an underdeveloped understanding of the gospel. What I lacked in theological sophistication, I made up in energy and enthusiasm.

I was given more opportunities than I could manage, so I developed fifteen to twenty messages that I preached and then preached again and again. To begin with, pastors invited me because they knew of my father, but then they began to invite me for reasons that to this day I do not fully understand. One reason was because revivals were an accepted congregational and denominational practice of the time. In these revivals I was immersed in a subculture that seemed to be immune to what was happening in the broader culture, at least for a while. Churches gathered in revival services on weekends and weeknights because they loved God and longed for God to renew their fervor and awaken both saints and sinners alike to the experience of grace (see appendix A).

For me, this time of youth evangelism was both a gift and a quest, with unusually enriching and exhilarating experiences. I learned that local churches are amazing, and often exasperating, organizations. They survive because of God's goodness working through human agency. I learned during my adolescence what has been foundational for the years that followed, and that is the centrality and diversity of local churches in the Baptist faith tradition.

Congregations are a laboratory where faith is discovered, experienced, nurtured, and sometimes damaged. Congregations are a community where life is shared and character is shaped. Denominations, conventions, and associations exist to serve churches and extend their ministry, not the other way around. Seminaries, schools of theology, and academic institutions are of little value if they do not educate and nourish leaders for congregations. Nonprofit and parachurch organizations, benevolent institutions, and mission-sending agencies are not the same as the church. All of these can be extensions of the church and partners with the church, but they are not the church.

And though the church is surely universal, global, and even cosmic, it is first contextualized in a particular place and time to embody the presence of Christ among a particular people. It is incarnational and it is local. As an adolescent, I learned this not in a theoretical way but in an experiential way. Without fully understanding at the time what I was experiencing, I fell in love with the life of congregations and saw in them an amazing and often maddening diversity. They were surely not all like Gambrell Street Baptist Church in Fort Worth.

Another gift given me as a young evangelist was the opportunity to meet men and women who served in these congregations without notice or notoriety. Week after week I was with pastors and laity, their names never to be known outside their local congregations, who exemplified love and showed grace. Many of them were examples of amazing Christ-likeness. Historically, Baptists have championed the priesthood of all believers. During my adolescence I experienced that theological truth in church after church.

While preaching a youth revival at Temple Oaks Baptist Church in Houston, I received from Pastor Johnny Barrett a *Thompson Chain Reference Bible*. It was my introduction to biblical study, and it became a constant companion during adolescence. Based on the King James Version, this study Bible placed themes and topics in the margins beside each verse and then connected them like "chain links" with an index of topics and texts at the end. It also offered brief analyses of biblical books, biographical sketches of biblical characters, summaries of the life of Jesus, archaeological aids, and maps. My love for the Bible and the study of the Bible had much of its origin in my mastering of the *Thompson Reference Bible*.

My experiences as a youth evangelist also satisfied, at least in part, my continued longings after God. I truly did believe the Bible I was preaching and the Savior it revealed. I did believe, with an adolescent sincerity, that God loved the world, answered prayer, had given the Son and sent the Spirit. I enjoyed the warmth of gospel music and the emotional satisfaction that came in service to a cause greater than myself. Although I was constantly warned by my parents that pride is sinful, I had enough self-awareness to recognize my ability to have influence on others, especially on young people.

I also had enough self-awareness to realize that my adolescent faith and ministry was just that, adolescent. My sermons were primarily about "the salvation of the lost," (the language of my father), "making a decision for Christ," (the language of Billy Graham), or "beginning the Christian life" (the language of my denomination). I knew there was more, which only increased my "longing after." A few years later at Baylor University, I was a student host for Earnest Campbell, the senior minister of Riverside Church in New York City. I recounted my heritage to him, and he gave me a warm smile and kind words: "Conservative and fundamentalist churches are the nursery of the church. Many people are born into the kingdom of God through their witness." I would later learn that Campbell himself was a graduate of Bob Jones University, a fundamentalist school in South Carolina. I remember that at the time his words were a great affirmation and encouragement, because even while a student at Baylor I was preaching youth revivals.

On another occasion while at Baylor, I was student host for Elton Trueblood, a Quaker philosopher and author. I told him I wanted to get a PhD in Bible, and he answered with words I have never forgotten: "We should give a PhD to every seminary student on the first day of class, and then they can forget about getting a degree and concentrate on learning. Be a lifelong learner, young man, be a lifelong learner." Good advice.

The Love of My Life

In between youth revivals I met Earlene Paulette Black at the Gambrell Street Baptist Church during a Wednesday night supper. From that first encounter I have been attracted to, fascinated with, and amazed by Earlene. She is a person of inner strength and beauty. She has always had a pure heart and the most beautiful smile in the world. I have often thought that I live for Earlene's smile. She is my best friend and the love of my life. The intersecting and intertwining of our lives has shaped and formed me more than anything else.

The story that led to our romance is quite remarkable. Earlene's mother, Rebecca Jane Allen, was born one of nine children in rural Madison County, Georgia. Not long after her high school graduation, she married Harold Thomas Black, a local boy who had joined the US Navy. Soon they had a daughter and traveled extensively until Harold suffered a severe heart attack and died at the age of thirty-seven. Rebecca was now a young widow. She returned to her family home with an eleven-year-old daughter. Within a year she felt a call and conviction of the Spirit to attend seminary and prepare for Christian ministry.

Rev. Bud Shivers, pastor of First Baptist Church, Commerce, Georgia, was on the board of trustees at Southwestern Seminary. He recommended that she attend seminary in Fort Worth, so she packed up her few belongings and drove 1,000 miles from home without knowing one person in Texas. It was a courageous act and a bold step of faith. It was also a move that would change the direction of her life, Earlene's life, and my life.

In coming to Fort Worth, Rebecca and her daughter brought the family dog, and since animals were not allowed in seminary housing they had to search for a home. Someone recommended a seminary professor whose home on the edge of campus had an attic apartment. The professor was T. B. Maston, a beloved professor of Christian ethics and a progressive voice in the Southern Baptist Convention for social, racial, and economic justice. Rebecca and Earlene moved into that apartment and became like family to the Mastons. Rebecca Black lived in the Maston home for thirty years, and after her seminary graduation she became director of circulation at the seminary library. Since the Mastons were members of Gambrell Street Baptist Church, Rebecca and Earlene became members, and that is how we met at the Wednesday night supper. We dated through high school and college and were married in 1966. We both were young. I was twenty-one. Earlene was twenty.

Rebecca Black was a woman of Christian courage and character. She became like a second mother to me, and I became like the son she never had. She also became like a mother to hundreds of seminary students, especially international students, in her role at the seminary. She was an exemplary personal minister and friend to people in need. She was also a great support in our marriage, and when Earlene and I had children she was an invaluable help, especially after I became a pastor. In 1988, when we moved to Atlanta with her as part of our family, she reflected on her life's journey: "I left Georgia thirty years ago with a daughter and very little else. I have returned with abundance, a son-in-law and three grandchildren."

Earlene and I are often asked about the secret of our marriage and ministry together. I am convinced that one secret has to do with our companionship and friendship as equals. Earlene's childhood experience of grief with the death of her father was traumatic. It prematurely ended an idyllic childhood and forced her to grow up quickly. By the time we met, she clearly exhibited a maturity and inner strength of character far beyond her years. I was never attracted to anyone else like her. Our friendship was almost instantaneous, and it has only grown in the years that have followed.

I am convinced that another secret to our marriage, which is really not a secret at all, has to do with the influence of our parents and the influence of the Mastons. We saw in each of them a commitment to the will of God, as they understood it, resulting in faith, hope, and love lived out first and foremost within the context of family. That commitment also resulted in self-denial and sacrifice.

For me, I observed my mother and father live separated from one another thirty weeks out of a year and yet remain faithful and devoted to one another. I remember asking my mom, "Why is Dad gone so much?" She would respond, "It's a privilege for us to share our daddy with others." I never heard my mother murmur or complain, although I know it was hard. Earlene observed her mother bear the grief of her husband's death, uproot her life, leave her family, and move to seminary because of a deep conviction of God's call. It was hard, but she persisted. Both of us observed the Mastons live out their Christian commitment in their home with great courage and grace.

When Earlene and I began our courtship, I would walk through the Mastons' back door, through the kitchen, and into the stairwell that went up to Earlene's apartment. To say that I was in the Mastons' home often would be an understatement. I saw a lot of them as they lived their life together. I also saw their son, Tom Mac, who lived his sixty-four years in the home with his parents. Tom Mac had cerebral palsy and could not clothe or feed himself. He required constant care from his parents. To observe the Mastons provide that care while managing extensive responsibilities outside the home was a great influence on Earlene and me. T. B. Maston maintained a vigorous schedule of teaching, writing, and mentoring. Essie Mae Maston was active as a Sunday school teacher, gardener, and participant in the seminary community. But their first priority was in their home. They were amazing to observe.

What we both observed in our families of origin and in the Maston home made it clear that faith does not make us immune from human hardship. Indeed, at times faith creates hardships. The living of life within family is about adjusting and adapting to what is given, and often what is given includes a mixture of pain and pleasure. It requires resilience, creativity, and courage. Most of all, it requires love.

In Retrospect: Conscience and Conviction

My childhood and adolescence were not typical, if there is such a thing as a typical childhood and adolescence. I had a desire, almost a compulsion, to be a preacher for as far back as I can remember. That desire, no doubt, was in part the result of watching my father. But it only increased and intensified because of early opportunities to stand in front of people and recite Scripture or tell Scripture stories. Then, as I was invited to preach youth revivals and youth rallies in Baptist churches, my love for proclamation grew. I wasn't a prodigy, but I did realize that my desire to preach and my ability to preach were gifts. This made me feel special.

This also made me feel a sense of responsibility and obligation. My conscience was sensitive to right and wrong. Since I loved my parents, I watched them intently and wanted to please them. Both were people of moral integrity with dispositions of kindness, and that only intensified my aspirations to do what was right. I unconsciously learned lessons about virtues and values as I observed the way they lived. I didn't want to fail in their expectations of me.

I grew up with clear boundaries about moral behavior. I was taught to always tell the truth, to refrain from vulgarity or profanity, to respect those in authority, to keep my body free from sexual sin and my mind free from sexual fantasies. My parents practiced regular tithing to the church. They would often divide their tithe between me and my siblings for each of us to put in a Sunday offering. My parents were scrupulously honest. They paid their bills and didn't incur a lot of debt. They were generous in giving to others, even though their income was modest.

There was a phrase I often heard my father use to describe his moral conscience: "Others may. You cannot." My mother was a woman who loved God and served others with her whole being. My parents had deep convictions, but they also had a tenderness and kindness that made their convictions and character attractional. My home was a place of laughter and love, not condemnation and judgment.

Earlene's mother was also a person with strong convictions who had the courage to follow them, and I never wanted to disappoint her deep trust in me. T. B. Maston's influence was important in the formation of my moral consciousness. He wrote a popular book in 1955 to help Christian young people navigate their moral and ethical decision making, *Right or Wrong*. It clearly reflects the culture of the 1950s, but it is amazing how much of its reasoning is still relevant to today. He dedicated the book to the youth of Gambrell Street Baptist Church. Maston, along with other leaders in my home church, instilled in me a desire to be honest, to speak the truth, to accept responsibility for my behavior, and to treat others with respect.

Lindle Marie Savage Vestal, my mother

Rebecca Jane Allen Black, Earlene's mother

Evangelist Dan Vestal and Daniel Vestal at an outdoor revival
(1951)

Evangelist Dan Vestal and Daniel Vestal (1957)

Newspaper ad from 1956

Youth evangelist

BRISTOL VIRGINIA-TE

Young Revivalist

Dan Vestal, left, 16-year-old evangelist from
Texas, arrived here yesterday for a revival at Gateway Baptist Church. He is shown being greeted
by Jim Murry of the Gateway congregation.

Youth Revival (1960)

Program cover for Youth Revival (1965)

Chapter 2

Doubt, Deconstruction, Formation

Faith and Experience

The theological soil that nurtured my childhood and adolescent faith was rich with ingredients of the subjective and experiential. I was taught to experience God, know Christ, and feel the Spirit. Faith was not so much mental assent to dogmas or doctrine as it was personal acceptance of Christ with a sincere heart. One must have a relationship with Christ and experientially receive his love and forgiveness to call themselves Christian. Believing was a matter of the whole person: mind, emotion, and will. We were not creedal, but we were certainly confessional, that is, we were not required to cite a doctrinal statement in order to be baptized, but we were required to profess publicly why and how we trusted in Christ for our salvation.[1]

The faith of my childhood culture, evangelical and evangelistic, was celebrated corporately in music and preaching. Congregational music was robust because we were singing about our experience with Christ. Gospel songs and hymns had a profound influence on my early theology. I memorized them because we sang them over and over again. Congregational singing is itself a religious experience, unequaled by few others when participation and exuberance are high. I still love congregational music more than the musical performance of a few.

At certain times in our corporate worship, there was an intensity and spirituality that bordered on the sacramental. The holiest moment in an evangelical worship service was the invitational hymn after the sermon. It was a call to decision, a time for personal and public response, a summons for people to come forward and greet the pastor with a commitment or confession. It was a holy moment when everyone believed that eternal transactions were taking place before our very eyes. And often, that is exactly what happened.

After I became a pastor, I stood at the front of congregations too many times and prayed with individuals too many times not to acknowledge the sanctity of the "altar call." I also know that pastors and evangelists alike have misused this ritual to manipulate emotions and pressure guilty and troubled souls in order to satisfy their own insecurities and ego needs. Today the hymn of invitation, or time of public decision, is no longer used in many Baptist or evangelical churches, even in emotionally charged worship experiences where the theology is intensely experiential. It is now considered by many a relic of the past. Perhaps it is. But in the culture of my early life, it was essential.

Other corporate rituals that shaped my early theology were baptism and communion. Again the focus was on the subjective, with strong appeals to remember what Christ has done for me, what Christ means to me, and what Christ has promised me. The emphasis was on personal dedication and devotion, and there was always the possibility of personal transformation. Personal testimonies were welcomed and encouraged because those who gave testimony were icons revealing the power of the gospel.

Doubt

What was missing from the theological soil of my childhood and adolescent faith were ingredients of critical reflection, serious study, and honest doubt. These elements were not considered helpful to the central mission of the church, and many were convinced they could hinder it. I was strongly encouraged to love God with my heart and soul but not so much with my mind. The pervasive fear in an evangelistic culture was that philosophical and theological engagement could undermine faith, if not destroy it altogether. Although my father was the greatest of all encouragers for me to get the formal education he never received, he was constantly warning me, "Don't let those liberals destroy your ministry." There was an implicit anti-intellectualism in my heritage, as well as a fear of academic study.

Before confronting that anti-intellectualism and struggling with many questions from such a confrontation, I experienced another kind of struggle. It was a struggle with personal experience itself, my own experience. Immediately after high school, and in the middle of my itinerant preaching as a youth evangelist, I hit a spiritual and emotional wall. I felt myself flooded with uncertainty, doubt, and confusion. All kinds of questions bombarded me. Had I really been converted as a child? I could hardly remember the event, and this was supposed to be the most important event of my life. Did I have adequate faith then—or now? Though I knew I was sincere, I couldn't find assurance or comfort about the efficacy of my own experience.

I was desolate. I asked to be rebaptized in a youth revival I was conducting in Houston. I sought counsel from Arthur Travis, the pastor of my home church. My parents were supportive but unable to offer consolation. In fact, no one seemed to offer consolation. I felt plunged into a darkness of mind and emotions. It was like a downward spiral I could not stop. One doubt led to another. I was disconsolate and plagued with disturbing thoughts: "Perhaps it is not possible to have assurance." "Perhaps the Bible is not true." "Perhaps there really is no God." "Perhaps life itself is an illusion and religious faith is foolish." This continued for months with an intensity that was frightening.

When I started at Baylor University at age seventeen, I entered into a broader and bigger theological world. And though that world did not help me with my experiential struggle, it did introduce me to the rich traditions of faith and the many pioneers and pilgrims of faith before me. I learned of their struggles and doubts and found some comfort in knowing that I wasn't the first to question aspects of my faith. I experienced more liturgical forms of worship that gave me permission to continue worship while living with my doubts. For the first time, I heard preachers and teachers who were much more candid about their questions and uncertainties. And perhaps most importantly, I found friendships with fellow students and Baylor professors who accepted me and encouraged me to persist in my doubts until I could find resolution.

Resolution did come, but it was slow in coming. Part of it came as I explored devotional writers who were certainly evangelical but were more focused on piety, prayer, and virtue than on heaven and hell. I read several writers from the Keswick movement and those who spoke about "a deeper Christian life," "a hidden life," "a Spirit-filled life," or "an exchanged life": J. Sidlow Baxter, Hannah Whittal Smith, Ian Thomas, George Mueller, David Brainerd. These writers helped me to affirm my faith even while doubting and to experience grace even while questioning the adequacy of my experience. Slowly but surely, I received comfort and consolation.

Assurance also came from two unexpected sources: the charismatic movement and friendships with fellow student evangelists. During the decade of the 1960s, it seemed that the world was coming apart with assassinations and riots, a counter culture of music, sex, and drugs, as well as the civil rights movement and the Vietnam War. But the decade was also a time of intense spiritual renewal, at least in certain places. The "Jesus movement," originating in California, had national impact on Christian young people. Accompanying it was a fresh awakening to the presence and power of the Holy Spirit expressed in various visible manifestations. I never spoke in tongues or practiced a "prayer language," but I had several friends who did. I was never "baptized with the Holy Spirit" as a separate experience from conversion, but I had several friends who gave strong testimony to such an experience. It was evident, even in mainline Protestant and Catholic churches as well as numerous Baptist churches, that something new was happening. It was increasingly clear among many that the Spirit was given not just to "Pentecostal" denominations but to all denominations. More and more Christians were discovering the "charism" (gift) of the Spirit and the "charisms" (gifts) of the Spirit.

I found myself seeking and searching for the Spirit in a way I had not done before. I gained a greater appreciation for Christians whom I had previously described as "holy rollers" or "Pentecostals." I acquired a greater freedom to talk about the Spirit, celebrate the Spirit, and submit to the Spirit, recognizing that the wind, fire, breath, and flow of the Spirit could not be controlled by human reason or human understanding. All of this resulted in my experience of a richer and more robust faith. It gave me a greater and deeper joy than I had known.

At the same time, to my surprise, I discovered that Baylor had attracted a number of young ministerial students whose passion and calling was evangelism. Michael Gott, a gifted student and fervent preacher from east Texas, spoke words to me that I have never forgotten: "I believe God is doing a great work in today's world, and I intend to be a part of it." Michael continues to travel the world as a vocational evangelist. Billie Hanks, the son of a prominent west Texas family and a protégé of Billy Graham's associate, Rev. Grady Wilson, founded an evangelistic association while a student and is still involved in a ministry of international evangelism and discipleship. Bob Saul collaborated with the administration to begin the Baylor University Evangelistic Association while a student and would later work for the Home Mission Board of Southern Baptists in their department of evangelism. Joe Atkinson, a gospel singer whose musical gifts were matched by a fierce commitment to evangelism, became a dear friend at Baylor. There were other young evangelists: Ben Loring, Stephen Leddy, Herbert Shipp. Even though there were other "preacher boys," for some reason Baylor had attracted a number of young men who shared a similar vocational identity. Our friendships were enriching, and we found community with one another.

As I gained assurance and consolation, the content and style of my preaching was changing. I still called sinners to repent and be converted, but I increasingly called on converted sinners to live like saints and celebrate their salvation and indwelling Spirit. My preaching was still evangelistic, but it was also becoming more pastoral. Theological transformation was taking place, although I didn't have the vocabulary to fully describe it.

One other life-altering experience that took place at Baylor brought me recovery from my melancholy, affected my preaching, and guided my vocational direction. I spent three months in the Philippines as a summer missionary. The Baptist Student Union invited me to participate in its annual missions program, and I accepted.

Accompanied by John Moeser, Bill Whittaker, and David Perkins, three other students from across Texas, I spent the summer preaching revivals in Filipino Baptist churches, similar to what I was already doing in the US. The dramatic difference was that I was immersed in a culture and country different from my own. It forced me to ask whether or not I would live out my calling as an incarnational missionary somewhere other than America. I concluded that I would not.

Deconstruction

Then something happened that inaugurated yet another transformation. I had an intellectual, academic awakening. While at Baylor I experienced an enlightenment so profound that I now see it as "an intellectual conversion." It was as if a light dawned, and suddenly I gained a passion for study and an insatiable desire to learn. As a religion major I had done well, completing the required courses under the tutelage of a very good faculty. The faculty in Baylor's religion department were excellent teachers, and they took a personal interest in me: Glenn Hillburn, James Wood, Kyle Yates, John Davidson, Bob Patterson. Also, Richard Cutter, a professor in the classics, instilled in me the discipline necessary to learn Greek. These professors became mentors and later became friends and colleagues.

But it was in an elective New Testament course ("Hebrews to Revelation") that I really "woke up" intellectually and academically. The course was taught by Ray Summers, chair of the religion department and a recognized New Testament scholar. My desire to learn became as intense as my desire to experience. Much of this desire I attribute to Ray Summers, who helped me believe in myself as a student. He inspired in me not only a desire to learn but, perhaps more important, a confidence that I had the critical faculties and mental capacity to learn, and to learn much more than I had done up to the present. He, along with the other professors, taught me to think, to question, to explore. He also gave me tools that were necessary to learn in a more robust way.

For the first time I began to see the Scripture as a human book as well as a divine book. I learned the methods of the historical-critical study of Scripture as well as the biblical languages of Greek and Hebrew. I became fascinated with the biblical text itself and began to engage questions of its authorship, transmission, and interpretation. My love for the Bible increased, as did my belief in its authority and centrality to faith.

But I experienced a real change in how I viewed the Bible. This involved a kind of deconstruction from a simple "biblicism" to a reconstructed understanding of the Bible as a rich collection of ancient documents written from different historical and theological perspectives. It began what would become a lifelong quest to learn those perspectives and also discover the amazing unity that binds them together.

I never lost my faith in the divine inspiration of these documents, but I did lose faith in a simplistic way of reading and interpreting them. I also lost faith, at least for a while, in many of the accepted interpretations I had received from childhood and became less sure that my own interpretations were correct. Loss of certainty is painful, just as loss of naivete is humbling. So, to say the least, my experience of theological formation at Baylor involved a good measure of discomfort and doubt. But it also involved discovery. I was becoming a learner. New horizons were opening up. New mentors and new conversation partners were being introduced to me, and it was transformative.

After I graduated with a degree in Religion, Ray Summers offered me a scholarship to stay at Baylor and pursue a master's degree in New Testament with the possibility of pursuing a PhD. I felt honored by the offer and gladly accepted. Earlene and I had just married and she required another two years at Baylor to graduate, so I plunged into graduate school with enthusiasm. The seminars in biblical studies and biblical theology were not only challenging but exhilarating. I had never studied so hard in my life, and I had never been confronted with so many new ideas in such a short period. I relished the collegiality of other students, most of whom were older than me and farther along in their formation. They were kind and thoughtful even as we had vigorous discussion. Seminars were based on each student preparing and presenting a research paper or a book review that was followed by conversation. Professors joined in the conversation with an occasional lecture and at times to act as a referee.

Debate and argumentation were not only accepted but encouraged, always to be done with mutual respect. This methodology was as important in my theological formation as the material we were studying. I was no longer just listening to lectures, taking notes, and asking occasional questions. I was reading, researching, and entering into active conversation with others who were doing the same thing. In these seminars I learned the value of dialogue and even disagreement in the learning enterprise. These seminars also created in me a resistance to fundamentalism, whether it is a fundamentalism on the "theological left" or the "theological right."

I concluded that fundamentalism is more of an attitude or a "mindset" than anything else. It is a worldview that closes in on itself and shuts out any possibility of error. A fundamentalist arrives at a position of belief and then stubbornly declares, "It's my way or the highway." A fundamentalist is so certain of their own interpretation, conviction, or perspective that they simply will not allow room for honest disagreement without excluding the one with whom they disagree. A fundamentalist cannot admit the possibility of another person being right and their being wrong. For a fundamentalist, there is no ambiguity, no uncertainty, and no humility. A fundamentalist refuses to accept that our ability to apprehend truth is always partial and limited. In these early years of my theological formation, I became less certain about a lot of things while becoming more certain about a few things. And even about those few things, I came to realize how little I really knew and how much I had to learn.

Social Conscience

Another dimension of my formation during college and seminary had to do with an awakening of my social conscience, which resulted in another deconstruction and dislocation. My parents were Democrats primarily because of FDR's New Deal. Dad enlisted in the CCC camp after completing high school and lived in the congressional district of Sam Rayburn, the longtime Democratic Speaker of the House. But I never heard my parents talk politics, and I never heard any political conversation in my home church even though T. B. Maston was a member. I was in a middle-class family living in an all-White neighborhood, attending all-White public schools, and worshiping in an all-White church. I was in a political, racial, social bubble unaware and unconcerned about poverty, racism, or any other societal ills.

Dwight Eisenhower was president, and though I vaguely remember his reelection campaign in 1956 when he defeated Adlai Stevenson, I remember that I felt comfortable in Ike being president. As far as I was concerned, the USA was the greatest country in the world. While in junior high school I won an oratorical contest sponsored by the Optimist Clubs of America. I memorized my speech, which was titled "Freedom, Our Most Precious Heritage," and it was what one might expect for the late 1950s, a glorious tribute to the American way of life.

The election of John Kennedy in 1960 was a surprise to me but made little impact on my consciousness. Life seemed good, and I couldn't imagine why that might change. The only social problems I heard much about were the dangers of organized crime because of J. Edgar Hoover's warnings and the threat of communism from the USSR.

That threat became existential with the Cuban missile crisis in 1962 during my first semester at Baylor. I recall listening to Kennedy's speech on the radio with my roommates and realizing that war was possible. But after the crisis passed, so did any personal or social angst I might have had. A year later, President Kennedy was assassinated, and though I was riveted to the television coverage of the event I didn't see how it might affect me. Like everyone else at the time, I can remember when Kennedy was shot. I was conducting a youth revival that was only a few miles from Dallas. But soon afterwards my social consciousness returned to dormancy, and I went about my life of studying and preaching.

This is the way it was for me until 1968, when suddenly and dramatically my dormancy vanished, and I was born again with a new social consciousness and conscience. The events of that tumultuous year are seared in my memory and imagination because they created new awareness, new dissatisfactions, and new convictions inside me. The assassination of Martin Luther King Jr., the assassination of Robert F. Kennedy, the riots that broke out across the nation, and the TET offensive in Vietnam resulted in a fierce mixture of emotions: anger, sadness, fear, and determination. For the first time I realized my complicity in racial injustice and my ignorance about a multitude of social concerns.

Just a few years earlier I had become good friends with John Westbrook, a fellow student at Baylor and the first African American to play football in the Southwest Conference. He was also a ministerial student, and we connected as young preachers. He went with me to meet my parents, and we often prayed and talked together. But even in that friendship my own social conscience and consciousness remained dull. It's sad to say that there was a disconnect between the gospel I was preaching in churches, and even the gospel I was studying in the classroom, and the racial and social revolution that was going on around me.

The disconnect ended in 1968, and I experienced a dramatic change in my social consciousness. Several events converged to bring about this change. While preaching a revival in Oklahoma City at the time of Martin Luther King's assassination, I wept as I watched his funeral. My grief was partly the result of a disturbed conscience and the recognition of my complicity in racial injustice. When the riots broke out across the nation, I remember praying in fear, "Lord, is this the beginning of the end of America?" When Robert F. Kennedy was shot, I felt hopeless. The events that unfolded that year have been analyzed and televised numerous times, but for me they were life changing. I became awake and aware in ways that were at the time difficult to comprehend. Suddenly I was as concerned about social morality as I had been about sexual morality.

Also in 1968, I discovered Sherwood Wirt's book, *The Social Conscience of the Evangelical*, and read it quickly because Wirt was the editor of *Decision*, a publication of the Billy Graham Evangelistic Association. About the same time, I discovered the writings of Richard Niebuhr and Reinhold Niebuhr, and for the first time I explored the impact of systemic and structural evil on society. My ethics course in seminary, under C. W. Scudder, introduced me to social ethics as a discipline of study. A few years later during my doctoral work, I had a homiletics seminar under Clyde Fant where we explored the relationship of societal sins on preaching. In all these experiences I could feel myself changing and being changed in ways that would shape my future ministry.

Research and Writing

Completing a thesis for the Master of Arts degree took twelve months of research and writing. It was the most ambitious academic project I had ever attempted, and it would become one of the most fulfilling experiences of my life. Under the tutelage of Ray Summers, I decided to write on "The Christology of Miracles in the Gospel of Mark." I settled on Mark's Gospel because it is considered to be the earliest of the four Gospels. I settled on the study of miracles because they comprise almost a third of the Gospel. And I settled on Christology because I wanted to explore what this primitive Christian document conveys about Jesus' self-understanding as well as the early church's understanding of him. I struggled with the meaning of miracle itself, the historicity of the miracles as events, how the miracle stories were formed, and what they communicated about Jesus. Why did Jesus perform miracles, and what was their meaning both then and now?

In the process of writing, I confronted questions about my calling and vocation. Should I continue as an evangelist? Should I become a teacher? Should I become a pastor? I was still active with itinerant preaching almost every weekend. But my preaching was changing even more as it was informed by my academic studies. My earlier doubts and desolations were subsiding, and I had found satisfaction in the rhythms of being a student, being married, and being a preacher. I applied to the University of Edinburgh for more graduate work but was denied admission. I considered continuing at Baylor for a PhD, with my father's strong encouragement, but my heart wasn't in it. I concluded that my gifts and temperament were pointing toward the pulpit rather than the classroom, and that probably meant becoming a pastor. I set my sights on earning a seminary degree with the intention of pursuing a doctorate in theology.

Southwestern Seminary was the only option I even considered. It was in my hometown, and I was deeply rooted in Texas Baptist life. Earlene and I made the move easily, and I completed my Master of Divinity in twenty-four months and then was admitted into the Doctor of Theology program. After the rigor of research and writing in graduate school at Baylor, I found the adjustment to sitting in large classrooms and listening to lectures very difficult. Attending seminary in the 1960s was similar to a person needing a "union card" to work in certain industries. A seminary degree was considered a requirement to becoming a pastor, so I accepted the learning environment at the MDiv level with two expectations. The seminary degree would "certify" my credentials as a minister, and the courses that focused on the practices of ministry would help me: worship leadership, pastoral care, religious education, and especially preaching.

I relished the study of homiletics, recognizing that I needed yet another deconstruction and reconstruction. Even though I had preached far more than most of my peers, I attempted to put it aside. I determined to become a student both of preaching and of preachers. Under the tutelage of H. C. Brown and Clyde Fant, I committed to the discipline and craft of preparing and delivering sermons. I have never seen myself as an exceptional preacher but have felt that I had a measure of natural talent and spiritual gifting to exegete and expound Scripture in the context of a worshiping congregation. For almost as long as I can remember, my self-understanding has included a desire to preach and a desire to preach well.

Seminary not only fueled my desire to be a good preacher but also fueled my desire to preach a good gospel that was relevant to society. My acquaintance with evangelists and my own experience as an evangelist made it logical to study Christian apologetics in my doctoral studies. John Newport was the professor at Southwestern whom I wanted to mentor me. I asked if I could study philosophy of religion under his guidance, and he agreed. Newport was not so much a philosopher himself as he was an excellent analyzer of philosophy and the questions philosophy asks of faith. Newport was a called a "Renaissance man," and he was the most widely read person I had ever encountered. Stories abounded about the breadth and scope of his reading and his voracious appetite to consume information. There was no subject in philosophy and theology for which John Newport did not have a bibliography.

Seminars in my ThD program were challenging and a welcome return to a research-and-writing way of learning. They included Evil and Suffering, Hermeneutics, Philosophy of History, Science and Religion, Art and Aesthetics, Anthropology. The subjects we explored created lively debate marked by real differences of perspective. Learning to think and speak philosophically required that we address the difficult questions every human being asks: Where do we come from? Where are we going? What is the meaning of life? What is the true, the good, the beautiful? We compared worldviews and world religions. One cannot wrestle with these questions without being changed. I was being changed during those two years of seminars though I didn't know where these changes were leading.

The decision about a doctoral dissertation was guided by John Newport. The decade of the 1960s was coming to a close, but already there were academic efforts to analyze and interpret this tumultuous time in American culture. Newport suggested that I make such an effort by researching two prolific and popular Christian writers with widespread influence. Their books sold into the tens of thousands. One was Francis Schaeffer and the other was Alan Watts. Schaeffer, a conservative evangelical author who lived in Switzerland, had significant intellectual influence with the emerging "Jesus movement" and in the broader culture of evangelicalism. Alan Watts was an Episcopal priest who sought to combine Christian faith with Zen Buddhism. He became an intellectual guru to many in the "counterculture" of the 1960s, including Timothy Leary and Lawrence Ferlinghetti. Both of these apologists had enormous appeal among young people, and both were responding to the existential questions of the day, although with different epistemological, ontological, and metaphysical perspectives. I spent two years reading them and then writing a dissertation titled "A Comparative Study of Representative Emphases in the Thought of Alan Watts and Francis Schaeffer." It was a satisfying study that became invaluable for future ministry.

As I was completing my dissertation, the seminary administration asked me to become a teaching fellow in Biblical Backgrounds and Evangelism. Although I enjoyed the experience, I knew that my future was in the local church as a pastor and not in the academy as a professor. My twelve years of theological education, six at Baylor and six at seminary, were coming to a close, and as rewarding and challenging as they had been, the next chapters in life were to be even more rewarding and more challenging.

Chapter 3

Being a Pastor

Few words are as meaningful to me as the word "pastor," and few words describe a more difficult and demanding vocation. Before completing my theological education and before leaving itinerant evangelism, I had been recognizing an internal attraction to pastoral ministry. It was not as though I experienced a sudden shift in my thinking or received a sudden call, but rather I felt a gradual turning to a different way of life than what I had known.

Being a pastor is definitely a way of life. It involves serious theological study (sermons combine research, reflection, and writing) as well as regular preaching and teaching (at that time it meant three preparations a week). But unlike a professor in the academy or an evangelist on the road, a pastor is immersed in the daily life of one congregation, for better or for worse, for an extended time. The life of a pastor is all-encompassing, both for the pastor and the pastor's family, day in and day out, living as an exemplar to the congregation and in turn being accountable to the congregation. It is a "fishbowl" kind of existence where everyone is watching, or at least it felt that way.

I have been pastor of six Baptist churches, five of them in succession for a total of twenty-seven years, and one of them for another eight years after my tenure at the Cooperative Baptist Fellowship. Each congregation was "home" for me and my family. We found nurture and nourishment, love and encouragement in all of them. But being a pastor is also hard work. I consider it to be the most difficult and demanding job in the world but also the most satisfying and fulfilling. I have now lived long enough to see many pastors burn out or give up. I have also seen pastors stumble and fall because of money, sex, or power. But more than anything else, I have seen pastors quit simply because they grew weary and discouraged.

Those who have influenced my pastoral ministry did so without my ever having met them. I was given all of the books that B. H. Carroll wrote in my adolescence and absorbed his influence as a Texas Baptist pastor. He was at FBC Waco for thirty-five years, having profound impact on Baylor University and founding Southwestern Seminary. George W. Truett considered Carroll to be "the greatest personality I ever touched."[2] Truett himself, who was at FBC Dallas for forty-four years, was a personality that touched me through his writings, recordings, and example. He is reported to have said that he wouldn't "step down" from the pulpit to be president of the US and that he had long sought for and been given the heart of a pastor. I held both of these Texas Baptist pastors in an almost reverential awe in my earlier pastorates.

While a student at Baylor, I was a member of Seventh and James Baptist Church and enjoyed my friendship with the pastor, Riley Eubank. He was a gentle soul with a keen mind who taught me by example how to preach in the context of a worshiping congregation. For one year I was in charge of the Baylor Religious Hour, a weekly worship service for students, where I had the responsibility of hosting guest speakers. A number of those speakers were effective pastors who could communicate in winsome ways. I listened and learned about the high calling of pastoral ministry just by informal conversations and observation.

A few years later, I discovered Eugene Peterson, a Presbyterian pastor and author whose prolific writings were forged from a life-long commitment to being a pastor. As I read and studied his books, Peterson, only a decade older than me, profoundly influenced my understanding of vocational integrity and identity (see page 43 for recommended reading).

Meadow Lane Baptist Church, Arlington, Texas (1970–1972)

I became a full-time pastor at the age of twenty-five just as I was beginning my doctoral program. The surprising interest of Meadow Lane Baptist in Arlington, Texas, converged with my internal urges to convince me to make a vocational change. This neighborhood congregation with about 500 members took a chance in calling a young preacher with no pastoral experience. All of the deacons were old enough to be my father or grandfather, but they embraced and loved me in such a way that would not let me fail. Here I began to learn the rhythm and routine of sermon preparation, hospital visitation, funerals, weddings, church conferences, pastoral care, and counseling. My theological education had prepared me for this.

What it did not prepare me for was resolving conflict between members, working with staff, equipping laity for ministry, managing a budget, and leading a building program. I learned early to set some boundaries and priorities. I reserved my mornings for study and found, to my amazement, that the church family respected the decision. It was a practice I would continue into the future. I

Books by Eugene Peterson
that influenced me

Under the Unpredictable Plant: An Exploration in Vocational Holiness

Five Smooth Stones for Pastoral Work

Working the Angles: The Shape of Pastoral Integrity

The Contemplative Pastor: Returning to the Art of Spiritual Direction

The Pastor: A Memoir

Take and Read: Spiritual Reading, An Annotated List

Leap Over a Wall

Subversive Spirituality

Christ Plays in Ten Thousand Places

As Kingfishers Catch Fire: A Conversation on the Ways of God Formed by the Words of God

A Long Obedience in the Same Direction: Discipleship in an Instant Society

took one night a week for "visitation," going into homes to evangelize. This is not a practice I continued in the following years, but at the time it was very effective. A number of families became Christians and joined the church from those visits. I limited the number of individuals to whom I would offer pastoral counseling and the number of times I would schedule an appointment with the same person. I arrived at the church most mornings by 8:30 and stayed until 5:00. I was usually involved in a church event at least one other night of the week. Saturday was my Sabbath. Life was busy but good.

During our time at MLBC, both of our sons were born: Philip and Joel. These births were two of the most profound spiritual experiences of my life, and I was overwhelmed by the prospect of being a father. Earlene and I made a deliberate decision to give the highest priority to one another and our children. We decided early in our marriage that the home is the most important institution in the world and that our home would, as far as we could determine it, be a little bit like heaven and a laboratory of Christian community.

Family life is not easy under any circumstances, but it is especially challenging for a pastor's family. It requires intentionality, prayer, and hard work. I had witnessed so many pastors' families sacrificed on the altar of ministerial success or professional ambition that I pleaded with God early in my life to protect me and my family. I asked God to turn my heart as a father toward my children, to turn their hearts toward me as their father (Mal 4:5), and, most importantly, to turn all of our hearts toward God. I asked for grace and experienced grace because I realized that there is no such thing as a perfect family. Whatever success Earlene and I have had in our family is because of God's goodness and grace.

Because of grace, our family has been blessed through the years with support and sustenance from our extended family and each of the church families where we served. Earlene's mother took great pride in our children and spent extensive amounts of time with them. My parents were a source of exemplary kindness and encouragement. In each of our pastorates we discovered an incredible amount of love for our children and a desire to help them. Although I never expected the church to provide for our children what only we as parents could provide, I discovered that the relationships, programs, and ministries of the church were allies offering them community, instruction, and formation. Both of our sons, and later our daughter, grew up loving the church and desiring to serve the church. I believe part of that is because the churches we served loved children, not just our children, and gave priority to children's care in their budgeting, programming, and ministering. I shall forever be grateful.

Southcliff Baptist Church, Fort Worth, Texas (1972–1976)

Southcliff Baptist in Fort Worth issued me a call in August 1972, and I accepted. Southcliff was a suburban congregation strategically located on an interstate and near the seminary. Its membership of 2,000 was composed primarily of middle- and upper-middle class families who expected the church programs to be administered effectively, the preaching to be nourishing, and the worship services to be conducted with evangelical warmth. Southcliff was a recent merger of two other congregations and had experienced explosive growth.

I was eager and energetic. I was also naive. It was the first time I encountered entrenched power structures in congregational life. At a personnel committee meeting where we were considering a part-time minister of youth, I commented that the young man being considered would be temporary since he was a seminary student. A committee member quickly responded, "As far as I'm concerned all ministers are temporary." Of course, he was right. Ministers come and go while the church with its systems remains. But the tone and implication of his remarks sobered me. Later I would learn more about internal power struggles in ecclesiastical life.

On another occasion the deacons were making a decision about embarking on a major building program. I argued passionately for it, while the most respected deacon in the church, James Riddle, spoke against it, arguing that the church couldn't afford to complete the project. Amazingly, the deacons voted to proceed. Later that night, James Riddle called me and said something to the effect, "Pastor, I want you to know that I love you, and even though I voted against the building program, I will support the majority vote and continue to support you." As it turned out, we only had enough money to complete the exterior and one floor of the interior. The second floor was completed a few years later. Through all of this experience,

Jim Riddle was a humble, gracious, and supportive influence. He used his considerable power for the common good of the church. His behavior and attitude taught me some important lessons about leadership.

Southcliff was also the place where I discovered a gifting that I had not yet realized. This was the aptitude and ability to form genuine friendships with businessmen and professional leaders in the community who were seeking to grow spiritually. All of them were men, and most of them were professed Christians, but they were unsatisfied with their faith journey. These laymen were either already members of the church or interested in becoming members, and they wanted more in their lives than financial success or career advancement. They were seeking to make a difference for good and for God in their work, in the community, and in the world. Some of them were struggling with the relevance of faith to life, the challenges of marriage and family, and various temptations in the world.

All of them were older than me (though not by much), but I was drawn to them, challenged by them, and genuinely desired to help them in ways beyond my preaching and teaching. They also seemed to have been drawn to me and sought me out for friendship. I began having breakfast or lunch with many of them. Earlene and I became friends with some of them and their wives and socialized as couples. I invested in frequent conversations and discovered that, although I was a pastor, I was first a man like them in need of Christian friends. Adair Ratliff, Gene Eatherly, John Travis, Ben Woolery, Tim Penland, Pete Simon, Jim Hart, and many others became friends to me and I to them. I found great satisfaction in the ministry of friendships.

I honestly don't know whether I mentored them or they mentored me. I learned as much from these lay Christian leaders as I might have taught them. I invested time and energy in them, but they also invested time and energy in me. Together we experienced spiritual growth and opportunities for shared ministry. I had more biblical and theological training than they had, but they had more experience in business, politics, and social interactions outside the church. They viewed the world with different perspectives than I did, but we learned from each other and our friendships enriched us and strengthened the church.

The experience of Christian friendships has been extremely important both in my life and my ministry. Whatever success I have had in local congregational leadership has been, in large measure, because of the effectiveness of lay leaders within the church and community. I am comfortable being around Christian laity (or even non-Christians) who have strong personalities or have achieved success in their professional life. I am also comfortable being with Christian laity who have little or no success as the world measures success. I learned to seek friendship for friendship's sake. I enjoyed spending time with non-clergy and even non-religious or non-churched individuals. I grew from friendships with those who are different from me just as with those who are similar to me.

Most of the literature that defines pastoral leadership does so in terms of tasks: preaching/teaching, pastoral care, and administration. Tasks, however, as important as they may be, are not as important as human and personal interaction. Prior to all other roles and responsibilities, a pastor must relate to everyone in a spirit of friendship and nurture authentic friendship with as many as possible.

First Baptist Church, Midland, Texas (1976–1988)

In 1976 at the age of thirty-one, I became pastor of the 6,300-member First Baptist Church of Midland, Texas. It was the nineteenth largest church in the Southern Baptist Convention. I was not the first choice of the pastor search committee and perhaps not even the best choice, but I believe I was the right choice. All eleven members of the committee had agreed on my candidacy, except one named Johnny Brown. Johnny, a successful west Texas oilman, had been unable to attend the final meeting of the committee. A time was determined for us to meet personally. He was an affable and warm person but had an intimidating emotional and spiritual intensity. He came to Fort Worth to question me. I had an intuition that this particular conversation would likely determine if the committee would extend me a call.

After visiting for several hours, Johnny looked me straight in the eyes and asked, "Daniel, what do you bring to First Baptist and the city of Midland that makes you think you could be our pastor?" I remember my answer because it startled and surprised me even as I was speaking: "The only thing I bring is my naked soul for the Holy Spirit to use." The response was not premeditated or rehearsed but an honest confession of how I saw myself at the moment. I knew I had a good education, some natural and spiritual gifts, and a few years of experience, but I knew before the beginning of my time in Midland that I was "over my head." I felt in desperate need of divine grace and guidance if I were to be an effective pastor of this historic church.

My trial sermon a few weeks later was based on the confession of the Apostle Paul to the church in Corinth:

> When I came to you, brothers and sisters, I did not come proclaiming the mystery of God to you in lofty words of wisdom. For I decided to know nothing among you except Jesus Christ, and him crucified. And I came to you in weakness and in fear and in much trembling. My speech and my proclamation were not plausible words of wisdom, but with a demonstration of the Spirit and of power. (1 Cor 2:1-4)

In the following twelve years I never forgot the words I spoke to Johnny Brown. As time passed, I did grow and mature in my preaching and leadership, but I was always conscious of my weakness in need of God's sustaining and guiding grace.

Evangelism

I invited eleven different evangelists to preach and conduct revivals at First Baptist during my tenure: my father Dan Vestal, John Bisagno, Richard Jackson, James Robison, Gene Williams, Jay Strack, Junior Hill, Angel Martinez, Jack Taylor, Ron Dunn, and Arthur Blessitt. The spiritual impact of these revivals on the church and city was profound. It is not an exaggeration to say that scores of new church members were added and hundreds of lives were changed.

One of the first revivals was conducted by John Bisagno, pastor of First Baptist, Houston. Early in the week he asked me for the names of some men in the community who were known (or notorious) for not being Christian or members of any church. Two of them were Ed Darnell and Jack James. The following Sunday morning, both of them made public professions of faith and requested baptism. Ed had recently retired as the Sheriff of Midland, a position he held for thirty-five years. He was a giant of man, and he was legendary throughout west Texas. Jack James was the owner of the Budweiser distributorship in west Texas and had a reputation of not liking preachers or churches. I presented them to the congregation and later baptized them to the amazement of everyone. Their baptisms became the talk of the town and in many ways legitimized my leadership as pastor in the eyes of many.

A few years later, in 1982, I invited an evangelist whom many considered to be eccentric, Arthur Blessitt. I had placed a number of calls to his phone, but he never responded. When he did respond, he told me that he was a "street evangelist," not a congregational or mass evangelist. He was renowned for carrying a nine-foot cross on his shoulder and walking across continents. I asked him to come to our affluent city, and he told me the only time he could come was for five days in December, two weeks before Christmas. I considered it wise to ask the church for permission before confirming the invitation. The church agreed. With their consent, Arthur stood in the pulpit of First Baptist on a Wednesday night before a sanctuary that had filled to capacity an hour before the service began. It was electric. We had never experienced anything like it.

He wore blue jeans, and I wore a suit. He was free and fresh. I was reserved and apprehensive. He told stories of his travels and his conversations with rich and famous people as well as poor and power-less people. He recounted his encounters with the good, the bad, and the ugly of humanity. He preached for at least an hour each evening, and it captured the imagination of an entire city. He led a downtown "March for Jesus" on Friday for all who wanted to participate, and it was featured on the front page of the *Midland Reporter Telegram* on Saturday morning. He had personal conversations with some of

Midland's most prominent citizens, including George W. Bush, who at the time was experiencing his own spiritual and personal renewal.

The final service of the revival was on Sunday night, and we had already planned our annual Christmas concert with full choir and orchestra. It was always a highlight of the year. We decided to proceed with the music to be followed by the message. The music lasted for an hour. The message lasted for an hour. Time for prayer and response lasted for almost an hour. But nobody was keeping time. We were standing on holy ground, and everybody knew it. It was a most remarkable event, unlike any other we had experienced. The choir with robes and the orchestra with tuxedos surrounded a "street preacher" whose persona and passion disarmed the most cynical. Oil executives sat next to oil field workers. Women with fur coats were laughing and crying alongside the homeless. Cultural and class barriers were broken down. We were more than a crowd. We were a congregation, a community.

The following year, 1983, the SBC had its annual meeting in Pittsburgh, Pennsylvania, and Arthur was scheduled to preach at a preconvention event. I met him in a restaurant overlooking Pittsburgh the night before the convention and asked if he would return to Midland the next year for a citywide evangelistic event. He agreed, and in April 1984, more than thirty churches across denominational and racial lines co-sponsored six nights of worship and witness. We gathered each evening at Chaparral Center on the campus of Midland College. The spiritual and social impact was profound, demonstrating an ecumenical unity never before experienced in Midland.

In October 1983, the First National Bank of Midland went bankrupt. It was the largest independent bank in Texas and was considered to be invincible as a financial institution. The bank's collapse meant the collapse of careers, a financial and existential threat to many in the oil and gas industry, and a sobering reminder that life is fragile and little in this world is certain. A couple of Sundays after the bank collapsed, I preached from Ecclesiastes 3:1: "There is a time for everything, and a season for every activity under the sun." The title of the message, which was broadcast live on television throughout west Texas and eastern New Mexico, was "What Time Is It in Midland?"

It created quite a response and opened doors for the church to offer support and friendship to people who had never before attended.

The bank crisis created a personal crisis for hundreds of families. It also created a "kairos" moment for an entire region of the country that prided itself on self-sufficiency and self-made millionaires. Suddenly nobody felt sufficient. Suddenly everybody realized how interconnected we were as a community. Some, not all, began to seek a different kind of security and found their way to faith in Christ and membership in the church. I found myself thrust into a place of influence within a troubled city with opportunities to counsel scores of individuals who were impacted by the failure of one of the city's most important institutions.

Social Ministry

Midland was and is a city of affluence with one of the highest per capita incomes in America. But it had its share of problems. One of them was drug and alcohol abuse among adolescents. Under the courageous leadership of the church's youth minister, Charlie Dodd, we began a twelve-step recovery program titled PDAP (Palmer Drug Abuse Program), named after the Palmer Episcopal Church in Houston where the program originated.

In the deacons' meeting where a decision was being made whether we would open our building and our hearts to young people struggling with addiction, there was a poignant moment of soul searching and courageous action. One of the deacons, Willie Du Bose, was also a county judge. He knew that the problem of adolescent drug abuse was rampant. He made a passionate appeal for the church to take action, knowing that there was risk. Several civic and social organizations had requested that we allow the PDAP program to be housed in our church building. The deacons responded with courage and voted to allow this non-church, non-Christian program to use our Sunday school rooms for nightly meetings, knowing that cigarette smoke would fill the rooms and filter to other parts of the building.

They also knew that it would open the church to possible vandalism and perhaps threaten the safety of our members. It was a bold step for a traditional congregation to make, and it communicated volumes to the community. Buildings are a symbol of power, and when we use our church buildings compassionately for the good of the community, we gain considerable good will and influence within the community. The PDAP program was an immediate success. Scores of young people "sobered up." Many of them flooded into First Baptist for the first time, followed by their parents and entire families who were also suffering because of drug addiction. Equally important, the church itself experienced changes in its attitude to a marginalized segment of society.

As is often the case when a collective conscience is awakened and a communal consciousness is created, the results were transformative. First Baptist became increasingly aware of other pressing needs in the city, and its people determined to use their considerable influence to address those needs. We responded to a shortage of low-income housing by participating in a specially created "Commission for Housing" and donated $40,000 to it. We responded to the plight of poverty by beginning a daily feeding program administered by members of the church. We responded to some gaps in the mental health care delivery system by beginning a robust counseling program within the church and another counseling program outside the church as well as a chaplaincy program at Midland Memorial Hospital.

We responded to racial divisions by helping create a public trans-portation system and a "Human Relations Council" that became a forum for dialogue and activism. Under the leadership of Susan Edwards, a member of the church and a licensed social worker, we began the Midland Crisis Center to provide food, clothing, and other social services to a diverse population. Under the leadership of Bob Hopkins, the church's minister of education, we nurtured partnerships with African American and Hispanic congregations. We significantly expanded our efforts to offer financial assistance to indi-viduals and families for rent, utilities, and medical needs. More of our members became involved in efforts to improve public education by serving as members of the MISD board, as volunteers, as tutors, and as leaders in the PTA and in various sports programs throughout the city.

The human and financial resources of the church refocused exter-
nally without consideration of how this might "grow the church" or
increase its membership. Priorities of the budget shifted to ministry
and mission away from the benefit of our own congregation. The
shift was gradual, but it was dramatic. By the time I left Midland,
44 percent of the church's undesignated receipts were going to mission
causes. We were giving 30 percent of our budget to the worldwide
ministries of Southern Baptists through the Cooperative Program,
which meant we were giving more to that program than any other
church in the Southern Baptist Convention.

We were also giving another 14 percent of our budget directly
to evangelistic, educational, and benevolent ministries throughout
the world. The distribution of these gifts was determined by a group
of lay leaders. In addition, we collected three annual offerings a
year for missions (state, national, and world), the sum of which was
often in excess of $200,000 a year. The generosity of the church was
increasing, as was the involvement of its members in mission projects
and programs.

All of this thrust FBC into national prominence within the SBC,
which resulted in my first book co-authored with church historian
and seminary professor Robert A. Baker, *Pulling Together: A Practical
Guide to the Cooperative Program.* The following is an excerpt from
that book. For me the book was a confession of my own commitment to the centrality of the local church in God's plan for world
redemption.

> The local church is an agent of the kingdom of God; therefore, its
> identity is tied to the extension of the kingdom. Kingdom of God
> is a worldwide kingdom that breaks down all human barriers. It
> knows no racial or geographic boundaries.
>
> The kingdom of God is not confined to any political ideology,
> an economic system, or any social structure. It exists in the world,
> but it transcends time and space. The kingdom has people in it,
> but the kingdom is not a human institution. The progress of God's
> kingdom is dependent on human involvement, but the final victory
> of God's kingdom is not dependent on human involvement.

The local church is to be an embodiment of the kingdom and an instrument of the kingdom. Its methods are to be kingdom oriented. Its message is an announcement and an invitation about the kingdom. Its motives are to be kingdom inspired.

The time has come for pastors to ask the sobering question, "Am I a kingdom person?" The time has come for us to face the issue, "Are we really committed to the kingdom? Are we more committed to the kingdom than we are to personal interest?" There is nothing wrong with the pastor's quest for excellence, aggressive leadership, or the use of promotional skills, but all this must be subordinated to a consuming concern for the kingdom.

We need to be more concerned about the kingdom of Jesus than denominational and institutional loyalties. I owe an unpayable debt to my own denomination and its institutions. But first and foremost I'm a follower of Jesus Christ, and whoever else follows Jesus Christ is my brother. Even though we may differ doctrinally, if we acknowledge Jesus is King, we are in his kingdom together. But our denominational churches are not the kingdom. We're servants of the kingdom. We must not identify our churches as the kingdom. The kingdom is much bigger than any of our denominations.

We also need to be more concerned about the kingdom than politics. I love this country and feel stronger every day about our freedoms. But the USA is not the hope of the world, the Savior of the world, or the model for the world. The only hope for salvation is the kingdom of God, and the model for this world is the kingdom of God.

Perhaps the matter of congregational identity is one of focus and priority. Surely no one would deny the importance of multifaceted ministries, electric-like worship, deeper Christian experience, congregational growth, denominational loyalty, and social involvement. But when any of these, or any combination of these, takes a priority over extension of the kingdom, the identity of the church becomes confused.

When a passion for anything less than the kingdom of God becomes the passion of a pastor and church, they will be considerably less than God intended. When the primary energy of a pastor and church are consumed with anything other than the kingdom, they will in some way become warped and wayward.[3]

Church Growth

Amazingly, FBC itself continued to grow in attendance, additions, and spirit. More than 1,500 new believers were baptized, and another 3,000 members were added to the church during my twelve years as pastor. One reason for growth was the functioning of our Sunday school led by our minister of education, Bob Hopkins. The adults were divided into departments, which functioned like small congregations of thirty to sixty. The departments were then divided into smaller classes, or cell groups, of ten to twenty where a lay Bible teacher conducted a forty-five-minute Bible lesson with application to daily life. Each Wednesday night these leaders met for an hour to plan and pray. We were constantly adding new departments and classes with new workers enlisted and trained. This methodology provided an effective and practical way to organize the church for learning, fellowship, and ministry.

The youth and children were also organized into smaller groups led by clergy and lay leaders who loved them, prayed for them, and worked with them. My own children, like so many others, were impacted by the influence and investment of these leaders, especially Mary Dorchester, Izora Browning, Jack Green, and Lois Rogge. First Baptist gained a reputation as a place that cares about children and youth. Families, with all kinds of configurations and needs, came to experience such care. It was a season of fruitfulness and flourishing.

Yet I was growing restless at FBC. The Southern Baptist Convention was now engaged in an intense struggle for its soul, and I was increasingly drawn into that struggle. By 1987, I had served on three major convention committees: a Cooperative Giving Study Committee (1981–1982), a Committee on Nominations for Boards and Agencies (1984), and a Peace Committee (1985–1987). The divisions in the convention were growing deeper, and I knew a defining crisis was ahead. I kept the church informed of my denominational activities, and they gave me their blessings partly because I had remained politically unaligned and I had not involved the church in denominational controversy. But at times I felt that I was living in two parallel worlds, congregational ministry and denominational conflict. It was exhausting.

The greatest source of my restlessness, however, was that I was being drawn to ministry in a larger urban context. Midland is a city of about 150,000 in the plains of west Texas. It is located in the Permian Basin, a geological term to describe one of the richest oil and gas fields in the world. This mineral basin produces great wealth, and it also produces a "bubble-like" environment of privilege and isolation. I longed for a more heterogeneous environment with greater racial, economic, cultural, and political diversity. I felt an increasing desire to lead a congregation facing the complex problems of a large population center and the mission challenges of urban America. Both the restlessness and longing within me were factors as I discerned the possibility of relocation. Several opportunities to move presented themselves, but I felt a particular prompting of the Spirit to respond to the call of Dunwoody Baptist Church in Atlanta, Georgia, to become their pastor.

I left Midland in 1988 with remorse and grief but also with clarity and conviction. I had experienced a Camelot kind of life for twelve years with an incredible support system, deep friendships, and a fruitfulness that had exceeded all my expectations. Our daughter, Anne Elizabeth, was born in Midland, and the entire church welcomed her into the world. I wore a pink boutonniere every Sunday morning for nine months anticipating her arrival without knowing whether Earlene would give birth to a boy or a girl. When she was born, there was a communal gladness that bordered on giddiness. All three of our children were loved by the church, and Earlene was celebrated and respected for being the pastor's wife that she is, a woman of exemplary character and deep spirituality. But leave I did, to go to a church about half the size of First Baptist in a city where no one watched me on television or even knew my name. In the middle of a denominational storm that was part of a larger cultural/political storm, I said goodbye to a church and city that I had grown to love.

Dunwoody Baptist Church, Atlanta, Georgia (1988–1991)

Going to Dunwoody Baptist in Atlanta did not lead to the ministry I had anticipated, nor did it result in a tenured time of pastoral leadership. I only stayed three years. I left Midland for Atlanta with only one thought in mind: to lead an urban congregation in its witness for Christ in one of the great cities of America. I was fully prepared to immerse myself in the challenges of a mission-hearted congregation with great potential. I imagined, perhaps naively, that I would escape continued involvement in the denominational conflict since I had made efforts to bring peace by serving on three SBC committees in the previous ten years. In my own mind I was finished with giving time and energy to the convention and was eager to give all my time and energy to a local congregation that felt poised for an exciting future.

The search committee from DBC was composed of intelligent and capable lay leaders. We talked excitedly about possibilities for the future, and they promised me their full support. They even granted me six weeks of transition to complete my second book, a doctrinal study book for Southern Baptists titled *The Doctrine of Creation*. I began my ministry at DBC in September 1988, with high hopes and great expectations.

In only a few months, however, the direction of my life and ministry changed dramatically as I faced an internal struggle of conscience. I was torn between a lifelong love affair with the Southern Baptist Convention and an opportunity of ministry offered by a loving church. I was torn between two loves, and within three years I walked away from both. During the three years at DBC, I made two unsuccessful bids to become president of the Southern Baptist Convention (1989–1990), and I helped in forming the Cooperative Baptist Fellowship (1991), leaving the SBC behind. All of this was done out of conviction and with the support of the church. But it wasn't easy, and I realized that some in the church were disappointed in my denominational involvement. In 1991, I accepted the call of Tallowood Baptist Church in Houston, Texas, leaving Dunwoody Baptist behind.

Both departures, though born out of conviction, were accompanied by deep grief. My grief in leaving DBC was my own disappointment for such a brief tenure. I never felt anything but love and support from the leadership and membership, but I know there was disappointment that we did not achieve the high hopes and great expectations we had shared earlier. I too felt that disappointment.

My grief in leaving the SBC behind was a kind of grief unlike anything I had yet experienced. My father had died several years earlier and I grieved his loss, but this was different. The denomination that contributed so much to my formation had died. At least it had died to me. Its character had changed so dramatically that I could no longer support it. I had given much of my life to keep this from happening, but it was simply not to be. I felt sadness and failure.

In coming to DBC I had expected to avoid continued convention involvement. I was naive. The SBC controversy not only followed me to Atlanta but seemed to pursue me. Within three months I made decisions that would shorten my tenure at Dunwoody Baptist and thrust me into roles of SBC leadership that I could not have imagined. I did not regret those decisions, but I did regret the impact those decisions had on Dunwoody Baptist and the consequent failure to fulfill the dreams that the church and I had shared for the future.

In leaving Dunwoody, I also felt gratitude for the brief time we enjoyed together. Located in affluent suburbs of north Atlanta, the church had become regional in its outreach and was recognized as creative and innovative in its ministry. Cecil B. Day, founder of Days Inn, was a longtime church member, and after he died his wife gave generously to build a Wellness Center complete with a swimming pool, racquetball courts, exercise rooms, and spas. It became the face of DBC for many in the city. The church had begun a School for the Arts that offered private music lessons and tutoring services. They sponsored an extensive sports program for children with softball, basketball, and volleyball leagues. They also had a quality weekday early education program, a strong senior adult program, and a ministry to adults with disabilities. The church deserved its reputation as a "good neighbor" and a family-friendly congregation.

I was proudest of colleagues who served alongside me as effective ministers. Under the leadership of Dave Briley and Glenn Sloan, the church created an outstanding music ministry with choirs, orchestra, ensembles, concerts, and dramas. Under the leadership of Marjorie

Norton, the church organized itself into Bible study groups that increased and grew significantly. Under the leadership of Greg Smith, the church saw extensive outreach through recreation and a wide range of family activities. Under the leadership of Allan Jackson, the church invested heavily in a youth ministry that impacted the lives of hundreds of teenagers. Under the leadership of Marcy Cotton and June Webb, the church developed a prayer ministry that enlisted scores of members in intercession.

Under the leadership of capable and courageous laity, DBC earned its reputation as a missional church. We funded several new church starts and a wide range of benevolent and outreach ministries. I found a cadre of lay leaders who were deeply committed and visionary Christians: Arthur Turner, Varion Spear, Suzanne Dabney, Charlie Drake, Bill Delk, Carl Lindsey, Roland Wilson, Jim Jennings, Jerry and Bev Wilkinson, Ted and Diane Kennedy, George and Sue Haynes, Walter and Era Weeks, and Steve and Judy Kyle, along with many others. To paraphrase the words of the Apostle Paul, "I thank God every time I think of these and their partnership in the gospel" (Phil 1:3-4).

Other laity in Dunwoody inspired me, encouraged me, and reinforced the conviction that nothing in the world is as powerful as committed and compassionate Christians living in their homes, their church, and in society. Roy Overstreet, Carl Norton, and Lee Baggett were especially gifted Bible teachers. Dean Day, the widow of Cecil, was and is a remarkable woman of Christian character and influence. Jim Strawn used his accounting skills "to the glory of God." Bob Cloer, a real estate developer, was a strong Christian influence and like a brother to me. Marty and Betty Dicken are lay leaders who opened their lives and home to Earlene and me in ways I will never forget. I could go on and on in naming those at DBC who were Christian exemplars.

Tallowood Baptist Church, Houston, Texas (1991–1996)

My arrival at Tallowood coincided with an intense debate occurring in Southern Baptist churches and other evangelical churches across the country. It had to do with the nature and style of corporate worship, especially music. The "worship wars" were between those who wanted "traditional" music led by organs, choirs, and hymn books and those who wanted "contemporary" music led by praise bands, praise music, and video screens. This is an oversimplification of a much more complex conflict, but it captures, and perhaps caricatures, what was a controversy in many congregations. It was a hidden conflict in Tallowood.

Tom Mosley was the beloved and respected minister of music, and he led worship in what many would call a "blended style." It included both traditional and contemporary elements, but he was silently pressured to maintain an even balance between the two. He did it in a masterful way, but always a hidden tension was present to move the church more in one direction than the other.

The growing influence of dynamic student ministries, like Louis Giglio's "Passion" conferences, and mega-churches like the Hillsong Church in Australia and the Willow Creek Church in Chicago was increasing and eventually would "win the day" in most evangelical worship services. The "worship wars" largely faded away because most churches adapted and changed, some with significant conflict, until a "contemporary" model prevailed. Those who chose a more traditional or liturgical style have become a distinct minority. Tallowood maintained a blended balance.

The vision that captured my heart at Tallowood emerged from within the congregation itself and the urban context in which the congregation is located, Houston, Texas. Houston is one of the most diverse and dynamic cities in the world. It is the fourth largest in America, the center of its oil industry, and the busiest port in America in terms of foreign tonnage. It encompasses over 650 square miles and has a population that is 40 percent non-White. The energy and synergy of the city is overwhelming, as is its heat and highway system. I had a love/hate relationship with Houston. I hated the traffic and the weather, but I loved the people and the diversity.

When I arrived, the church was strong and stable with a membership of 4,500 composed primarily of White middle- and upper middle-class professionals. It was also composed of four smaller language congregations that had their own pastors. All met in space provided for weekly worship, each in their own language: Hispanic, Chinese, Japanese, Korean. The children and youth of all five congregations were integrated into the Bible study program on Sunday morning and other church activities during the week. I viewed myself as Tallowood's senior pastor and viewed each of these four pastors as equals and co-pastors. We met regularly for prayer and planning on how to make Tallowood a multicultural congregation.

Our goal was that all five congregations would see themselves as comprising one church with a shared ministry. The most visible expression of this vision was, ironically enough, worshiping together on several occasions through the year, especially at Christmas. Under the leadership of Tom Mosley, we moved beyond "worship wars" and joined together in some amazing experiences of multicultural worship. With a combined choir and special ensembles, we offered ourselves to God, spent time learning each other's traditions, and developed a unity of spirit that transcended our racial and cultural differences. It was a little bit of heaven.

This developing unity made it easier for us to join together in ministry to a racially and culturally diverse city. Tallowood's urban mission initiative, administered and implemented almost entirely by laity, was a wonder to behold. It is no exaggeration to say that hundreds of our members engaged weekly in ministry to nursing homes, apartment complexes, and community centers. They repaired and built homes and offered clothing and food as well as medical services throughout Houston. Every Sunday school department had a mission leader. The church not only had a missions committee that dispersed considerable funds to mission partners but also had a missions development council charged with the responsibility of strengthening communication and coordination between the various mission outreaches into the community.

At Tallowood, music and missions became allies instead of competitors, and both grew because of it. We never completely broke "the color line" in attracting and involving African Americans in our congregation, but we were in the early stages of serious conversation, trying to discern what might be required of us if we did. I was happy at Tallowood and envisioned myself completing my active ministry as its pastor.

––––––––

One of the hopes I harbored in the recesses of my heart in coming to Houston from Atlanta was to heal from the bruising and battering I experienced in the SBC conflict of recent years. I especially felt the need for emotional and spiritual replenishing from having been involved in convention politics and in the early stages of beginning the Cooperative Baptist Fellowship. The SBC meetings in Las Vegas (1989) and New Orleans (1990) were difficult for me. My natural inclination is to avoid conflict and confrontation. I much prefer collaboration and cooperation, but for the better part of the previous three years I was immersed in almost constant conflict and confrontation with a fundamentalist coalition that was engaged in a hostile takeover of the SBC. After my defeat in two convention presidential elections, which was in itself draining and diminishing, I chaired the steering committee charged with the responsibility of beginning a new Baptist denominational organization. I was exhausted.

The renewal I sought did come during my time at Tallowood, and it came in a most unexpected way. What renewed me more than anything else was an introduction and immersion into contemplative prayer and several spiritual practices different than those from my own faith tradition. Rev. Melvin Gray, Rector at the Holy Spirit Episcopal Church, was just across the street. We became good friends and met regularly for prayer and conversation. I discovered a retreat center only a few miles away, "The Cenacle Retreat House," administered by an order of Catholic nuns who offered me hospitality and friendship. I visited them often.

Shortly after arriving at Tallowood, I conducted a revival at FBC of Charleston, South Carolina. Rev. Tom Newbolt, a former Catholic priest, was minister of education, and he suggested that I read William Clemmons's book *Discovering the Depths*. The book was published by Southern Baptists, and Clemmons was a respected Southern Baptist professor. His book was a helpful and significant introduction to the contemplative practices of Christian spirituality integral to Catholic, Orthodox, and Quaker traditions.

In my earlier years I had read extensively about prayer and spirituality from my Baptist/Reformed/Evangelical tradition, so it felt "safe" to read Clemmons's book, which was subtitled *Guidance in Personal Spiritual Growth*. This book awakened in me a receptivity to literature that could help me tend to my personal spiritual growth. In seminary I had taken a class from John Newport on "Christian Mysticism," but it was presented in such a critical and analytical way that I never really considered becoming an experiential student of the mystics. We studied various mystics with a rational methodology, comparing and contrasting them to one another and outlining the strength and weakness of each.

This academic approach to spiritual formation created a fear in me of anyone who wrote on prayer whose doctrinal or theological perspective was different from my own. The possibility that I might learn from spiritual masters even if we differed on subjects like baptism, the Lord's Supper, purgatory, and the status of the Virgin Mary was foreign to me. I did not grow up anti-Catholic, but I was guilty of a deep suspicion and reluctance toward all things sacramental. I remember hearing Baptist rhetoric that questioned the salvation of anyone who was Catholic. Clemmons's book removed a lot of my fear and suspicion. It also opened a door for me to learn about prayer from Christian pilgrims through the centuries whom I had largely ignored.

Tom Newbolt made another important suggestion besides recommending Clemmons's book. He suggested that I read the book slowly, only one chapter per day. He suggested that I read with an open heart to hear what the Spirit was saying through what I was reading. He recommended that I read not so much for information as for formation, not as much for rational analysis as for spiritual transformation. This kind of reading in itself becomes prayer, listening prayer. Since seminary I had become a voracious reader of books, theological books in particular. I devoured information. I consumed it. I enjoyed it. Now he was suggesting that I read with the simple and single purpose of listening to God.

My discovery and practice of contemplative prayer was transformational. The greatest transformation came from a new experience of God's love. It enabled me to receive God's love and rest in God's love in a deeper way than ever before. The fuel that causes the fire of prayer to burn is love. The passion that compels fervent prayer is love. The power that sustains persistent prayer is love. Ultimately and long term, we must not make prayer a way of life because of guilt, duty, or fear. We must love, and the more we love, the more we pray.

But we cannot love and pray without being loved. We cannot give love without receiving love. In fact, our love for God and for others is a result of experiencing God's great love for us. This is what contemplative prayer did for me. It taught me to open my mind and heart to God's self-giving love, to always be receiving love.

In the evangelical tradition of my youth, the emphasis of prayer was on talking to God. Even my quiet times were structured around saying the words recorded in the model prayer of Jesus: words of praise, adoration, submission, confession, and petition. My practice was to speak to God verbally or mentally, believing that God listened. Surely, this is valid and an important aspect of prayer, but there is another side of prayer. God wants me to listen. God wants to speak, commune, and communicate with me. What God wants to communicate most of all is how great God's love and grace is towards me.

The practice of listening prayer set me on a journey of almost daily discovery and introduced me to some pioneers of prayer who then became my mentors and teachers. Most of them were alien to my faith tradition. Clemmons's book introduced me to Thomas Merton, and though much of his writing was difficult to understand, I persisted in reading slowly and reflectively. In my visits to the Cenacle Retreat House, I discovered Henri Nouwen, the spiritual exercises of Ignatius, and the Desert Fathers. Several Quaker writers became spiritual guides to me, especially Thomas Kelly and Richard Foster. Other spiritual masters would follow, both ancient and contemporary, especially Thomas Keating and Basil Pennington, who taught me "centering prayer" as a way to pray beyond words and even beyond thought. Soon, I began to explore the spirituality of Orthodoxy, especially "the Jesus Prayer."

From all of these I learned how important it is to listen to God. I learned some new disciplines that helped me to receive, to release, to rest. I am still learning. I am still learning how to release to God my competitiveness and my need to be in control. I am still learning to surrender to God my anxieties and my ambitions and to abandon my temper and tongue to God. I still struggle with compulsions and a performance-based religion. Slowly and painfully, I began learning how much God loves me, treasures me, values me. This learning has created an incredible freedom and joy that brings forth both love for God and love for people.

The contemplative dimension has taught me to speak of prayer as way of life, which means that the act of praying cannot be separated from an attitude of attentiveness. It is a disposition that learns to listen, listens to learn, and, most importantly, listens and learns to let God communicate love. Prayer as a way of life involves a continuous receiving of what I need more than anything else in the world: the free and unconditional love and grace of God. I need to experience that love, realize that love, be refreshed by that love, and be healed by that love. I need that love all the time.

Several years later I wrote an article that described my discovery of contemplative prayer as a way to experience God's love.[4]

> David writes in Psalm 142: "I cry aloud to the Lord / I lift up my voice to the Lord for mercy / I pour out my complaint before him / before him I tell my trouble."
>
> How wonderful it is to be able to speak to and into the divine presence and unload one's mind of troubles and difficulties. Indeed, we are commanded, "In everything by prayer and petition with thanksgiving present your requests to God." There are other forms of spoken prayer: praise, confession, and intercession.
>
> However, there are times in life when words, whether framed audibly or mentally, are simply inadequate in the presence of the holy. We simply don't know how to pray as we ought, so we express to God in inaudible groans or sighs what is beyond words. Or perhaps we weep or laugh, or do both at the same time, as acts of devotion.

But there is yet another form of an inaudible prayer that nourishes and enriches devotion. Some call it contemplation. Others call it contemplative prayer or meditative prayer. This act is a deliberate refusal of words, as well as thought, in order simply "to be" in the presence of God. The presupposition behind such prayer is that human language confines God to our understanding and restricts the infinite to our finite capacities. So, at least for a time, one relinquishes all constructs and ideas about God so as to give attention to God, who is beyond all constructs and ideas. The only act required is a loving attentiveness to the one who is present.

This form of prayer is not the only one for a Christian, and I would not presume to say it is even the highest form of prayer. But it is a practice that has strengthened my conviction of God's reality, love, and mystery. It is a discipline that has deepened my faith in the one God as Father, Son, and Holy Spirit. Prayer without words has deconstructed many of my false notions and uncovered many places where I have needed healing.

I do not consider myself a mystic, and I am surely not a recluse or a monk. In fact, I am an extrovert and activist by temperament. But I've experienced great benefit from this practice and commend it as a way to help us find community. We live in a tumultuous time, a challenging time, much of which is caused by our own anger, greed, and fear. One of the results, to quote Rudyard Kipling, is that "we shout at each other across seas of misunderstanding."

It seems that we are bombarded with words. Everybody around us has an opinion they want to give. Everywhere are analyses, editorial comments, lectures, articles, sermons, and critiques. Words, words, words. They scream at us from television and the Internet: texting, emails, YouTube, Facebook, Google, Twitter, and Instagram—a continuous stream of information and ideas.

How difficult it is to be still and know God. How challenging it is to find a quiet center, to nurture that center and then live from that center. How hard it is to listen, at the deepest part of our being, for the still, small voice that brings assurance, clarity, courage, and compassion. How humbling it is to admit that perhaps we don't know the right answers, or that we don't even know the right questions. How can we promote unity between us when there is such little unity within us? How can we be instruments of peace when we experience so little of it in our own lives?

Another Psalm of David that seems appropriate for our day is Psalm 131: "My heart is not proud, O Lord / My eyes are not haughty / I do not concern myself with great matters / Or things too wonderful for me / But I have calmed and quieted in my soul / Like a weaned child with his mother / Like a weaned child is my soul within me."

My time at Tallowood was truly a renewing time. At first I spoke of that renewal discreetly and only to a few friends. I was aware of how much I had yet to learn and also that there is a temptation for pastors to speak too quickly of their own experiences when those experiences have not yet been adequately assimilated and absorbed. The church had a strong intercessory prayer ministry under the leadership of a good and godly lay leader, Donna Dee Floyd. I invited her and some others to the Cenacle Retreat House with me, where I shared what I was experiencing. The response was encouraging. Soon there would be more retreats, followed by sermons and lessons on spiritual formation.

Two other important lay leaders were Margaret Campbell and her husband Justin. Together they walked with me in my journey of spiritual discovery, and we began a planning process that resulted in an invitation to Richard Foster, the Quaker author, to come to Tallowood for a "Renovare" conference. Richard Foster had only recently founded "Renovare," a non-denominational effort to nurture prayer and spiritual renewal. Melvin Gray from Holy Spirit Episcopal Church joined me in offering the invitation to Richard and in preparing for the weekend event. It was a great success with 1,400 people in attendance. It would become a prelude to a national gathering of Renovare only a couple of years later at the Houston convention center, attended by more than 5,000. Margaret would later become the chair of the board of directors for Renovare, serving as a leader in a spiritual renewal movement across the nation.

When I left Tallowood in 1996 to become executive coordinator for the Cooperative Baptist Fellowship, I knew I had experienced a spiritual and vocational renewal. The church itself was responsible for much of it. They had been a responsive and loving community. The lessons I was learning about prayer and spiritual formation would not only change me but also go with me into the next chapters of life.

In Retrospect

Pastoral Leadership

During my years as a pastor, I saw enormous changes take place in congregational culture, denominational culture, and societal culture. I also experienced enormous personal change. But there were also some constants, some abiding truths that sustained and guided me. Since my background was so highly focused on evangelism and evangelistic outreach, I always considered my pastoral ministry as evangelistic. The churches where I was pastor were fruitful in baptizing new believers.

But from the beginning of my pastoral ministry, I was convinced that the calling and role of a pastor was different from that of an evangelist. I took seriously the responsibility of "shepherding" the congregations that were entrusted to my care. The guiding text and imagery for my pastoral leadership has been John 21 and the words of Jesus to Simon Peter, "Feed my sheep." These three words have been the "north star" of my vocational identity and practical ministry in all of the churches where I have been pastor, even though each church was different from the others and the culture has constantly changed.

Jesus said, "Feed *my* sheep." Jesus makes clear that the sheep belong to him. Christ is the head of the church. The church is not the property or possession of one person or one group of people. Christ alone is the great shepherd of the flock. There is a tendency in all of us to be possessive and controlling, to act as though we can set the agenda for the church. But if we realize that the church is owned by Christ, it affects how we live within it. The temptation is strong for a pastor to feel entitled or privileged and try to exercise control over what belongs only to Christ.

Jesus said, "Feed my *sheep*." Why sheep? Why refer to God's people as sheep? Clearly Jesus is drawing on the analogy from the Old Testament where Yahweh refers to himself as the shepherd of

Israel and to the people of Israel as the sheep of his pasture. But why sheep? It is because sheep must be cared for both as individuals and as a flock. In his most famous psalm, David makes a personal declaration: "The LORD is my shepherd" (Ps 23:1). Jesus, the chief shepherd, loves and cares for each individual member of his flock, just as God cares for each one of us as individuals. But the ministry of the pastor is also to care for the church as a whole, to provide spiritual nourishment to the whole congregation, not just one group or one segment.

Pastors must tend to the well-being of all God's people, not just a privileged few or the most gifted, talented, rich, or influential. The reason for the sheep analogy is that a flock of sheep is vulnerable to danger. Thieves can steal them. Wild animals can kill them. They can get lost. Sheep need a shepherd, and without a shepherd they will not survive. Similarly, the church needs pastoral leadership that cares for God's people, both as individuals and as a whole.

Jesus said, "*Feed* my sheep." For a shepherd to feed the flock means to provide what nourishes and sustains people in their lives with God. Pastors preach and teach the written word so that people can be nourished by the living Word, Jesus Christ himself. God's people need wise counsel and sound instruction from Scripture. They need to be encouraged, exhorted, and sometimes rebuked by the truths of Scripture. And the "feeding" is always to be offered in love, since members of the flock are not numbers or statistics, names on a roll, or demographics on a chart. They are beloved children of God. They are people redeemed by Christ. They are human beings indwelt by the Holy Spirit. This means that pastors must treat those in the congregation with tenderness and care because each has great worth and value.

This pastoral commission has been both the foundation and compass for my understanding of congregational leadership. It has grounded and guided other functions that I believe all pastoral leaders should provide. Pastors have many other responsibilities. They should equip the saints and do the work of an evangelist as well as perform a variety of tasks such as leading in worship, administering the ordinances, and organizing and overseeing ministries. But all responsibilities of pastoral leaders are to be fulfilled in a pastoral spirit and in compassion for God's people.

The Church as Organization and Organism

As a human organization, the church must structure itself to function and fulfill its mission in the world. Like other human organizations, it is imperfect because it is composed of imperfect people. I do not believe the New Testament is clear on exactly how the church is to structure itself organizationally. I do not believe there is one normative organizational pattern for the church that fits all contexts and all cultures for all time. History, it seems to me, has demonstrated this confusion as it has also demonstrated that the church can be an instrument of the Spirit in various organizational structures. At no place is this confusion more evident than in church governance.

I am a Baptist by conviction, which means I believe in local church autonomy. Any connection that a local church has beyond itself is purely voluntary, not mandated by a hierarchical system or structure that requires obedience. Baptist churches do connect with one another by forming themselves into denominational structures, such as associations, conventions, fellowships, and unions. But they do so voluntarily. And always the denominational structures cannot impose theological or ministry constraints on the local church. A Baptist church is free to choose its own minister, craft its own worship, and organize itself for ministry however it chooses, without interference from a bishop, synod, or presbytery.

Baptist churches, however, organize and govern themselves in a variety of ways. Some are governed almost exclusively by the pastor, who sees himself or herself as an "overseer." Some are governed by a small group of laity who form themselves into a diaconate, a church council, or an informal power structure of a few individuals. Still other churches are governed by a more democratic process with regular church meetings guided by documents such as a constitution and "rules of order."

I view healthy church governance as a blending of all three of these perspectives, with some necessary tension between them. The New Testament uses three words that form the basis for these different perspectives of church self-governance. The words are *episkopos* (bishop), *presbuteros* (elder), and *laos* (people). I believe that one can make a strong case for the theological legitimacy of each of these perspectives, but ultimately one must give preference to one of them.

The "clergy-governed" form of governance gives preference to the *episkopos*, requiring that the senior pastor or bishop or lead elder have final authority. The "small-group" form of governance gives preference to the *presbuteros*, requiring that the elders or presbytery or council have final authority. The democratic form of governance gives preference to the *laos*, requiring that the entire membership have final authority. I prefer the congregationally governed church, guided and supported by both other clergy and lay leadership. This is a cumbersome way of church governance, but it is based on a conviction that every member in the local church has direct access to God and should participate fully in the important decision-making of the church.

Throughout my years as a pastor, I embraced congregational governance but also embraced my role of assertive leadership through pastoral preaching, equipping of laity, and personal relationships. I can't say I always enjoyed church conferences and the conversations they generated, but I believed them to be essential for authentic congregational ownership of the church's ministry. I have never bought into the mega-church or seeker church model of governance because they feel more like a corporation or a well-run business than a family. Neither have I bought into a Roberts Rules of Order model of congregational governance because it feels more like governance in a political caucus or a city council than a family.

The church is much more than an organization. It is an organism. It is a spiritual, mystical reality unlike any other grouping. The church is a living, breathing community of people who are indwelt by the living Christ through the presence of the Holy Spirit. The New Testament word that describes the church is *koinonia* (fellowship or communion), meaning that we partake of and participate in a divine life with one another and with God. "Fellowship" means that we experience and enjoy human relationships in ways that transcend time and space, because the eternal God is in the making of them.

The closest human analogy to the nature of the church is that it is like a family, where people are bound together by biological kinship. But the church is different from human families because the church is not bound together by biological kinship but by a spiritual communion and covenant with the Creator and Redeemer God who is Spirit. The church is composed of individuals and families connected not by flesh and blood but by the eternal life within and among them.

Our fellowship with one another happens because we have fellowship with God. Our sharing in one another's lives happens because we share in the divine life of the triune God. It is a holy, sacred, and even supernatural dwelling place for the Spirit, an organism. As such, the church is a living tabernacle or temple through which the Holy Spirit works in mysterious ways. Among the many ways through which the Spirit works mightily is in the church's proclamation (*kerygma*), its teaching (*didache*), and its service (*diakonia*). These tasks are as important today as when the church began. They remain the unchanged tasks of the church that desperately need to be recovered and renewed, regardless of societal and cultural upheaval.

The church is entrusted with a message of good news, and the proclamation of the good news, *kerygma*, is a divine mandate. Some are especially gifted and equipped to proclaim, but the message and ministry of proclamation belongs to the whole church. And what is this good news? It is that the creator God loves the world and has acted in history to redeem it and reconcile it to God's own self. To that end, God chose, liberated, and formed Israel through whom he would reveal his character and purposes. When the time was right, God sent Israel's Messiah, God's only Son, to be the world's Savior and Lord. Proclamation of this message results in people repenting, believing, and being incorporated into Christ's church. The church, and the church alone, is charged with the task of proclaiming the gospel to the whole world. It must not refuse or neglect this task.

The church also is entrusted with the task of teaching and instructing all those who repent and believe the proclamation. This is *didache.* Again, some are especially gifted as teachers, but instruction in Christian discipleship is the responsibility of the whole church. And what is the teaching of Christian discipleship? Jesus commanded that we teach disciples to observe all the things that he commanded. This is what the apostles did to the new believers after Pentecost (Acts 2:42). This is what the Apostle Paul did in his missionary journeys when churches were formed with new disciples. He instructed them in the way of Christ. This is why Paul's letters and the letters from other apostles are included in our New Testament. They teach Christian disciples how to grow into maturity. The neglect or refusal to fulfill this task results in a church that is full of "babes in Christ," prone to error and conformed to the world's system.

The church is also entrusted with the task of *diakonia*, serving one another and everyone around us in humility and compassion. Just as Jesus went about doing good, so the church's mission is to do good and create good through service. Service in the name of Christ involves both acts of mercy and works of justice. Service in the name of Christ involves bringing "good news to the poor, freedom for those who are imprisoned, recovery of sight to those who are blind, and release for the oppressed" (Luke 4:18-19). Like Jesus was anointed by the Spirit for service, so are we anointed for service. Again, some are uniquely gifted for service, but the task of serving a hurting, broken world for its good is entrusted to the whole church. We can join with those outside the church who serve others, but even if no one else joins in, the church is mandated by Christ to be a servant to others.

In a time when the church seems paralyzed by analysis, uncertain about itself, and acting at times as if it is in near despair because of the onslaught of evil around it, we would do well to recover the apostolic vision of the church's nature and mission. The church is a living organism, a fellowship (*koinonia*) created for the tasks of proclamation (*kerygma*), teaching (*didache*), and service (*diakonia*). Transformation still happens when the gospel is proclaimed and taught, accompanied by selfless service. Now is not the time for pastors to lose confidence, boldness, or theological nerve. I only wish I were just beginning to be a pastor.

Meadow Lane Baptist Church
Arlington, Texas

First Diaconate
Meadow Lane Baptist Church

First Baptist, Dallas, Texas, 1970
Dallas Cowboys quarterback Roger Staubach, seated,
gave testimony before the sermon

"Our New First Family"
THE DANIEL VESTALS
Earlene, Bro. Daniel, Joel, & Philip

Southcliff Baptist Church, Fort Worth, Texas
First Sunday (bulletin for October 8, 1972)

First Baptist Church, Midland, Texas

First Baptist Church, Midland, Texas, 1976

Midland mayor honors Southern Baptist missionaries,
John and Martha Adams

First Baptist Church, Midland, tenth anniversary with
Dr. & Mrs. T. B. Maston with their son, Tom Mac

First Baptist Church, Midland, Texas, 1987
Philip, Joel, Daniel, Anne, Earlene, and Muffin

Dunwoody Baptist Church, Atlanta, Georgia

Dunwoody Baptist Church, Atlanta, Georgia

Tallowood Baptist Church, Houston, Texas

Tallowood Baptist, Camp Tallowood

Chapter 4

Southern Baptist Convention: Community and Controversy

In 1978, I stood on the floor of the Southern Baptist Convention in Kansas City, captivated and captured by a vision for world evangelization. Jimmy Allen, pastor of First Baptist in San Antonio, was the convention president. He embodied a dual passion for evangelism/ missions and social justice. He challenged the convention to fulfill "the great commission" and "the great commandment" in a way that stirred my imagination. Jimmy Carter, a fellow Southern Baptist, was president of the United States at the time, and he addressed the convention via satellite from the White House. We inaugurated an ambitious, and perhaps triumphal, effort called "Bold Mission Thrust," the goal of which was to mobilize all of the convention's resources to proclaim the gospel to every person in the world by the year 2000.

We inaugurated a two-year program modeled after the Peace Corp and titled "Mission Service Corp," which asked adults, young and old, to volunteer two years of their lives in mission work. The enthusiasm of Southern Baptists, including my own, was palpable. I stood on the floor of the convention and wept. As a young pastor, I promised God that I would give my life to this cooperative effort. I returned to Midland determined to use whatever influence I had to increase our financial support for world missions, and I determined to lead First Baptist in a way that would make missions the "stack-pole" of our programming.

It is difficult for those who never knew the SBC before the fundamentalist takeover to appreciate the affection and attachment that many of us felt for our denominational home. It was in many ways an extension of our love for our local congregations. In Baptist polity every church is autonomous and independent, so whatever connection or community it chooses beyond itself is completely voluntary. Growing up at Gambrell Street Baptist, I realized early the importance of that voluntary connection because of its proximity to Southwestern Seminary. The close proximity of the seminary and the presence of so many faculty and students were visible icons of the value of cooperation between Baptist churches. I would later attend that seminary with almost no tuition because of the support it received from the SBC.

I often heard missionaries return from their assignments and praise the SBC for its cooperative funding of salaries and ministries. I participated in retreats, conferences, and numerous events throughout my early life that were in some way connected to the ecosystem of SBC life. I heard sermons and lessons on the value of cooperation based on mutual trust and respect in spite of differences. I was persuaded that unity was better than division, shared decision-making was better than autocratic decision-making, and churches could do so much more when they worked together for a common good. The SBC was a meaningful and authentic community beyond my local church. So when I attended the SBC annual meeting in 1978 and saw the unity and energy around Bold Mission Thrust, my imagination was captured and I felt that a *kairos* moment had arrived.

Little did I realize that this gathering would be the last convention with a traditional Baptist to serve as its president and that events were already unfolding for a fundamentalist takeover. The takeover, or what is often called "the conservative resurgence," was a well-organized plan to elect fundamentalist pastors as presidents who would ensure that only those who believed in the inerrancy of Scripture would serve on the governing boards of all agencies. The plan, beginning in 1979 and continuing until 1990, was devised and directed by Paige Patterson (a pastor) and Paul Pressler (a lawyer). The plan was then implemented by a powerful cadre of charismatic pastors from Southern Baptist mega-churches: W. A. Criswell, Adrian Rogers, Bailey Smith, Jimmy Draper, Charles Stanley, Ed Young, and Jerry Vines, all of whom would serve as convention presidents. These were then supported by a host of lesser-known but equally committed "true believers" who were convinced that the convention had become liberal and that a "conservative resurgence" was necessary.

In the ten years between 1979 and 1989 (while I was in Midland), I resisted the takeover but did not become involved in any organized effort to defeat it. My resistance to the takeover was primarily born out of extreme discomfort with the methods and means by which the fundamentalists were seeking to make theological corrections in the seminaries. I myself had identified with the "inerrancy movement" because I believed it reclaimed a high view of Scripture and rejected what I felt was an increasing distrust in the authority of Scripture due to an overreliance on the historical-critical tools of biblical interpretation. The coalition that formed to implement theological changes in the convention, however, determined from the beginning that they would use secular political methodology to achieve what I felt should be accomplished through prayerful dialogue, honest debate, and wise corrections by administrators.

Both Paige Patterson and Paul Pressler recruited me to be a part of their efforts. Pressler came to Midland and encouraged me to participate. I refused, expressing my concerns about the organized efforts to "get out the vote" at the convention meetings and the harsh rhetoric used against professors who were labeled as liberals or non-Bible believers. Trying to use whatever influence I had, I urged cooperation and caution. I also refused to become involved in the counter efforts by traditional Baptists to "get out the vote" because I honestly believed the continuing conflict would die away. My reasoning, though faulty, went something like this: "Surely whatever theological problems we have are not so great but that reasoned and thoughtful conversation between individuals of goodwill can solve them." I wrongly believed that somehow, someway, we could find a middle ground of compromise and the passion for total control would subside.

Cooperative Program Study Committee (1981–1982)

In 1981–1982, I served on a select committee, appointed by the Executive Committee of the SBC, to study the giving trends and patterns of Southern Baptist churches and then bring recommendations that would increase the funding for missions. It was essentially a committee to fund Bold Mission Thrust. What was significant about my serving on this committee is that it introduced me to Adrian Rogers, pastor of Bellevue Baptist in Memphis and the first elected SBC president with the Patterson/Pressler coalition supporting him. Adrian Rogers was a larger-than-life personality, and I found myself in awe of his voice, his rhetorical gifts, and his charm as well as his ability to fill a room with his presence. He talked incessantly with no self-doubt or nuance in any statement he made. Adrian Rogers, more than anyone else, dominated the fundamentalist takeover of the 1980s. As we became acquainted, I realized how powerful a personality he was and how much influence he could exert.

He was always cordial and complimentary to me and knew exactly what to say when we were in a private conversation. A couple of years later I happened to be at First Baptist in Dallas, where W. A. Criswell was pastor, and also happened to be in a private conversation between Criswell and Rogers. Criswell, often called the "godfather of the takeover," was senior to Rogers in age and tenure, so Rogers deferred to him. Criswell, however, was well aware of the emerging power that Rogers was exerting and was extravagant in his praise and predictions of the future. These two men were the icons and titular leaders of a political/social/cultural "tidal wave" that swept over America's largest Protestant denomination and then over the nation itself.

Committee on Nominations for Boards and Agencies (1983–1984)

In 1982–1983, I chaired the SBC committee with the responsibility to choose the individuals who would govern all the SBC seminaries and institutions. I was returning home from a preaching mission in Brazil when I received a message in Miami to call Jimmy Draper, a prominent Texas pastor who would eventually become SBC president and then president of the Baptist Sunday School Board after the takeover was complete. Draper was chair of the Committee on Nominations, which had been appointed by the convention president. Our conversation was brief but pointed. Draper asked if I would be chair of the Committee on Nominations for Boards and Agencies. I was surprised. Evidently the Patterson/Pressler coalition felt comfortable with my being selected. I was considered conservative enough for them, and since FBC Midland was giving such large amounts to the Cooperative Program I was viewed as a denominational loyalist. I agreed to serve.

The Committee on Nominations for Boards and Agencies is a fifty-three-member committee composed of two representatives from each state convention. By 1983, the takeover was gaining momentum and had been successful for five consecutive years both in electing a president at the annual meeting and in placing fundamentalist trustees on the various boards. But the traditional Baptist leadership remained in place both at the executive level and the board level. The committee I chaired was almost evenly divided between the two factions, now called "conservatives" and "moderates."

This naming and labeling of the groups was itself a victory for the fundamentalist faction because, by any standard of measurement, the vast majority of Southern Baptists considered themselves theologically conservative. To be named a "moderate" implied half-heartedness or tentativeness in conviction, and to be named a "liberal" was simply anathema in Southern Baptist culture. Those who wanted to be identified as "conservatives" not only needed to be committed to an inerrancy view on the nature of Scripture but also needed to be a committed participant in the plan to place in leadership only those who held a similar view.

This meant that the selection process was limited to those who held one view on the nature of Scripture and then would ensure that those selected for any kind of leadership also held to that one view.

All others were excluded from participation in the selection process and the governing process.

This conflict was not just about theology. It was also about power and control. For me this controversy defined what constitutes a fundamentalist mentality and methodology. It excluded from meaningful involvement in the convention anyone and everyone who didn't agree with one particular view on the nature of Scripture. This mentality doesn't allow for any disagreement or dissent. Neither does it allow for significant involvement of those who hold differing views on the nature of Scripture. Even those who hold a high view of Scripture but choose not to use the word "inerrant" in defining their view of Scripture were excluded.

When our committee met in Nashville, it was clear that the composition of the committee was almost evenly divided between the two groups. Emotions were intense. Two representatives from one state had such animosity that they turned their chairs away from each other during the deliberations. Others were angry, frustrated, and hurt. I determined to chair the meetings as equitably as possible. When we brought our final report to the convention, I felt that I had done the best I could do in a difficult situation.

SBC Peace Committee (1985–1987)

In 1985, I was elected to serve on a twenty-two-member committee charged with the responsibility of bringing peace and reconciliation. Our purpose was "to determine the sources of the controversies in our convention, and make findings and recommendations regarding those controversies, so that Southern Baptists might effect reconciliation."

The Peace Committee was intentionally composed of individuals who represented different constituencies. I was chosen as a theologically conservative pastor who was politically nonaligned. I had resisted the "fundamentalist takeover" publicly and privately but had not engaged in any organized effort to stop it. If anyone came to the Peace Committee assignment with a sincere desire for reconciliation, it was me. And I honestly thought we could achieve that goal. However, after a year on the committee making sincere efforts and being "a man in the middle" reaching out to both sides, I realized that only one side really wanted reconciliation. I realized that the fundamentalists only desired control, total control, absolute control, and they wanted no participation except with those who had that same desire.

My experience on the committee was a difficult one, perhaps the most difficult one in my life. I began with the genuine hope that we could resolve differences and create some kind of "middle ground" where substantive changes would be made in institutions while the organized political efforts to elect the convention president each year would cease. At the time, I didn't think I was unrealistic, but in retrospect I realize that I was naive.

Each meeting of the committee began with prayer and devotion. Everyone was cordial and polite. As time progressed and as individuals spoke passionately, it became clear how deep was the divide and how strong were the convictions. Adrian Rogers dominated the committee and was relentless in his insistence that the only issue before the committee and the convention was that everyone agree to the fact that the Bible was "truth without mixture of error." He was insistent that no one, absolutely no one, could teach in the seminary or serve as a missionary or lead an institution who did not subscribe to that statement.

This then led to contentious discussion of what "truth without mixture of error" meant when it came to interpretation. No one could counter or debate with Adrian Rogers effectively except for Cecil Sherman, the singular most important leader in the moderate network and pastor of FBC, Asheville, North Carolina. Others were equally intelligent or academically credentialed, but only Cecil Sherman had the mental acuity and verbal skills to "hold his own" with Adrian Rogers.

On one occasion Cecil Sherman offered a commentary that sought to interpret the plagues inflicted on Pharaoh and Egypt prior to the exodus. He read from the commentary, which offered several plausible explanations of how the plagues might have been accomplished through natural phenomena. One example was that perhaps the blood running through the Nile River was caused by some change in the red clay on the banks. Adrian Rogers was incensed and said, "That's exactly the kind of false exegesis I'm rejecting, because it comes from a false understanding of the nature of Scripture as inerrant." At that point in the conversation, Cecil Sherman laid the book on the table and said, "These are explanatory notes in the *Criswell Study Bible* written by W. A. Criswell himself." It was one of those rare moments when I saw Adrian Rogers silenced. He smiled at Cecil Sherman, congratulated him for his brief rhetorical victory, and then proceeded as if it had never happened. He continued to argue why adherence to "truth without mixture of error" was essential.

On one occasion I raised the issue of the numerous discrepancies in biblical narratives that give historical record of the same event, such as the chronology of the temptations that Satan set before Jesus. Other examples were cited, but all were brushed aside as irrelevant and inconsequential to the fact of inerrancy. Any suggestion that Bible-believing Christians might disagree on interpretation was rejected and given as proof that such an interpreter did not believe in Scripture as "truth without mixture of error." The discussions were futile and frustrating, endless and exasperating.

The only time I felt that I made a credible recommendation that might lead to reconciliation was deep into the committee deliberations. I suggested that perhaps we try to clarify what "truth without mixture of error" might mean for today and particularly in our context. I suggested that some phrases might be helpful that affirm both belief in the historical and factual truthfulness of biblical narratives and belief in the miraculous and supernatural truthfulness of biblical narratives. When I made the suggestion, Adrian Rogers paused and pondered before a positive response: "This is good. This is good." For a brief moment I had hope that the committee could reach some kind of compromise. It might send a signal that belief in the truthfulness of Scripture requires belief in the historical and miraculous, while not trying to be so exact that such belief would stifle or limit serious interpretation.

It seemed that we might have a breakthrough. Then Adrian Rogers said, "This is good, but we need to give some examples so that people will know what we mean." At that moment I knew that whatever hope there might be for reconciliation was hanging in the balance. If we cited specific examples, then that automatically would preclude any interpretive differences and would necessarily force only one interpretive possibility. Without the examples, I hoped that the affirmation could be seen as a confessional statement that allowed differences in interpretation. With the examples, I knew that the affirmation would become another creedal statement requiring all interpretations to conform to the examples. Perhaps this moment wasn't as tense for everyone as it was for me, but for me this was a defining moment.

When Adrian Rogers began to write and then read the example, I cringed at his phrases: "the direct creation of Adam and Eve as real persons," "the attribution of authorship to the named author of all biblical books," "all miracle stories as supernatural events," "the accuracy of all historical narratives as they are written." Adrian Rogers looked at Charles Fuller, the chair of the committee, for approval, and Fuller responded, "That's fine with me." That was when I knew that any hope of finding theological common ground had passed. I knew there could be no theological compromise or any way the committee might bring theological recommendations that could be implemented with integrity. I was despondent.

Another defining moment for me had to do with the conversation about organized political activity within the convention. About halfway through the Peace Committee experience, a press conference was convened in Nashville to bring a progress report to Southern Baptists. I was sitting at one end of the table next to Winfred Moore, while Adrian Rogers was sitting at the other end of the table in front of fifty journalists. Adrian Rogers spoke extensively about the theological problems in the SBC and the need to address them. As he had done repeatedly, he insisted that the only issue facing the committee and the convention had to do with theology. An editor of one of the state Baptist papers asked if the committee had discovered any evidence of organized politics that might be contributing to the conflict.

Adrian Rogers responded with a straightforward denial that any such activity was happening. Since the question was asked to the entire committee and no one else seemed willing to counter Adrian

Roger's answer, I felt compelled to do so. I thought Winfred Moore would respond since he was the senior moderate leader who had only recently been defeated for the presidency. I whispered to him, "Someone needs to give another answer." When he did not respond, I did. My statement to the press was that if the political methods presently being used in the SBC were used at FBC Midland, it would split the church. These methods were not only inappropriate but immoral.

After the press conference concluded, the committee reconvened and Charles Stanley, pastor of FBC Atlanta, spoke directly to me: "Daniel, I wish you had not used the word 'immoral' to describe what is happening. You should have used the word 'inappropriate' or 'unfortunate.'" I then said directly to Charles Stanley, "Charles, I wish I could use another word, but I believe these political tactics are wrong, sinful, evil. I believe you could cause them to stop, if you wanted." It was a tense moment, and Charles Fuller called for a brief recess. Charles Stanley and I intentionally stood, made our way to each other, and embraced. I told him that I loved him as a brother in Christ, and he offered me a similar expression.

My words created a headline in many Baptist publications the following week. A short time later I received a letter from Paige Patterson threatening legal action for defamation of character if I did not retract my words. I quickly issued a statement of apology to Baptist news organizations saying that I did not intend to identify any fellow Southern Baptist as an immoral person. Only a couple of years later I was nominated for the SBC presidency, and I traveled extensively to meet with small groups and appeal for support. Since then, I have often questioned whether what I did was also "inappropriate" and "immoral." I have struggled and asked myself if there was any difference between what the Patterson/Pressler coalition did for twelve years and what I did for two years. These questions have haunted me, and I acknowledge that I am accountable to God as well as to others for my actions.

Bill Moyers Interview (1987)

The Peace Committee brought its final report to the St. Louis Convention in June 1987. I sat on the platform, almost numb after the Peace Committee experience, next to a trusted friend as the committee report was being given. I looked at him and saw that he was crying. He said to me, "This is not the SBC I have always known." And indeed it wasn't. Shared decision-making, open communication, and acceptance of diversity were gone. In their place was a political machine that governed committee appointments, trustee selection, platform speeches, and even floor debate.

I left the 1987 convention in a state of depression and grief. Our family had already planned a vacation, and I was never so glad to have a period of rest and renewal. As we embarked on our vacation, I sought comfort and direction, not for the SBC but for my own life. The answer to that prayer came in a new discovery of the biblical prophet Jeremiah. I immersed myself in his life circumstances and prophetic actions. Jeremiah became a companion to me for several months.

As much as any Old Testament figure, Jeremiah embodied and epitomized a man of personal and spiritual religion. But he also embodied social religion. He faced a disaster of overwhelming proportions. The very fabric of Judah's existence was being altered—governmental rule, societal institutions, economic patterns, and even family relations were being changed. The collapse of the monarchy, the capture and deportation of the leading citizens to Babylon, and the desecration and destruction of the temple altered the fabric of society. And yet Jeremiah refused to give up hope.

Jeremiah acted in a symbolic and prophetic way. He purchased the title to a piece of family property (Jer 32:6). It was a tangible demonstration of his faith and hope for the future restoration of his people. In what Jeremiah did, God was speaking to him, to Judah, and to me. And the essential message from God was that in times of social upheaval we are to have hope. Our hope is an anticipation of salvation and deliverance that only the God of history can bring to pass.

I found great hope from Jeremiah because he did not run from the present or try to escape the consequences of the past. From my immersion in Jeremiah in the summer of 1987, I knew that even though the denominational home that I loved was embroiled in what seemed to be a hopeless controversy, I could not quit, retreat, or give up. There was too much at stake. I returned home not knowing what was ahead, but with renewed energy and strength to use whatever influence I had to foster reconciliation.

In August of that same year, Bill Moyers, the respected journalist and TV commentator, contacted me about participating in a PBS documentary, *God and Politics*. He informed me that this documentary would explore the causes and consequences of the SBC conflict and would be broadcast on national television. He asked if I would agree to an interview and also asked for permission to video our worship service.

I took the request to the deacons and then the church, and they gave their blessing. Moyers brought his film crew and recorded the following interview:

Moyers: (Introduction of FBC Midland, with the visual of us sitting in the sanctuary)

Vestal: We have always disagreed. We've always been able to debate. Serious theological debate, I think, is healthy. But the difference now is that it's not enough just to try to influence one another. What's happening is that if you do not agree with me, if you do not believe what I believe, and even more than that, if you will not participate with me in changing these institutions, you can't really be a part of Baptists anymore. And that will destroy us, that will destroy us.

Moyers: Daniel Vestal earned his doctorate in theology from Southwestern Seminary and is pastor of the FBC in Midland.

Vestal: Put yourself in the place of a man who maybe has taught in a Southern Baptist seminary for twenty-five or thirty years. And let's say he does believe the Bible as the authoritative word of God and does teach in accordance with our statement of faith, "The Baptist Faith and Message." But say he doesn't like to use the word "inerrantist" in describing his position on Scripture. That man is often called a liberal or a non-Bible believer. His reputation is discredited. His name is slandered. That hurts, that hurts.

Moyers: You yourself are a theological conservative.

Vestal: I'm very much a theological conservative and have long believed that some theological changes need to take place in our institutions. We need some renewal, theological renewal. We need a return to some biblical fundamentals and basics.

Moyers: Then why are you not part of this [conservative] faction?

Vestal: Because I don't believe that you achieve the kind of renewal and change that needs to be made in the convention through these political methods. In other words, the end does not justify the means. It's our side against your side. We win, you lose. Now that may be valid in the world of secular politics, but I contend that in the work of the kingdom of God, there's no place for that.

Moyers: What caused you finally to speak out? What caused you to stand up and register your dissent?

Vestal: I listened to a tape that Judge Presser produced, in which he basically recounted the political plan and strategy that he set forth back in 1979. I listened to that tape and physically was affected. I couldn't listen to all of it at one time. It had such an emotional impact on me, causing me to grieve, to be sad. It wasn't that I heard anything different. I knew that this was going on. I heard that it was going on. But it was now that it was being stated in a rather triumphal, victorious kind of way. And I know the people who have been hurt and the lives that have been wounded and the reputations and careers and ministries that have been slandered and slurred. Good people have been called names because they wouldn't play this political game.

Moyers: So what's at stake?

Vestal: Well, the very meaning of freedom, in my opinion, is at stake. A great institution is at stake. A great denomination is at stake. The effectiveness of an institution to join together.

Conference on Biblical Interpretation (1988)

In 1988, I was invited to speak at a conference on biblical interpretation, sponsored by the six SBC seminary presidents. It convened at the Ridgecrest Baptist Conference Center in Ridgecrest, North Carolina, as the second of three conferences: A Conference on Biblical Inerrancy (1987), A Conference on Biblical Interpretation (1988), and A Conference on Biblical Imperatives (1989).

The announcement to conduct these conferences was made when the Peace Committee met at Glorieta, New Mexico, in October 1986 with all the SBC seminary presidents in attendance. These three conferences were announced as part of the "Glorieta Statement" issued by the presidents to demonstrate their strong commitment to dialogue, compromise, and reconciliation.

At the beginning of their statement, they wrote,

> We believe that Christianity is supernatural in its origin and history. We repudiate every theory of religion that denies the supernatural elements in our faith. The miracles of the Old and New Testaments are historical evidences of God's judgment, love and redemption. We believe that the Bible is fully inspired; it is God breathed (II Timothy 3:16), utterly unique. No other book or collection of books can justify that claim. The sixty-six books of the Bible are not errant in any area of reality. We hold to their infallible power and binding authority.

It was this statement, as much as anything else, that confused and angered Cecil Sherman, leading him to resign from the Peace Committee. I experienced this in a different way. I viewed the seminary presidents' statement as a sincere effort to bring the controversy to a close or at least move toward reconciliation. They also committed themselves to fairness in selecting future faculty, lecturers, and chapel speakers who reflected this confession.

The 1988 Conference on Biblical Interpretation was important for me because it featured one of the foremost theological scholars in the world on biblical inerrancy, James I. Packer. Packer was a reformed theologian from England and often cited as an example of the kind of teachers needed in Southern Baptist seminaries. He delivered three lectures and participated in a panel discussion. He was gracious in spirit and was well received by all who attended.

Packer had been a theological mentor and model for me in earlier years, even though I did not agree with his views on election and predestination. His book, *Knowing God*, had made a profound spiritual and theological impact on my life and ministry. I considered it an honor to preach at the same conference where Packer was presenting. One of his presentations at the Glorieta conference was on creation. At the time of the conference I was completing my own book on creation, which would become the doctrinal study book for Southern Baptists in 1989. I found both inspiration and encouragement at the conference because I was in general agreement with Packer in his views of Genesis. The following is an excerpt from my book, *The Doctrine of Creation*. It affirms what I believed then and what I still believe now.

> A summary perspective of Genesis 1–2 is that we have an account of the origin of all things. We shall see later how different people have interpreted these chapters and how differing perspectives view the details; but let it be clearly stated that these words of witness affirm God as the origin of the universe.
>
> Matter is not eternal. It had a beginning. The beginning is not the result of blind chance, a random process, or an impersonal accident. Rather, the beginning of the universe is the result of a personal and good God. The opening chapters of Genesis give us a theological statement of origin.
>
> However one interprets the witness of Genesis, the witness is that the origin of the universe was according to a progressive and orderly plan. Sequence, progression, and purpose are according to a divine design. The strong Hebrew words used in Genesis 1 describe God's activity. "Bara," the word for create (1:1, 21, 27), and "asah," the word for made (1:7, 16, 31), punctuate the narrative at appropriate times, making clear the definite word and action of God.
>
> In a brief fashion Genesis 1–2 offers a historical narrative of the origins of the universe, the earth, and humankind. Of course, understanding and interpreting the narrative are not simple tasks.

But they are not made easier by denying the authenticity or accuracy of the narrative. Neither is the task made any easier by calling it mythical, or legendary, or folklore, either in a technical or popular sense.

There is historical continuity throughout the early chapters of Genesis. The origin of the universe, the origin of evil, and the origin of God's redemptive purposes in Israel are introduced in these chapters. Genesis clearly intends to portray historical flow that is foundational to the entire biblical message.

Creation of the universe and particularly the creation of humans begins a story. That story is called history. Man and woman, as the crowns of creation and as moral and spiritual beings, had a beginning. Genesis 1–2 tells us of that beginning, and Genesis 1–2 is an account of the dawn of history.

Some persons would call Genesis 1–2 a prologue to history. Indeed some persons would call Genesis 1–11 a prologue to history. It is true that it is a prologue to the particular history of a particular nation—Israel (Genesis 12). But it is not a prologue to history itself. Questions of where humankind began, how and why there is sexual differentiation, and the origin of language and love are answered in Genesis 1–2. These questions relate to the beginning of history.

Some persons would call Genesis 1–2 primal history or primeval history because these chapters address the universal questions asked by all nations and all cultures in all times. Such a description is acceptable if, at the same time, we would describe Genesis as particular history or real history. The drama of redemption recorded in Scripture is rooted in space-time history. Some of the earliest heresies in the Christian church attempted to remove historical reality from Christ's person and work. Many attempts have been made to remove Genesis 1–2 from historical reality.

The history of redemption is a whole, unity. It is actual. Jesus never spoke of Adam and Eve by name, but he clearly believed the Genesis account of God's direct creation of male and female. Jesus quoted Genesis 2:24 as the foundation for marriage (Matthew 19:4-6). Paul built his whole theology of redemption on sinfulness from Adam and redemption from Christ (Romans (5:12, 18). He also argued for certain practices in worship based on the creation account in Genesis (1 Timothy 2:11-15). Luke's genealogical table traces the ancestry of Christ through historical figures all the way to Adam, linking the redemptive purposes of God to a continuance of time back to the beginning of time (Luke 3:23-37).

To contend for Genesis 1–2 as historical narrative is not to contend for a wooden or literalistic interpretation of the narrative. As we shall see, there is legitimate disagreement, even among those who hold to the historicity of Genesis, as to details of the account. What kind of literature it is, what may be taken as figurative and what may be taken as literal, and what structure the account assumes are all questions open to discussion difference.[5]

In Retrospect

Exclusion

During the 1980s, I witnessed a fundamentalist takeover of the SBC in which I saw no desire for reconciliation among those who considered themselves conservatives. I only felt a desire to conquer, to win, to exclude those who were considered liberals. What I experienced was a spirit that did not reflect the spirit of Christ—one with reconciliation and renewal as its goal. It was rather a spirit of suspicion, bitterness, and rancor. I heard too many sermons that scolded and castigated fellow Southern Baptists as being instruments of Satan to call it any kind of reformation.

I read too many articles and newsletters that cast aspersions on professors, denominational leaders, and even pastors to dismiss it simply as theological disagreement. I heard too many angry accusations and too much unkind rhetoric both in public and in private to call it "righteous indignation." I saw too much shrewdness and secrecy in planning and organizing to describe what happened as a "conservative resurgence." What happened was not only a takeover. It was a hostile takeover, full of bitterness and animosity. I saw little that could honestly be called "the wisdom that comes from above," which is "first of all pure, then peace loving, considerate, submissive, full of mercy and good fruit, impartial and sincere" (Jas 3:17). I know of too many careers that were ended prematurely and too many ministries that were damaged because of false statements. I told Paige Patterson after the St. Louis convention in 1984 that his political efforts had unleashed a spirit of division and destructiveness that no one could control. From the first time I became aware of the Patterson/Pressler coalition, I felt an unease, even a repulsion. It was wrong, misguided, and mean-spirited.

At first, I was assured that the controversy was all about theology, not politics. I was told that there were only informal gatherings across the convention that were for prayer and discussion. For a long period of time, I accepted these assurances as truth, but then I heard reports and rumors of a more organized and coordinated effort. Finally, I heard a recording by Paul Pressler in which he proudly chronicled how he had traveled extensively speaking to small groups and building support for the takeover. I became so emotionally and viscerally upset that I turned off the player to gather my composure. The recording devastated me. It was not only a clear statement of what so many had denied but also a proud and triumphal account that seemed alien to the way churches, or a convention of churches, should function.

The 1980s were a time of painful conflict within the SBC. My pain was the result of sadness, and then anger, at the fact that many good and gifted individuals were falsely maligned because they would not define and describe their belief in the Scripture by using the word or concept of inerrancy. They were not only ridiculed but were excluded from meaningful involvement and participation. They were brutally shut out.

As large numbers of Baptists were excluded, the SBC culture and ethos itself began to change. The change was so dramatic that it became unrecognizable to its previous character. It was becoming more and more authoritarian and rigid in its governance. It was becoming much too aligned with secular politics and the Republican party. As the largest non-Catholic denomination in the country, the SBC was becoming the most significant institutional platform for expanding the agenda of partisan ideology.

The SBC changed its doctrinal statement to exclude women as pastors, and it refused to welcome any church that called a woman as pastor. It changed its mission focus to an almost exclusive emphasis on church starting and moved away from a holistic missiology that included social ministry and social justice. It removed itself from the Baptist World Alliance, the only Baptist ecumenical body in the world. It lost its concern for Christian unity, interfaith dialogue, and other global issues such as climate change and world peace. Most of all, the SBC lost its vision and passion for unity in diversity and cooperative mission.

Church/State Marriage

Also during the 1980s and beyond, I witnessed a marriage of the American evangelical community to the Republican party and the damage it did to the Christian witness. Most of the activists and advocates in the fundamentalist takeover of the SBC aligned with Jerry Falwell, Pat Robertson, Ralph Reed, and the "religious right" to ensure the election of Ronald Reagan, George H. W. Bush, George W. Bush, and Donald Trump as presidents. At first, many of these SBC leaders were quiet about their alignment but later became more visible and open about it.

They were then followed by a new generation of Southern Baptist leaders who also aligned with Republican politicians: Jack Graham, James Jefferies, and Jerry Falwell Jr. Their endorsements and engagement in the campaigns of Republican candidates has played a significant role in American culture for the past forty years. It was the cornerstone of the White evangelical base for Donald Trump and his presidency. This is a great sadness for me.

In the Moyers documentary, evangelist James Robison was featured for his fiery endorsement of Ronald Reagan in 1980 at the Dallas "National Affairs Briefing." I have known and loved James Robison since we were both teenagers. I was preaching a youth revival Memorial Baptist in Pasadena, Texas, when James answered God's call to ministry. I have followed his ministry through the years and prayed for him often.

It was not until 2018, when he sent me a copy of his autobiography *Living Amazed*, that I knew about one particular meeting between SBC leaders and other evangelical leaders planning their endorsements of Reagan. James Robison recounts the meeting in vivid detail and describes the interaction between Adrian Rogers,

Charles Stanley, Bill Bright, Rex Humbard, Jimmy Draper, and others. James Robison was asked to meet with Ronald Reagan and encourage him to seek the presidency. He was also asked to arrange a "Washington for Jesus" prayer meeting.

> During that same time of prayer at the hotel in Dallas, Pat Robertson had looked across the table at me at one point and said, "James, I want to ask you something. We have a Pentecostal pastor, named John Gimenez, who wants to organize a Washington for Jesus prayer meeting on the National Mall. It's Pentecostal and charismatic."
>
> He turned and looked at Bill Bright, as well, and said, "Would the two of you consider joining with John, as tri-chairmen of Washington for Jesus, and make it a total-church prayer meeting? James, maybe you can bring in these mainline Bible Baptist leaders and Southern Baptists. And, Bill, with the Campus Crusade influence you've got all over the world, can we turn this into a real prayer meeting for the whole body?"
>
> I said to Bill Bright, "I'll do it if you will."
>
> "I will," he said.
>
> I looked at Adrian Rogers and Charles Stanley and said, "Do y'all understand our doing this?"
>
> When they both nodded, I asked if they would speak at the meeting, and they agreed. Jimmy Draper also said he would help, and he spoke at the rally as well.
>
> The night before the gathering on the Mall, in April 1980, I preached a service for the pastors at Constitution Hall. Maybe three thousand pastors were there, and I preached on spiritual unity and working together, which I was just beginning to learn something about. But it was a powerful message, and the whole place responded.
>
> Washington for Jesus drew something in the neighborhood of half a million people for a prayer meeting on the National Mall.[6]

I do not doubt the seriousness or sincerity of the men who participated in this prayer meeting, planning the endorsement of Ronald Reagan, or in the "Washington for Jesus" prayer rally on the National Mall. But I do doubt their judgment and strongly disagree with their actions. Their endorsement of a political candidate for public office was purposely set in the context of Christian worship and proclamation, giving it more credibility. These men viewed the world through the lens of their similar identities. They were predominately White, male, and privileged. They were conservative evangelicals in their theology, immersed in a faith-based culture with strong egos and significant financial resources. To be sure, there were some differences between them, but their similarities far outweighed their differences. It is little wonder that when these powerful and charismatic leaders gathered for a meeting, they would assume the collective mantle of what they perceived as prophetic action.

They identified their action as ordained by God. Perhaps it was. But what does that say to the rest of us, who as Christians support other policies and other politicians? Are we then against God's ordination? Shall we simply repent of our errors and submit to what they identify as divinely given revelations? Many equally sincere Christians, myself included, believed that Jimmy Carter's vision for America was much closer to the Sermon on the Mount and the social ethic of Jesus than was Ronald Reagan's. But even if that were true, it didn't give us the right to use our pulpits and positions of pastoral leadership to claim God's singular choice and anointing on Carter to be elected. And it surely didn't give us the authority to pronounce the judgment of God on those who differed with us.

For me, the problem with the "religious right" and "Christian nationalists," which from the beginning have been so closely tied to the fundamentalist takeover of the SBC, is that they identify their political, economic, and social ecosystem as the only Christian way or the only biblical way for America. This ideology is presumptuous in claiming that it speaks for God.

And then there is an even greater problem: it harms more people than it helps. It offends many non-Christians and those with no faith. It causes them to stumble and prevents them from truly hearing the gospel of the crucified-risen Christ. The offense caused is not from the gospel message itself but from the close alignment of the gospel message with a partisan political ideology. Christians have long differed on economic theories for civil society, on the structures necessary for effective government, on the justification for war, on the best ways to address social ills, and on many other political issues. And they will continue to do so. But Christians can and should agree on the message and ministry of the church: "For we do not proclaim ourselves; we proclaim Jesus Christ as Lord and ourselves as your servants for Jesus sake" (2 Cor 4:5).

Should Christians be engaged in politics? Yes. Should Christians be informed and involved in the social issues of the day? Yes. Should Christians use their influence to persuade and argue for causes and candidates they believe are best? Yes. But when Christians, or any other religious group, contend that their perspective is the one that God blesses and ordains, they are acting in presumptuous and dangerous ways. History is replete with examples where religious leaders have influenced political decisions with the conviction and pronouncement that their influence was from God. As I read history, I find these influences a "mixed bag," where at times it was good and at times it was bad.

The significance of the meetings and rallies that James Robison so closely chronicled is that they set a precedent and pattern for the next forty years. These events wedded a large segment of the Southern Baptist community and an even larger segment of the broader evangelical community to power politics. In the decades that followed, there would be many other meetings between evangelical leaders and secular politicians. Perhaps the subsequent meetings were not as significant as the first one, but clearly there has been a pattern and plan that has shaped American culture and divided the church during my lifetime.

These meetings have co-opted and corrupted the Baptist and evangelical witness for more than a generation. From them, millions of sincere evangelical Christians have been persuaded to believe that the core of the gospel is to save America from godless liberal politicians. I remember hearing Jerry Falwell say to a large gathering of pastors, "Pastors, your job is to do three things. Get people saved. Get people baptized. Get people to vote." There is a direct link from the DFW meeting and Jerry Falwell's "moral majority" to Franklin Graham's "Prayer March: 2020" in Washington, DC. These meetings were effective and instrumental in mobilizing the evangelical Christian community to endorse a presidential nominee and equate their endorsement with the gospel. What a tragedy.

These meetings, and the alliances they represent, have shifted the priority and passion of the church from world evangelization, formation of Christian character, nurturing of families, compassion and justice for the poor, and worshiping the triune God to partisan politics. As with all distortions of the gospel message and the church's mission, there is an element of truth in this distortion. Christians should be good citizens of Caesar's kingdom, but Christians belong to another kingdom, and their singular focus is to seek it, embody it, serve it, wait for it, and work for it. Christians should never substitute Caesar's kingdom for Christ's kingdom nor confuse the two. Rather, Christians seek and work for a day when Caesar's kingdom, in all its earthly manifestations, "will become the kingdom of our Lord and of his Christ" (Rev 11:15).

Also, the marriage of church and state confuses the power of the state with the power of the church. The state's power is coercive, even violent. It holds a sword that it can wield with impunity. The church's power is persuasive and peaceful. It too holds a sword, but it is the sword of God's word and Spirit that pierces the conscience. The tragedy of the "religious right" (or any other alliance that joins church and state together) is the delusion that the church accomplishes its mission with coercion and force. (In appendix D, I offer a sermon titled "Religious Liberty and Christian Citizenship" that provides an alternative to the marriage of church and state.)

Chapter 5

Southern Baptist Convention: A Failed Quest for Reconciliation

SBC in Las Vegas (June 1989)

My appearance on the Moyers program, which aired across America in December 1987, thrust me into a public spotlight I had not known. Even though my interview was brief, I received hundreds of responses saying, "You should do something more than you are now doing." Since I had not been involved in the moderate political network, I was at a loss as to what I should do. In February 1988 (only a few months after the interview and my arrival at Dunwoody Baptist), a press conference was scheduled in Nashville, Tennessee, to announce renewed efforts to elect a moderate SBC president. John Baugh, a Houston lay leader, called me and urged me to attend.

This was a crisis for me because I knew what attending the press conference would mean. I knew it would involve me politically in a way that I had not been involved. I prayed about the request and consulted with several friends as well as the deacons at Dunwoody Baptist. I decided to attend. The Nashville press conference was important for another reason, although at the time I didn't realize how important it would be. It was my first real encounter with John Baugh, another larger-than-life personality who would later become a dear friend and trusted mentor. He was responsible for convening the press conference.

Gus Niebuhr, a religion reporter for the *Atlanta Constitution*, was present. He asked me directly if I would be nominated as SBC president at the June convention in Las Vegas. His question was a total surprise. It was the first time anyone, especially anyone in the press, had said anything to me about political leadership. I responded by saying that I expected Richard Jackson, pastor of North Phoenix Baptist in Phoenix, Arizona, to be nominated again as the moderate candidate.

In only a few weeks I received a call from Herb Reynolds, president of Baylor University, asking if I would allow my name to be placed in nomination before the convention. Again, his call was a surprise. There was no person for whom I had more respect than Herb Reynolds. As president of the largest Baptist University in the country, he had enormous influence. He pledged his support if I would accept and suggested I take some time to consider. After prayerful deliberation, I consented.

My willingness to be nominated was motivated by the same desire that caused me to serve on the Peace Committee and appear in the Moyers program. I genuinely wanted reconciliation. I had come to the conviction that there could be no reconciliation without political reconciliation. I came to believe that there had to be inclusion of all Southern Baptists in the decision-making process. I made the open pledge that if elected I would purposely choose individuals from both sides of the controversy to serve on committees. I promised that an equal number of fundamentalists and moderates would be appointed. I promised inclusion instead of exclusion with the desire for genuine renewal.

I made the announcement of my decision to Dunwoody Baptist on Sunday night, April 16, 1989, and the church was supportive and encouraging. They paid for the reproduction and mailing of the message to all 36,700 Southern Baptist churches at a cost of $26,000. The mailing list was obtained by Rick Fisher, associate pastor. Church members addressed and stuffed the envelopes. Thirty-one deacons signed a letter that said,

> We would like to introduce to you someone who is very special
> to us, our pastor, Dr. Daniel Vestal. On Sunday evening in April,
> Dr. Vestal shared his heart with our church family concerning the

Southern Baptist Convention. It is our prayer that you will listen to the enclosed tape of that evening and read the transcript. We would further trust that what you hear and read will bring you to a time of prayer and meditation about your involvement in our convention.

I was fully aware that my chances of being elected in the Las Vegas convention were slim. Jerry Vines was an incumbent president and a popular mega-church pastor. The Patterson/Pressler network was much more organized than the moderate network, and the majority of Southern Baptists still believed the controversy was simply about defending the Bible from liberals. During May and June, I responded to a number of speaking invitations from pastors and laity who believed, as I did, that new leadership was needed to end the crisis.

When the convention convened in Las Vegas, a city I had never visited, I was at peace with my decision to be nominated but was not optimistic. David Sapp, a fellow pastor in Atlanta, nominated me as president. I lost the election to Jerry Vines by a vote of 10,754 (56.58 percent) to 8,248 (43.39 percent). It was a decisive defeat. I had already determined that if I were defeated, I would seriously consider another effort the following year in New Orleans.

At a press conference, I promised Jerry Vines my prayers and, when asked about being nominated again, I responded, "I wouldn't rule it out." Earlene was with me at the press conference, and our two sons, Philip and Joel, stood beside me. It was a bittersweet moment. I returned to Atlanta disappointed but not discouraged. Many were already urging one final effort. I had announced my candidacy only a few weeks before the Las Vegas convention, and it was thought by many that I should announce another candidacy in only a few months, giving me time to get better acquainted with Southern Baptist churches outside of Texas. In August, the Baptist Sunday School Board tried to fire its president, Lloyd Elder. Lloyd Elder was a dear friend of my family and former pastor of my home church in Fort Worth. It was yet another brutal example of how the fundamentalist leadership was discrediting and demeaning good people. That event sealed my decision to be nominated again.

SBC in New Orleans (June 1990)

On Sunday, September 24, 1989, I announced to Dunwoody Baptist that I would allow my nomination the following year in New Orleans. I acknowledged that it was unprecedented for any candidate to announce publicly so early, but I stated my conviction that we were living in unprecedented times. I told the church my desire to be open, honest, and transparent in all I did and not be coy and pretend an action that was not true.

The months between the two conventions were busy ones. I preached at the European Baptist Convention in Switzerland and at Southwestern Seminary for the campus revival. My book on creation had been published, and so I was asked to teach in a number of conferences and congregations. I asked four respected Baptist laity to counsel and advise me: John Baugh from Houston, Jim Lacy from Midland, Tom Purdy from Waco, and Carl Kell from Kentucky. Their wisdom and support were invaluable since I was embarking on a quest into unknown territory. I talked often with Phil Strickland, director of the Texas Baptist Christian Life Commission; David Currie of "Baptists Committed," a network of moderate Baptists; and Jimmy Allen, a veteran Baptist leader. I viewed myself as a pastor, not a politician, yet I was intentional in a year-long effort to garner votes for an election to a position of power and influence.

I also met with a number of groups throughout the year to explain my candidacy and my vision for reconciliation. One group was composed of the presidents of Baptist colleges and universities affiliated with the SBC. Herb Reynolds arranged the meeting. Not all forty-five presidents were in attendance, but a significant number were present. Although they listened intently, I never felt much concern or support from most of them. One group that did have concern were Southern Baptist missionaries. Finley Graham, a longtime missionary to the Middle East, collected signatures of endorsement from more than 300 retired missionaries and presented them to me in Dallas. The resolution urged Southern Baptists "to join us in supporting Daniel Vestal in his efforts to unify the SBC and to direct it again toward its primary task of world missions." It was an especially meaningful endorsement.

My message before the New Orleans convention was the same as that before that in Las Vegas: reconciliation. I promised again that if I were elected, I would make appointments equally between fundamentalists and moderates. I offered "A Plan for Renewal and Refocus in the SBC," titled "Mission 2000," that called for comprehensive mission strategy, theological renewal, focus on major social and moral issues, a repair of relationships, and a recovery of authentic spirituality. I received a joint endorsement from eighteen former state Baptist convention presidents. Hopes were high that perhaps this year would be different than previous ones.

On the night before the New Orleans convention, I spoke to a gathering of Hispanic pastors along with Morris Chapman, pastor of FBC, Wichita Falls, Texas, who would be nominated as the fundamentalist candidate. I knew Morris as a colleague in Texas, but we were not close friends. A few years earlier he had called me with what I thought at the time was a strange request. He told me he had heard about my being influenced by the inerrancy movement and he wanted some information. He asked if I would suggest some books and authors that he could read to help him understand what inerrancy involved. I suggested several resources and never heard from him again.

My defeat at the New Orleans convention on June 12, 1990, was even more decisive than in Las Vegas. It was the third largest convention on record with 38,745 registered messengers. Morris Chapman received 57.68 percent of the votes. I received 42.32 percent. This defeat was difficult to accept. I had worked hard calling on Southern Baptists to reject the takeover, preserve Baptist distinctives, and rededicate themselves to cooperative missions. Others had worked much longer and much harder than I had. Disappointment and discouragement were everywhere. The most divisive controversy in the history of Southern Baptists was over. The outcome was clear. The struggle for the soul of the SBC between two competing visions had now been determined. No moderate Baptist had the desire or energy to continue it. The SBC that many of us had known and loved was now gone. What were we to do?

A Call for Convocation (1990)

On the evening after the decisive June 12 vote, I had a reception in my hotel suite for friends from Dunwoody Baptist and FBC Midland who were at the convention. They graciously offered their affirmation and affection. Jim Denison, my successor at FBC Midland, was present, and I asked him to accompany me on a visit to Jimmy Allen, the leader of the moderate network, "Baptists Committed." We went to his hotel room well after 10 p.m. Jimmy was already in his pajamas. The one question on our minds was, what are we to do now? I had not seriously asked that question earlier, nor considered possible options if I were to lose the election. Perhaps that was naive, but I had been cautiously optimistic that the New Orleans convention would be the beginning of the end of the takeover. That was not to be.

I do not remember who first made the suggestion, but the three of us decided that I should call for a gathering of concerned Baptists to plan for the future and that the gathering should be soon. I was already scheduled to speak at a "Baptists Committed" breakfast the following morning, so we determined that would be a good time and place to issue the call. I returned to my room and completed my address at 3 a.m.

The one overriding emotion I had that Tuesday night was hope. Of course, I was sad and disappointed. But beyond that sadness and disappointment was a genuine conviction that God was at work. I honestly didn't know what ought to be done, but I felt that in the collective experience of Baptist people we could discern the will and work of God. It was clear to me, and everyone else, that resistance to the fundamentalist takeover was over. I felt it was providential that the breakfast was already planned for Wednesday morning. It provided the perfect place to call for a convocation and to ask for Baptists Committed to convene and plan for the meeting. Its purpose would be renewal, and in it we would find ways to cooperate for the cause of Christ. The following is a portion of the message I delivered.

> I tried for the better part of ten years to be a reconciler without being involved in the political process of the denomination. Since

the beginning of this controversy, I stood in the middle; and for almost all of the 80s, I sought to reach out to all sides to bring peace. That failed. The main reason I entered the political arena and sought the presidency of the SBC last year and again this year was because I hoped it would give me a platform to work for reconciliation and renewal. That failed.

The election this year in New Orleans was not about who believes the Bible as the word of God. I believe the Bible is the word of God. Our presidents, administrators, professors, and denominational employees believe the Bible is the word of God. Rather the election this year was about our mission for the future—whether or not we will forge a united and inclusive denomination for world missions. On June 12, 1990, that vision failed. And to say that I am not disappointed would be dishonest. I am deeply disappointed.

Why did it fail? Why did we lose the election? I confess to you that I don't have all the answers. I've searched and questioned, but I am not emotionally or intellectually prepared at this time to offer an analysis. But this I do know: what we did was right. I will not say that everything we did was perfect, but it was right. We spoke to the issues that are crucial to our day: openness, fairness, missions, trust, and freedom. We resisted a political movement that excludes people from decision-making, assassinates people's character, questions people's integrity and commitment to the word of God. We resisted it, and we responded: it's wrong, it's wrong, it's wrong. We called for a return to Baptist distinctives: the priesthood of the individual believer, religious liberty, separation of church and state. We called for a return to our Southern Baptist heritage: cooperative missions, unity in diversity. . . .

Let me appeal to those who voted for Daniel Vestal and have resisted the movement that now controls the convention. Practice Christian charity. Focus your faith in Jesus Christ as Lord, and God as the sovereign One in creation, redemption, and history. Restore your faith in the Holy Spirit as comforter, enabler, and guide. Be hopeful about hope-filled tasks that God gives you.

I read recently about a tablet in an old English church that read, "in the year 1652 when throughout England, all things sacred were either profane or neglected, this church was being built by Sir Robert Shirley Bart, whose special praise is to have done the best of things in the worst of times, and to have hoped them in the most calamitous." Now is not the time to despair. Go back to where you live and work, and fill your life with hope-filled tasks.

Let me appeal to Baptists Committed to provide a forum soon where representative and interested individuals can meet for formal discussions about the future of Southern Baptists. I would like to ask this organization through its executive committee to initiate a retreat or conference to invited participants, but open to the press and interested observers, to discuss and deliberate the future of the denomination. I would like to ask that such a meeting occur before the fall, and I personally would like to participate in it.

More than 800 gathered for breakfast on the morning of June 13. It was a sober event. I remember the almost immediate response to the call for a convocation. It was a resounding affirmation that the time had come to move beyond political contest and theological debate. We somehow realized that the time had come to forge the future, to act instead of react, to find ways to cooperate without sacrificing our Baptist distinctives. We all felt the need for a collective and corporate experience that would seek renewal. I was tired of the conflict. All of us were tired. We needed ways to be healed and to give healing. We needed a place to be accepted for who we were, true followers of Christ with a worldwide mission vision. We knew we were Baptists who believe in the Bible but also believe in the freedom to interpret it. We needed a time to celebrate those convictions, a place to deliberate together on how to implement them into action. I left New Orleans weary yet confident of God's leadership.

In the following weeks, I received numerous letters expressing grief, piercing analysis, and hope.

Bill Blackburn from Texas: "A dangerous spirit has invaded the SBC. It is a spirit of power politics, the end-justifies-the-means ethics, and attempts to cover unholy behavior with the smokescreen of holy talk."

Nora Padgett from Tennessee: "I've been a Southern Baptist for more than half a century. I've never experienced darker days for our denomination. So many individual and group actions that are contrary to the Christian way of life: persons assuming the 'authority' to judge who is a 'Bible believing' Baptist."

Peter Rhea Jones from Georgia: "I feel exceedingly disenfranchised today. The message that I kept getting from the platform where we had no voice was as follows: We are entirely right. You are altogether wrong. We do not really want you."

Larry Baker from Louisiana: "Entrenched power and established political machines don't simply give up and their grip is not broken easily."

Foy Valentine from Texas: "Baptists everywhere can stand at peace with God for having tried to stop the fundamentalist evil. Thus far, we have failed. We can be sure, however, that Romans 8:28 has not been repealed."

Robert Ferguson from South Carolina: "New Orleans has represented a watershed for me, and now I am committed to facing the future confidently and to gathering with those of like mind and spirit in determining the future."

B. J. Martin from Texas: "One of my early lessons in Southern Baptist life was that our strength came from our diversity. I was preaching my belief in God's perfect word before some of these were born, and I resent their implications that I do not believe the Bible as firmly as they do."

In Retrospect: The Success of the Fundamentalist Takeover

Why was the fundamentalist takeover successful? To this question there are multiple answers. The fundamentalists themselves interpreted their success as a result of God's will. James Hefley's multi-volume account of the controversy is titled *The Truth in Crisis*, and he argues that the outcome happened because "the" truth, championed by fundamentalists, triumphed over the falsehood championed by moderates. Paul Pressler, a primary architect of the takeover, wrote much of the same in his book, *A Hill on Which to Die: One Southern Baptist's Journey*.

Baptist scholars from several disciplines have interpreted the controversy in different ways. Bill Leonard, a church historian, authored the popular book, *God's Last and Only Hope: The Fragmentation of the SBC*. He describes how cultural and historical factors converged to hasten the fragmentation already taking place. Unity in the SBC had been a grand compromise for a long time, held together by a theological "middle way," shared regional and cultural values, a few effective denominationalist leaders, and a successful programmatic and financial plan. With the takeover, the compromise no longer worked. Nancy Ammerman, a sociologist, wrote *Baptist Battles: Social Change and Religious Conflict in the SBC*, in which she chronicles the history of the conflict and offers extensive sociological research based on data collected from numerous surveys and questionnaires. Bruce Gourley's book *The Godmakers: A Legacy of the SBC?* contends that the SBC had created gods from its own cherished ideas that became ultimate realities guiding behavior. What happened in the 1980s was the result of 150 years of "overt racism, 'southernness,' and organizational arrogance." Gourley's interpretation is similar to that in Luther Copeland's book, *The SBC and the Judgment of History: The Taint of Original Sin*.

Rob James along with Gary Leazer and James Schwopes authored *The Fundamentalist Takeover of the SBC*, giving a concise historical account of events between 1979 and 1990. Carl Kell and Raymond Camp analyzed the rhetorical power of fundamentalist preachers in the takeover. In *Anatomy of a Schism: How Clergywomen's Narratives Reinterpret the Fracturing of the SBC*, public and practical theologian Eileen Campbell Reid interprets the conflict through the narratives of five clergywomen who provide a gendered, psychological, and theological way to understand what happened. Their stories also show how clergywomen reflected and navigated the Baptist struggles and then shaped an emerging renewal of understanding of what it means to be a minister, Baptist, and human.

A common thread runs through all of these accounts and analyses, the first of which is that the roots of the controversy we experienced go down deep in Southern Baptist soil and extend decades into its history. Serious stresses and tensions were pulling the denomination apart: theological, cultural, regional, social, and racial. Perhaps it is amazing that the SBC "held together" as long as it did. With the hindsight of more than three decades, I offer some of my own observations on why the takeover was successful.

First, the organized political network of the fundamentalists was effective. Perhaps it was more effective than they expected, but it accomplished what was intended. It mobilized thousands of Southern Baptists to come to conventions and vote. This required grassroots campaigning by Paul Pressler and many others. The network was inspired and motivated by numerous publications mailed regularly to Southern Baptists. These publications distributed information, and disinformation, that fueled the fire of political passion. This network also required money, and in ways that are unknown to me, it was able to secure a lot of money.

Second, what was happening in the SBC was also happening in America. Ronald Reagan defeated Jimmy Carter in 1980 and was reelected in 1984 with the help of Jerry Falwell, Pat Robertson, Ralph Reed, "the Moral Majority," and many of the same pastors who led the SBC takeover. The secular political culture was also poisoned by false accusations and fear, charismatic personalities, grassroots organization, and money. It resulted in a takeover of the Republican party by the "religious right" and success in subsequent elections.

Third, the power and persuasion of charismatic mega-church pastors and televangelists contributed to the success of the takeover. A pastor's conference convened on Sunday evening and all day on Monday before the SBC annual meetings. It featured the appearances of gifted fundamentalist preachers like Adrian Rogers, Charles Stanley, Ed Young, Jerry Vines, Jimmy Draper, James Robison, W. A. Criswell, and others. Few, if any, moderate pastors had the rhetorical ability to communicate as effectively, and they were never given a significant platform to do so.

Fourth, the narrative and message of fundamentalists was more singular and compelling than that of the moderates. Fundamentalists had one central message they repeated over and over: "We believe the Bible is the inerrant word of God." Every sermon, every speech, every article focused on the defense of the Bible and an attack on anyone who appeared to be a threat to belief in the inerrant Bible. Moderates had multiple narratives—freedom of conscience, priesthood of the believer, cooperative missions, church/state separation, denomina-tional survival. Our fragmented message was simply no match for a singular narrative.

Fifth, some, though not all, SBC leaders prior to 1979 were insensitive and indifferent to theological and biblical concerns at the grassroots level. Fundamentalists tapped into an anxiety that had been growing for several years. I heard too much anecdotal evidence to dismiss it. Institutional distrust has always existed in Southern Baptist life, but as the SBC grew in size and strength, so did the smugness and self-assurance of some of its leaders. They simply could not imagine that what was being threatened by the fundamental-ists could happen. They were out of touch with a large segment of Southern Baptist culture.

Other factors working in the 1980s were harbingers of what lay ahead. These factors might not explain why the fundamentalists succeeded, but they at least help me see the controversy through a different lens now than I could at the time.

First, the decline of centralized denominations in the American religious experience was beginning, even though at the time it was not obvious. Only a few months after the New Orleans convention, Nancy Ammerman, a respected sociologist and author, addressed the Alliance of Baptists, an earlier moderate breakaway group.[7] She perceptively described the SBC as the most "connectional" denomi-nation in America, despite its contention of local church autonomy and democratic practices at the convention level. She pointed out that Southern Baptist churches were amazingly similar in their alle-giance to Southern Baptist programs and ministries. However, such a strong connectional tie was beginning to wane, even though few could see it. Those who orchestrated the fundamentalist takeover promised that the denominational ties would flourish into the future and usher in a great revival because of the takeover. Of course, that didn't happen.

What has happened in the next thirty years was the exact oppo-site, just as Nancy Ammerman predicted. Local churches discovered new freedoms and are increasingly making new choices about how they will spend their missions money and where they will order their

Christian education literature. The denomination can no longer assume automatic allegiance. Denominations are not only declining, including the SBC, but are also increasingly irrelevant to a multitude of congregations. This was not evident at the time of the takeover, but the diminishing of denominations was at work in the 1980s.

Another factor both influencing and being influenced by the fundamentalist takeover in the 1980s was a burgeoning polarization in American culture. The public rhetoric used by the fundamentalists against the moderates was ugly, mean-spirited, and demeaning. The moderates were surely not without excess in their rhetoric, but nothing compares to fundamentalist diatribes against moderates as "skunks," "secular humanists," "heretics," and "instruments of Satan." This rhetoric was similar to the secular political rhetoric of the 1980s, when advocates for freedom of choice for pregnant women were called "baby killers" and AIDS was described as God's judgment on America for homosexuality. Harsh pronouncements that went beyond disagreements of conscience or intense debate were to become increasingly common in a polarized America. The language from the SBC was ugly, and it became part of a culture of ugliness in public discourse.

Yet another factor at work in the 1980s that becomes even more evident in the years following was the widening difference between fundamentalists and moderates on multiple issues: the role of pastor, women in ministry, separation of church and state, and mission methodology. Before 1979, a broader consensus existed on the priority of mission, helping Southern Baptists to hold together while allowing for differences. This consensus, "a rope of sand," was encouraged across theological, cultural, and geographical differences. The conflict of the 1980s fed a growing divide that took priority over mission consensus.

A final factor at work in the 1980s was a growing accommodation to authoritarian and autocratic rule in SBC life. Because of fear that the Bible was being abandoned, many good Southern Baptists were willing to give up on treasured ideas such as freedom of conscience, thoughtful dialogue, and civil discourse and embrace an enforced conformity administered by a few. If coercion was necessary to preserve theological integrity, so be it. If our siblings in Christ who had devoted their lives to SBC ministries needed to be fired and humiliated, so be it. More and more Southern Baptists became comfortable with an authoritarian and autocratic way of governance. The human and institutional consequences of that autocratic rule were dramatic.

Southern Baptist Peace Committee, 1985–1987

Bill Moyers Interview for PBS, December 1987

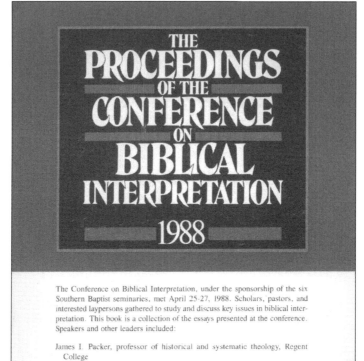

The Conference on Biblical Interpretation, under the sponsorship of the six
Southern Baptist seminaries, met April 25-27, 1988. Scholars, pastors, and
interested laypersons gathered to study and discuss key issues in biblical interpretation. This book is a collection of the essays presented at the conference.
Speakers and other leaders included:

James I. Packer, professor of historical and systematic theology, Regent
    College
Robert Johnston, dean, North Park College and Theological Seminary
Walter Kaiser, dean and professor of Old Testament, Trinity Evangelical
    Seminary
Grant Osborne, professor of New Testament, Trinity Evangelical Seminary
Ken Hemphill, pastor, First Baptist Church, Norfolk, Virginia
Richard Jackson, pastor, North Phoenix Baptist Church, Phoenix, Arizona
Jon Stubblefield, pastor, First Baptist Church, Shreveport, Louisiana
Daniel Vestal, pastor, First Baptist Church, Midland, Texas
Jerry Vines, co-pastor, First Baptist Church, Jacksonville, Florida

BROADMAN PRESS

COVER DESIGN: STEPHEN SMITH   ISBN: 0-8054-6005-5

Conference on biblical interpretation, 1988 (back cover)

Southern Baptist Convention, 1989, Las Vegas,
News Conference with Philip and Joel

Breakfast Gathering during the Southern Baptist Convention,
1990, New Orleans, during which I called for a
Convocation for Concerned Baptists

Chapter 6

Cooperative Baptist Fellowship: A Quest for Renewal

Convocation for Concerned Baptists (1990)

The ten weeks after New Orleans were weeks of anticipation and uncertainty. I received many letters with advice and counsel, condemnation and praise, anger and hope, fear and faith. Everybody had an opinion about what had happened, but no one knew what would happen next. Baptists Committed, under the leadership of Jimmy Allen, began immediately to implement the daunting and awesome challenge of putting together a national Baptist meeting in a time of crisis. What soon became apparent was that the meeting was to be larger than we first anticipated. In my initial challenge I called for "a forum where representatives and interested individuals" could meet for formal discussion. The plan was that it be for "invited participants, but open to the press and interested observers." Early in the planning stage, it was wisely decided to have an open meeting for any and all Baptists who wanted to attend.

The goal and intent of the intense planning was to devise a consultation that would provide opportunity for dialogue and discussion. For so long the closed and authoritarian environment of the SBC had stifled shared decision-making. For so long people had been subjected to decrees, manipulation, and criticism. Many were wounded and hurt, but all the while longing for freedom, cooperation, and unity.

The desire in planning was a format that combined worship, workgroups, state meetings, and plenary sessions. A schedule was set to balance large-group and small-group meetings, celebration and conversation, regional and non-regional fellowship. We sought diligently to have geographical, ethnic, gender, and vocational balance in leadership. We structured a setting where Baptists could address themselves to the crucial concerns for future witness: funding, missions, evangelism, theological education, ethics, public policy, and literature. We wanted to have genuine dialogue on legal issues, alternate information systems, local church and denominational relations. Hence, the idea was to have workgroup sessions and then reflections of those workgroups in the plenary sessions. We realized people wanted to talk to each other and listen to each other, to hear and be heard. So the meeting was planned, not knowing the outcome, with an emphasis on process and participation.

Many worked, planned, and sacrificed to prepare for the meeting that would eventually give birth to the Cooperative Baptist Fellowship. But one person deserves special credit. Oeita Bottorff was the chief architect of what was for me a "kairos" moment, a once-in-a-lifetime experience. She, more than anyone else, anticipated the significance of this event and labored to ensure that the details and logistics were tended to so that the movement of God's Spirit could be expressed in concrete action.

On the morning of August 23, 1990, I sat at a breakfast table with Oeita and two other friends, Jimmy Allen and Phil Strickland, finalizing plans for the consultation. What I remember distinctly about that breakfast was an experience recounted by Phil Strickland from Texas. Earlier that week Phil had been in conversation with some social service professionals and told them of his plans to attend the highly publicized gathering in Atlanta. One of them asked, "Do you realize the significance of that event?" Phil responded, "I know there will be a gathering of Baptist folk coming to discuss their future."

The next sentence in the conversation stopped Phil short. And at this point in his recount, Phil—not an emotionally expressive person—began to weep as he told us what she predicted: "You're going to a meeting in Atlanta that has to do with the renewal of the

Christian church in America." I desperately needed to hear that word of affirmation.

I then left the breakfast and walked down the street to where we would meet in only a few hours. There wasn't a person in the room. I suddenly felt afraid and asked myself, "What in the world have we done in planning this event?" Slowly people began to assemble. At 1 p.m. Jimmy Allen convened "The Convocation of Concerned Baptists" at the "Inforum" in Atlanta. As he did so, he too wept. The atmosphere was electric, and we sensed that we were at a historic juncture. The theme for the event was "For Such a Time as This." I delivered the opening address, beginning with the following:

> Why are we here? We're here to help, not hurt; to heal, not wound; to unify, not divide; to focus on the future, not the past. We're here to encourage each other, learn from each other, pray for each other, and listen to the voice of God through each other. We're here as Southern Baptist Christians to find ways we can get on with the work of God's kingdom, to spread the gospel of Jesus Christ, to minister to a hurting, hungry world, to be the people of God in our day.
>
> In a sense were here because we've been driven here, but also because we choose to be here. We've been driven here by a group of folks who have told us they don't want us to work with them in the cause of Christ. They call their movement the "conservative resurgence," and they have said for twelve years that if you don't believe in that resurgence and won't work for it, you have no place among them.
>
> They have not only maligned good and godly people, but they have caricatured and misrepresented them. They would take away our dignity and our freedom. I, for one, will not allow that to happen to me. I, for one, will not give that up. And so, in a sense I'm driven here to find people who respect me even if they disagree with me, and will allow me to cooperate with them in the grand and glorious cause of Christ.
>
> But do not pity me, for I also choose to be here. I choose because I believe in some principles and precepts that are foundational to my life: priesthood of the individual believer, religious liberty and separation of church and state, cooperative missions

based on the autonomy of every church, congregational polity, and moral integrity in decision-making. I am first and foremost committed to Jesus Christ. In that commitment, I believe in some principles and truths that are not only Baptist but biblical and Christian as well. The reason I have been a Southern Baptist is because this denomination has represented and embodied those principles. But now this denomination has not only abandoned those principles but is acting in violation of them. I am more committed to Christ and the principles of his kingdom than to any human institution.

I do not believe I have left the SBC, but rather the SBC has left me. But even more significant, it has left these basic foundational truths. I still believe in much of our missionary enterprise. I still believe in many of our institutions and ministries. So I'm looking for ways to support that mission enterprise and those institutions and ministries without violating these basic foundational truths. So why are we here? We're not here to form a new denomination. We're not here to plan political strategy. We're not here to wish anyone ill will or harm. We are here to explore how we can cooperate with each other for the cause of Christ in ways that do not violate our conscience or the principles that inform our conscience.

During the three-day convocation, more than 3,000 Baptists did indeed explore ways to cooperate with each other for the cause of Christ. We adopted an alternative funding plan, "The Baptist Cooperative Missions Program, Inc" (BCMP). We elected a sixty-member Interim Steering Committee and charged them with the responsibility to plan for another gathering the following year. I was elected chairperson.

Prior to the Atlanta Convocation in August 1990, the widespread feeling was one of uncertainty. During the convocation, the pervading atmosphere was one of joy, and afterwards the general mood was positive and hopeful. Personally I was elated. The three days in Atlanta exceeded my every expectation. It was the most exhilarating Baptist gathering I had ever attended. And I did not know I would serve as chairperson for the Interim Steering Committee until my name was called at the end of the event.

It is difficult to communicate the spiritual and emotional "pulse" of a gathering such as the Atlanta Convocation. Nothing about it was typical of previous meetings we had attended. Part of that was because of the context and circumstances of the past decade. An almost palpable momentum and anticipation for this event had been building since New Orleans, which was in itself an emotional event. Individuals and delegations came from thirty states with different experiences and expectations. Some came with anger and fear but did not want to sever ties to the SBC. Others had already moved beyond those emotions and were ready to do something bold and brave.

Nearly everyone arrived with some reservation because our ability to trust had been damaged by the takeover. Everybody had an opinion, an idea, a perspective; and it seemed that everyone wanted to express them. But pervasive throughout the meeting was a spirit of welcome, of hope, of gladness. It was like a family reunion where we were meeting cousins and aunts, some whom we knew well and some whom we had never seen. There were tears and hugs. Before and after plenary sessions, the halls were filled with lively conversation and laughter. The workgroups and regional gatherings were characterized by lively discussion, even disagreements. But it was healthy discussion where we each could be heard.

Both the secular and religious press gave extensive coverage to the convocation. The *New York Times* described the event as having "an air of finality on the end of a church's eleven-year battle," and concluded their coverage with these words: "Although those gathered here were moderate to very conservative in their theology they spoke warmly of a diversity of views, rejecting the concern of the denomination's leadership that constant vigilance was required lest traditional beliefs be watered down." The *Wall Street Journal* wrote, "Dissident Southern Baptists voted overwhelmingly to set up their own budget and government, in moves that fell just short of secession from the SBC at an unusual three-day meeting here." The *Christian Century* described Southern Baptist moderates as "aggressively responding to fundamentalists' takeover of their denomination," and then cited one specific incident: "During the final worship service, one woman remarked through her tears, 'Now I think I can remain a Baptist.'"

The *Atlanta Constitution* described the serious issues involved in what was happening:

> That the SBC has held together this long seems partly due to the belief of many ordinary Southern Baptists that what goes on in their own churches is unaffected by the doings of the national organization. In fact, however, the pastors available for them to hire, the Sunday school material they use, the home and foreign missions program they support, and even their ability to dispose of property (if they hold a denominational loan) are heavily influenced by those in control at the top.
>
> Leaving a denomination involves not merely breaking institutional connections but sundering deep psychological and emotional ties. And any real schism will inevitably create major conflict within individual churches, with the likelihood of substantial defections. It's easy to understand why a prudent pastor would be reluctant to plunge his congregation into such a maelstrom.
>
> But what the Atlanta meeting suggests is that moderate leaders are finally preparing to stand up and be counted.[8]

To use a biological analogy in describing what was happening, I would suggest that the Atlanta Convocation in August 1990 was a conception of what would be born nine months later as the Cooperative Baptist Fellowship. As moderate Southern Baptists, we were not yet able to act corporately and sever our ties to the SBC, but deep down we knew that such a severance was near. It would take a few more months of planning, praying, and preparing before a new association of Baptist Christians would come into existence.

Interim Steering Committee (1990–1991)

The election of an Interim Steering Committee was one important result of the convocation. Its composition was intentionally diverse. In addition to myself, there were six other at-large members: Jimmy Allen, Carolyn Cole Bucy, Richard Groves, Stan Hastey, Winfred Moore, and Cecil Sherman.

The other members represented various states: Ray Allen (Virginia), Nancy Ammerman (Georgia), Patsy Ayres (Texas),

Ken Chafin (Kentucky), Cherry Chang (California), Reba Cobb (Kentucky), Paula Clayton Dempsey (Virginia), Stephen Earlene (Oklahoma), James Graves (Florida), Joe Hairston (DC), Relma Hargus (Louisiana), Frank Heintz (Maryland/Delaware), John Hewett (North Carolina), Wink Hicks (Georgia), Jeanette Holt (DC), John Hughes (Missouri), David Hull (South Carolina), Jim Lacy (Texas), George May (Texas), E. W. McCall (California), Barbara McClain (South Carolina), Calvin Metcalf (Tennessee), Dwight Moody (Pennsylvania/New Jersey), Jamie Munro (New York), Virginia Neely (New York), Anne Neil (North Carolina), Dotson Nelson (Alabama), Mary Jane Nethery (Mississippi), Anne Nolan (Tennessee), Bill Owen (Oklahoma), Gabe Payne (Kentucky), Charles Price (New Mexico), John Roberts (Maryland/Delaware), Dot Sample (Michigan), Bill Sherman (Tennessee), Walter Shurden (Georgia), Ray Spence (Virginia), Joy Steincross (Missouri), Jon Stubblefield (Louisiana), Steve Tondera (Alabama), Bill Trautman (Illinois), Margaria Trevino (Texas), Joe Tuten (Mississippi), Charles Wade (Texas), Diane Williams (DC), Dan Yeary (Florida), and Rudy Zachery (Hawaii).

We were charged with the following responsibilities:

- Promote understanding, harmony, and community among those who choose to be a part of this fellowship.
- Plan a spring convocation for common worship and for further planning and action of this body.
- Develop proposals for the cooperative distribution of funds received by the BCMP, Inc. Also approve interim distribution plans for contributions, consistent with designation of donors.
- Develop a mission statement and necessary operating documents for consideration of the spring convocation, and take any further interim actions necessary to function.
- Receive, evaluate, and develop specific strategies related to concerns expressed in the workshops.
- Communicate to the churches, agencies of the SBC, and other Christian bodies our sense of renewal and hope and our commitment to seek and do the will of God.

• Develop a process for choosing a permanent steering committee to be elected at the spring convocation.

The Interim Steering Committee convened its first meeting in October 1990. We divided ourselves into committees and began to fulfill the charge given us by the convocation. We started with such basic decisions as voting to open a bank account and office as well as hiring part-time interim staff. We set the place and time for a second convocation (May 1991 in Atlanta) and began immediately to plan and prepare for it. We accepted the offer of *SBC Today* to be our communication tool to churches and individuals. We heard regular reports from the Southern Baptist Alliance and Southern Baptist Women in Ministry and enjoyed open communication with these organizations. We were kept up to date with the actions and development of the BCMP, Inc., all the while pursuing the goal of our own incorporation and tax-exempt status. This could not be accomplished until our constitution and bylaws were adopted. In four meetings, we prepared a constitution and bylaws, strategies for world missions, a multitrack funding plan, and a working budget all to be presented to the second convocation.

We deliberated and discussed with intensity and sometimes sharp disagreements. We debated issues from diverse perspectives because we were a diverse community. Each of us had certain areas where we had strong convictions and deep feelings, so we tended to make speeches to one another. It was a way of dealing with our grief over what had happened to the SBC, and it was a way of learning to relate to each other. We respected each other, but we really didn't know each other. We had to learn as we went along how to build consensus and community. Some of us were still emotionally tied to the SBC, and some of us were not. All of us realized how fragile our new fellowship was, how young our organization was, and how much we were dependent on God.

Presiding over the Interim Steering Committee was a stretching and growing experience. I had not sought the position, but neither had I run from it. I felt there were others more qualified than I was, but I also felt that I "had come to the kingdom for such a time as this" (Esth 4:14). I was apprehensive but sensed a deeper calm and peace that this was the right thing. The committee was composed of sixty strong personalities representing a wide spectrum of moderate Baptists. We were not only theologically diverse but also culturally and temperamentally diverse. I held everyone on the committee in highest esteem, and many of them intimidated me. Here were pastors and laity, male and female, scholars and businessmen who were assigned to make historic decisions as a committee. They responded to the challenge with grace and amazing unity. There were times of tension, but throughout each meeting there was a willingness and willfulness to do what we were asked to do.

John Hewett, pastor of FBC, Asheville, North Carolina, and CBF's first moderator, was a respected leader among us. His memories of the Interim Steering Committee still cause me to smile:

> Some of the early meetings of the Interim Steering Committee were painful therapy sessions for the disaffected and exiled among us. We talked and talked and talked, but couldn't find our way toward much action. Nostalgia for the SBC wonder years was often palpable. As one of those mournful episodes was peaking, I remember turning to a similarly frustrated friend and saying, "If Morris Chapman (the newly elected SBC president, who defeated Daniel Vestal in New Orleans) were to call right now and say, "We're sorry, please come back home," half this crowd would be on a plane to Nashville within the hour."
>
> Somehow, we muddled through. One of the biggest reasons was a gentle soul named Daniel Vestal, who was the right person at the right time. Daniel knew Baptists had forgotten how to do two important things: disagree and laugh. So he regularly asked us to look around the room, find someone with whom we might disagree on an issue, then go out for twenty minutes to talk together, heart to heart. When we reconvened, we always seemed to approve the next motion unanimously. After learning "holy war" in the SBC, we built this new organism from consensus to consensus.
>
> And Lord, how we laughed. We rediscovered the joy of our particular outcropping of the kingdom and the joy of our salvation. I experienced more authentic "church" in those meetings

than in any other religious gatherings before or since. Blest were
the ties that bound our hearts in Christian love.[9]

One of the most dramatic moments in the work of the Interim
Steering Committee came in its final meeting. Only a few hours
prior to the second convocation, Walter Shurden presented a document that he and Cecil Sherman had prepared, "An Address to the
Public." Cecil Sherman was the primary author of the document,
but Walter Shurden also contributed to it. The committee adopted
it without edits. Although I had wished we could have had time
for more discussion, I felt, then and now, that this was an eloquent
statement of the historical, theological, and practical reasons for the
formation of our fellowship (see appendix B).

First General Assembly (1991)

On May 9–11, 1991, more than 6,000 participants representing
1,556 churches gathered in the Omni Coliseum in Atlanta, Georgia.
For less than nine months, our fledgling organization had existed
under the name "The Baptist Fellowship." The Interim Steering
Committee had acted in good faith to fulfill its responsibilities. It
was prepared to challenge the participants to shape the future of the
Baptist witness. Those participants showed that they were more than
willing to accept the challenge.

Under the banner "Behold I Do a New Thing," a second convocation, which was the first general assembly, followed much the same
format as the first with a combination of worship, smaller discussion
groups, and plenary sessions for reports and business. The business
sessions were lively but cordial. I moderated each business session,
and at one point in a business session where there was debate and
discussion, I stopped and asked the assembly, "Isn't it good to be in a
Baptist meeting where we can talk and even disagree?" The assembly
broke out in applause and laughter.

Substantive decisions were made in an environment of freedom
and trust. The Interim Steering Committee recommended that we
name ourselves the "United Baptist Fellowship." During discussion
time, one dear brother came to a microphone and said, "Baptists

have never been united about anything. But we can cooperate. I recommend that we call ourselves the 'Cooperative Baptist Fellowship.'" His motion passed, and that's how we got our name.[10] A constitution was adopted. A coordinating council was elected with John Hewett, pastor of First Baptist, Asheville, North Carolina, as the first moderator. A missions proposal calling for a missions center and new directions in world missions was enthusiastically approved and affirmed. It was a glad and grand gathering.

A new association of Baptists had been born, but there was still a lot of uncertainty about the future. I knew I needed to take a break from the pace of life and level of denominational leadership I had experienced in the past ten years. When the May assembly adjourned, I returned to Dunwoody Baptist weary and relieved. Two weeks later, Tallowood Baptist contacted me about becoming their pastor, and in August I moved to Houston. I stepped away from active leadership in CBF, although I did serve on the search committee that recommended Cecil Sherman to be CBF's first executive coordinator. In moving to Tallowood, I was confident that I would spend the remainder of my ministry as pastor. It wouldn't be long before I was confronted with another surprise.

A Fledgling Fellowship

From its beginning, the Cooperative Baptist Fellowship was subject to blistering attacks and unrelenting efforts to undermine our legitimacy and even destroy us. Most of those efforts were not from official leadership in the SBC but from self-appointed critics, constantly ridiculing through well-funded publications. A stream of articles falsely accused us of being pro-abortion, pro-homosexual, and nonbiblical. We were portrayed by many as schismatic liberals who were simply "poor losers" in a struggle for theological integrity.

I was giving time and energy to being a pastor, so I escaped much of this early ridicule. But Cecil Sherman, who now was serving as the first executive coordinator, had to respond to these attacks and also give leadership to the fledgling fellowship. He did so with integrity and grace. In spite of the attacks, CBF was quietly and slowly growing both in numbers and in ministry. More and more churches were beginning to identify themselves with CBF without severing all ties to the SBC. Others were allowing individual members to contribute to CBF through their church budget, which enabled the church to be counted by us as a "partnering congregation." Our model of organization was not a "convention model," where a church sends messengers to the annual meeting based on the amount of money given. Rather ours was a "networking model" that both allowed and encouraged congregations to have dual affiliation.

In addition to our being attacked by adversaries, CBF was undermined by friends who strongly suggested that we were only a temporary organization and would soon morph into a Baptist organization much bigger and more of a rival to the SBC. These notions created a lot of conversations that then created a tentativeness and uncertainty about our future. Leaders from CBF and the Alliance of Baptists met together to discuss a possible merger or at least more ways to cooperate. These discussions were not without value, but eventually the two organizations went their separate ways.

A number of prominent voices also urged CBF to dissolve and join American Baptist Churches, USA, or to become a regional subgroup within ABC. These suggestions were strengthened by the fact that ABC had graciously allowed CBF staff and missionaries to secure their retirement benefits through its Ministers and Missionary Benefits Board (MMBB). The values and core commitments of the two groups were similar, but there was little enthusiasm or interest in a merger.

Still other conversations swirled about calling for a new confederation of Baptists created by CBF, the Baptist General Convention of Texas (BGCT), and the Baptist General Association of Virginia (BGAV). The notion was that CBF become the missionary agency in a combination of the three independent groups. Both the Texas and Virginia conventions had escaped a fundamentalist takeover, even though they were still organically and organizationally linked to the SBC. We did sign agreements with the two state conventions that allowed churches from these states to send money to CBF. Both were considered moderate in theology, but no serious efforts were ever made to merge them.

Herbert Reynolds, president of Baylor University, advocated for the creation of the Baptist Convention of the Americas that would encompass Baptists from the southernmost tip of South America to the northernmost tip of Alaska. He called on CBF, Virginia Baptists, and Texas Baptists to work toward a grand and great new venture that would not only rival the SBC but would exceed it in both size and influence. Although his appeals were passionate, no one seriously heeded the call.

All of these proposals came from well-intentioned Baptists. They each had merit and were offered in good faith, but they created rumors and counter rumors and caused a measure of uncertainty and apprehension about CBF's future. There also remained a residual sentiment in non-fundamentalist churches that since the SBC controversy was over, everyone should return to a pre-controversy normalcy and concentrate on their local ministries. A number of younger pastors began their ministries during the controversy but were never emotionally engaged in it. They had never known either the SBC prior to fundamentalism or the moderate effort to resist fundamentalism, so they had little emotional attachment to the old SBC, the new SBC, or the newly created CBF. Hence, they concentrated their energies almost exclusively on their congregations. Many of these non-fundamentalist pastors were capable and gifted leaders but simply were not sure of CBF's future.

In addition to these dynamics and developments, there were those across the theological and geographical spectrum who were cynical about the viability of CBF. They correctly identified the tradition and inertia in so many Southern Baptist churches and questioned whether those churches would sustain a new association of Baptist churches. Many, many pastors knew they were not fundamentalists in their theology or methodology, but they were fearful to lead their churches to identify with CBF. Many, many lay Baptists didn't want a fundamentalist pastor, but their ties to the SBC were strong and they were fearful of divisions in their churches if they identified with CBF. These were some of the challenges facing CBF and Cecil Sherman from the beginning.

Cecil Sherman

Cecil Sherman was chosen as CBF's first coordinator when he was sixty-four. He knew even before he began that he wouldn't be in the position of leadership for a long period of time. Others knew it as well. But his brief tenure of leadership was deliberate and decisive. He worked hard at telling the CBF story, answering critics, nurturing relationships with new ministry partners, and gathering a staff. These were strategic decisions because those chosen were proven leaders, convictional Baptists, and effective ambassadors. They, like Cecil Sherman, had a "life wish" for the fellowship and its future.

Cecil worked to secure Keith Parks as the first coordinator of Global Missions. This was a defining moment and, as much as anything else that had happened since the fellowship's beginning, it solidified CBF's viability and identity. I was conducting a revival at FBC, Columbus, Georgia, when I received a call asking what I thought about the idea. I was elated. Keith Parks embodied a passion for the gospel and a commitment to the worldwide missionary enterprise. His vision for reaching beyond geo-political boundaries to those who have the least access to the gospel was compelling. His administrative ability, pulpit ability, and impeccable integrity made a bold statement that CBF was legitimate.

A little more than two years after assuming leadership as coordinator, Cecil Sherman approached me in a confidential conversation about his plans for retirement. He asked straightforwardly, as was his custom, about my willingness to consider becoming his successor. It was the first time the subject had been mentioned to me, and it was a surprise. I had deep respect and great affection for Cecil, even though we were not close friends. He was fifteen years my senior, and we had ministered in different parts of the country, even though both of us were natives of Fort Worth, Texas. The most time I had spent with him was on the Peace Committee, and I watched him with admiration. He was courageous and able to articulate Baptist principles as clearly as anyone I had heard.

While serving on the search committee for the coordinator, I was reminded again of his convictions and eloquence. On the plane between Houston and Atlanta, I remember reading the resumes of the final candidates. Each was impressive, and each candidate was well qualified. During our interview with Cecil, he was so passionate and persuasive about the importance of CBF that there was little doubt that he should be our first coordinator. Cecil was the primary author of "An Address to the Public," adopted at our founding. He had been the most discerning and perceptive voice identifying the threat of fundamentalism for twelve years, and he had been the most visible leader of the moderate political network that resisted fundamentalism.

Clarissa Strickland began her twenty-three-year tenure as a member of CBF staff before Cecil became coordinator. Her memories of his first day in the Atlanta office are worth repeating.

> I had been employed for ten months when the most exciting thing of all happened. In April 1992, CBF's first executive coordinator was to begin work at CBF. This was, of course, Cecil Sherman, the one who for a number of years had so courageously tried to warn Baptists of what was happening in regard to the takeover of the SBC. In many ways, I saw him as a voice crying in the wilderness. For me, he already had hero status, and that perception would only increase in the years ahead.
>
> The first day Cecil was to visit the office in Decatur (when he was still living in Fort Worth), Sandra and I, with a great deal of anticipatory excitement, watched out our office window, where we had a clear view of the sidewalk by which he would arrive, walking from the nearby MARTA station. Pretty soon, his lanky, Ichabod Crane-like frame appeared, carrying only a briefcase. Cecil was to spend the night in Cartersville with my then-husband and me. When I asked him where his luggage was, he promptly opened the briefcase. On top was a neatly folded dress shirt. (I did not inquire as to what else might be under the folded shirt.) I thought of Jesus' command to the disciples to "travel light," taking neither two coats nor shoes nor scrip. Cecil was one who traveled light but seemed to carry a hefty stick.[11]

Perhaps most important for me, Cecil Sherman was a pastor who loved the church. He understood how Baptist churches functioned and how pastors can be agents of healing and change. After his retirement from CBF he was asked to teach at the Baptist Theological

Seminary in Richmond, where he influenced a younger generation of Baptists and taught on the life and work of the pastor. Cecil Sherman loved the Bible, and he loved to preach and teach the Bible. It is more than ironic that having been severely criticized by fundamentalists for not believing the Bible, he ended up helping more people study and interpret the Bible than nearly all of those who criticized him. While on the Peace Committee, I heard Adrian Rogers say directly to him, "Cecil, I wouldn't let you teach Sunday school in my church." Yet after his retirement from CBF, Cecil wrote Sunday school lesson commentary for Smyth & Helwys that helped thousands of Baptist laity understand the Bible.

Becoming Coordinator (1996)

I was happy as pastor of Tallowood for many reasons. The church was healthy and we were involved in so many ministries both in Houston and beyond. In my journal on April 9, 1990, I enumerated the various ministries in which we were involved and then wrote, "I believe God wants us to be a catalytic church that helps bring parts of the body of Christ together." It was a blessed time. Our children were close to Earlene and me. We were enjoying a season of fulfillment and fruitfulness. I was also in a time of spiritual and vocational renewal, learning the practices of contemplative prayer. More than 200 adults had participated in prayer retreats that I led personally. I was preaching with fervor and freedom.

All of this made it difficult to understand why I should leave Tallowood and become coordinator of CBF. I was content. The Spirit was at work. Since coming to Tallowood, I had opened myself emotionally to the possibility of a move only one time. When the presidential search committee at Baylor contacted me for an interview, I agreed. But I knew after the interview that this was not to be. The search committee didn't pursue me any further. Instead they asked my friend Robert Sloan to become president. I saw myself as a pastor, not as a president, of anything. So I was even more conflicted when Carolyn Crumpler, chair of the CBF search committee, called to ask if I would meet with them.

What followed were weeks of internal struggle. The search committee was a remarkable composition of Baptist leaders. I knew many of them well and admired all of them. My conversations with them were intense and inspiring, which only compounded my struggle. When Carolyn called to notify me that I was their choice to be the next coordinator, I was humbled and honored. But I had no peace about accepting. I simply didn't discern a divine call. It was difficult to do, but I declined the committee's offer. My immediate feeling was one of relief and a desire to refocus on being a pastor.

Several months passed and I didn't hear anything from the committee. I knew they would pursue other individuals for the position. When the General Assembly convened in June 1996 in Richmond, Virginia, Earlene and I made plans to attend. We had talked on occasion, but not frequently, about the decision and agreed that unless something dramatic happened we would put this possibility behind us. In fact, something dramatic did happen that changed my mind and heart. During the Friday night service Keith Parks brought a powerful mission challenge and the fellowship commissioned several new missionaries. During that commissioning time, I felt a clear impression that I should contact Carolyn and express a new willingness to accept the coordinator's position.

This was an emotional moment for me when the doubts and confusion seemed to evaporate, and I had a deep desire to give my life to the world missions effort of CBF. I wept silently and determined to make the call. After the service, Earlene and I were walking back to our hotel, and I told her what I was experiencing. She agreed. I called Carolyn almost immediately and told her that I realized the committee might be at a different place, but if they still wanted me I was willing to say yes. She did contact the committee, and the committee issued me another invitation. I wept again, this time with joy and confidence.

Anyone who has sought and received divine guidance in decision-making knows how difficult and subjective the experience can be. Although Scripture gives examples of individuals who experienced guidance, there is no one set pattern for all to follow. Scripture offers promises and guidelines for seeking guidance, but there are multiple means and methods by which God gives guidance. And there is always a human risk in making oneself vulnerable and receptive to guidance, as well as the real possibility of misinterpretation or misunderstanding any guidance as divine guidance. In other words, it is easy to confuse our personal desires with the will of God.

Scripture admonishes us, even encourages us, to ask God for wisdom (James 1:5), "to lean not to our own understanding" (Prov 3:5), and "in all things with thanksgiving let our requests be made known to God" (Phil 4:6). The working of divine providence is a mystery usually seen, if seen at all, in retrospect more than in prospect. The complexities and complications of our minds and motives are real. Yet we are privileged, as children of God who are created in the image of God and promised the Spirit of God, to seek discernment and clarity from God in all our actions.

In his famous prayer, Thomas Merton wrote,

> My Lord God, I have no idea where I am going. I do not see the road ahead of me. I cannot know for certain where it will end. Nor do I know myself, and the fact that I think I am following your will does not mean that I am actually doing so. But I believe that the desire to please you in fact pleases you. And I hope I have that desire in all that I am doing. And I know that if I do this you will lead me by your right hand, even though I may know nothing about it.[12]

I did arrive at a place of peace in my decision process to accept the invitation of the search committee. I trusted their judgment and confidence in me. I listened to the wisdom and counsel of friends and mentors, beginning with my wife. I measured my strengths and weaknesses, my temperament and personality, as well as the expectations and requirements set before me. I tried to discern the time, both in a "chronological" sense ("kronos" time) and in a "special" sense ("kairos" time) both for me and for CBF. I prayed for peace that passes understanding (Phil 4:6) in leaving the pastorate and going into denominational leadership. God gave me that peace. On September 9, 1996, I wrote following open letter to Tallowood:

For several months I've been seeking to discern the will of God for my life and future ministry. The purpose of this letter is to share some of that journey. In February a search committee for the Cooperative Baptist Fellowship asked me if I would allow them to nominate me as coordinator. I was honored and humbled, but did not feel I could leave Tallowood and accept their invitation. Both the committee and I moved in different directions. However, in May of this year I began to feel some stirrings in my heart that perhaps God was calling me to a new place of service in his kingdom. Earlene and I prayed earnestly and went to the General Assembly in Richmond knowing that we were facing a turning point. Sure enough it was during that June meeting that I came to a deep peace that I needed to talk to the committee. In the following weeks the committee again asked if I would allow my name to be nominated for the coordinator. This time I said yes.

The Coordinating Council of CBF will meet in Atlanta September 26-28 and will vote on the committee's recommendation. I'm asking you to pray in the weeks ahead for the unfolding will of God in my life, our beloved church, and in the CBF. I love this church and in turn have felt the love of this church for five years. It is because of that love that I desire to share personally with you what is happening and enlist your prayerful support. A time of decision by the CBF is close at hand, and it is important to me that you, as my church family, hear about all of this from me.

Deep in the heart of Baptist people is a desire for cooperative missions with integrity, vision, and freedom. The reason for this desire is because cooperative missions is woven into the fabric of the gospel. What we cannot do individually, we can do together. Cooperative missions and ministry is based on mutual trust and respect. It requires shared decision-making, authenticity, and honesty. God is at work around the world renewing a passion and romance for world evangelization through cooperation. Tallowood has long been a strong example of this desire, as this congregation has looked for ways to be involved in cooperative missions first to the SBC, and more recently through the CBF. As Tallowood looks to CBF to go forward cooperatively, I think other churches will do the same. I want to help those churches renew their focus.

Also, deep in the heart of Baptist people are some convictions about biblical truths. These truths have been foundational to our congregational life and our cooperative mission efforts. We have believed in the authority of the Bible for faith and practice. We have believed in the freedom and responsibility of every believer to interpret the Bible, to respond to God, and to discern the Spirit for themselves. We have believed in religious liberty and separation of church and state. We have believed in the autonomy of every church and servant leadership in those churches. God is also at work renewing an understanding and commitment to these bedrock principles of Baptist people. Tallowood's increased involvement in giving through CBF shows the desire of this congregation to return to those convictions, and I think other churches will do the same. I want to help those churches restore their convictions.

In the coming days let's covenant to pray earnestly, love deeply, live faithfully, and serve joyfully, remembering what Jesus said: "I will build my church and the gates of hell shall not prevail against it." I count it a privilege to be your pastor.

Convocation for Concerned Baptists, Atlanta, August 1990

Dr. Jimmy Allen
Convocation for Concerned Baptists
Atlanta, August 1990

Convocation for Concerned Baptists, August 1990,
News Conference

Convocation for Concerned Baptists, August 1990,
News Conference with Anne Vestal

Baptists Committed

June 1991

Cooperative Baptist Fellowship

6,000 Moderates Chart New Course

Some 6,000 Southern Baptist moderates gave birth to a new organization in Atlanta May 9-11, naming it the Cooperative Baptist Fellowship.

Meeting at the Omni Coliseum, participants charted a new course of denominational involvement which does not sever ties with the Southern Baptist Convention but which provides for "a coalition of churches and individuals who are tired of fighting fundamentalism and who want to get on with the mission of the church," said John Hewett of North Carolina who was elected moderator of the Fellowship.

Approved overwhelmingly at the convocation were the name, a detailed organizational structure as outlined in the constitution and bylaws, a budget and a plan to do missions together.

The attendance was about double that of a Fellowship consultation

Cooperative Baptist Fellowship
More than 6,000 participants, representing 1,555 churches, named themselves the Cooperative Baptist Fellowship (CBF) in recent Atlanta meeting.

held last August, also in Atlanta, to search for a new strategy after moderates lost their 12th straight bid for the SBC presidency. During that time, fundamentalists gained virtually total control of the convention.

It is unclear how many Southern Baptists and churches will identify with the Fellowship. More than 200 churches have contributed funds to the organization thus far. But Daniel Vestal, moderator of the interim steering committee which has met since August, said the new organization represents the sentiment of "hundreds of thousands" of Southern Baptists.

Vestal admits that the Fellowship has not resolved the tension between those who want to launch a new denomination and those who prefer to stay put, functioning instead as a convention within the convention.

He recognized that there is a "legitimate difference" of opinion, even among the Fellowship's leaders, about how far to stray from the SBC fold. But he called the tension "healthy."

"I want to link hands with those on either side of me in order to reach more effectively the world for Christ," said Ben Loring, pastor of

continued on page 2

In this issue

Founding General Assembly, Cooperative Baptist Fellowship,
May 1991, Atlanta

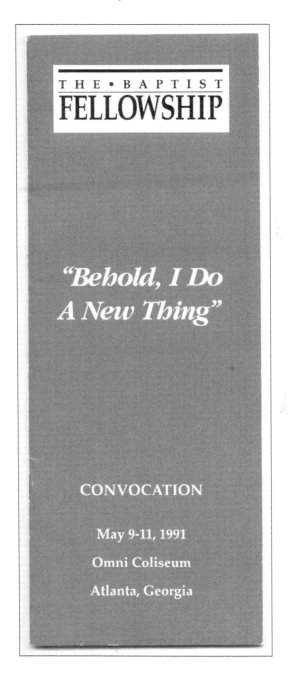

Program for Founding General Asssembly,
Cooperative Baptist Fellowship, May 1991, Atlanta

Chapter 7

Cooperative Baptist Fellowship: Relationships and Friendships

I came to CBF with some convictions that strengthened and sustained me for the fifteen years I served as coordinator. Among those convictions were that CBF was a work of God's grace and a renewal movement among Baptists. We were born out of controversy and conflict that was displeasing to God. Those of us who formed the fellowship had experienced exclusion and loss. God did not cause that exclusion, but God worked in it and through it to create something new and beautiful. Grace means that God brings good out of bad, joy out of sorrow, beauty out of ashes. Grace means that God's love is so rich and God's power is so great that God takes even what was meant for harm and uses it for our good and God's glory. Whenever God acts in grace, one result is renewal—spiritual renewal, ministry renewal, relational renewal.

I experienced all of these during my tenure as coordinator, and they were usually linked together. Over and over again, I witnessed and participated in the weaving of a beautiful tapestry of grace, resulting in new life, new forms of ministry, and new relationships. It's difficult to say which was the most meaningful, but I do know that I experienced friendships I would never have known were it not for CBF. The new friendships came in the context of new ministry, but they were more than working relationships. They were friendships with bonds of mutual respect and ties of trust.

CBF Leadership

Moderators

These friendships began with the coordinating council, CBF's governing body, composed of fifty-three individuals who were selected by the state and regional CBF organizations for three-year terms. The council set policies, approved an annual budget, and held me accountable for administering programs and staff. They structured themselves into ministry groups that focused on our initiatives: global missions, leadership development, and congregational life as well as the necessary administrative infrastructure of finance, personnel, and legal matters.

These council members represented a broad geographical spectrum in CBF life and were a blend of male and female, clergy and laity, young and old. They brought significant expertise and experience to their task of governance along with personal and spiritual integrity. I had respect and appreciation for all of them. We met three times a year, making it possible to move beyond casual conversation and create a sense of community. From the coordinating council, an advisory council comprising chairpersons for each ministry group was selected. The advisory council met additional times, allowing for even deeper relationships to form.

The four officers (moderator, moderator elect, past moderator, recorder) guided the work of the council and conducted my annual performance review. The moderator presided over all council meetings and the annual General Assembly. These officers were not selected by me but by a nominating committee of the coordinating council. I not only experienced grace through these friendships but also witnessed divine providence in their selection and in the unique gifts that each brought to the fellowship at the time they served. The moderators and recorders with whom I worked were authentic Christians, effective leaders, and true colleagues.

Moderators during my tenure were Lavonne Brown (1996–1997), Martha Teague Smith (1997–1998), John Tyler (1998–1999), Sara Frances Anders (1999–2000), Donna Forrester (2000–2001), Jim Baucom (2001–2002), Phil Martin (2002–2003), Cynthia Holmes

(2003–2004), Robert Setzer (2004–2005), Joy Yee (2005–2006), Emmanuel McCall (2006–2007), Harriet Harrel (2007–2008), Jack Glasgow (2008–2009), Hal Bass (2009–2010), Kristi McMillan-Goodwin (2010–2011), Colleen Burroughs (2011–2012), and Keith Herron (2012–2013). Recorders during my tenure were Bill Owen, Carolyn Dipboye, Paul Kenley, Susan Crumpler, Hal Bass, Jo Ann Carr, and Renee Bennett.

Colleagues

When I arrived in Atlanta, a small staff assembled by Cecil Sherman was functioning effectively: David Wilkinson (coordinator of communications), Bill Bruster (coordinator of networking), Gary Skeen (coordinator of administration), Keith Parks (coordinator of global missions), and Terry Hamrick (coordinator of church resources). These colleagues brought tenured wisdom and genuine passion to the newly formed fellowship. They each came from secure ministry positions and did so out of conviction and calling. After my arrival, Bo Prosser became coordinator of congregational Life and Ben McDade became coordinator of communications. Both brought their considerable gifts and experience to the leadership team. Each had a willingness to step into a fledgling organization, which was evidence of their courage and adaptability. An often-repeated expression in those early years was that we were building this plane while we were flying it.

What I discovered in these earliest colleagues would be a pattern of discovery with other staff through the years. Staff colleagues at CBF became friends, and their friendships were means of grace. I was privileged to work alongside a leadership team characterized by exceptional commitment and ability. The team changed through the years, and all was not perfect. As with any organization, mistakes were made, conflict occurred, and it was not always easy to work both effectively and efficiently. But what I value as much as anything from my time as coordinator are the relationships I experienced. I remember them fondly and say with the Apostle Paul, "I thank my God upon every remembrance of you for your partnership in the gospel from the first day until now" (Phil 1:3, 5).

David Wilkinson was a visionary leader who grasped just how unique CBF's identity and organizational model should be and how important it was for us to communicate clearly that we were "a new way to be Baptist." He stewarded the writing of our first mission statement along with significant input from two gifted pastors, George Mason and Greg Hunt. The first mission statement was adopted in 1995 as a bold and aspirational commitment to an unknown future. It was in itself a work of grace.

> OUR MISSION. We are a Fellowship of Baptist Christians and churches who share a passion for the great commission of Jesus Christ and a commitment to Baptist principles of faith and practice. Our mission is to network, empower, and mobilize Baptist Christians and churches for effective missions in ministry in the name of Christ.
>
> OUR PRIORITIES: Doing global missions in a world without borders. Championing Baptist principles of faith and practice. Affirming our racial, ethnic, and gender diversity as a gift of God. Networking Baptist churches and individuals for cooperation, encouragement, and exchange of information and ideas. Empowering churches through resources more than programs. Emphasizing strategic partnerships more than owning institutions. Cooperating through new ventures that encourage innovative and creative approaches to missions and ministry for the twenty-first century.
>
> OUR COMMITMENTS: We are committed to Baptist principles. We are committed to biblically based global missions. We are committed to a resource model as our primary means of serving churches. We are committed to a biblical vision of justice and mercy. We are committed to lifelong learning for ministry. We are committed to trustworthiness. We are committed to effectiveness.
>
> OUR INITIATIVES: Global missions. Resources for churches and church leaders. Partnership ministries. Baptist principles. New ventures. Fellowship.

I don't know how many people at the time fully appreciated how dramatically CBF was redefining itself and what it was aspiring to become as a movement of renewal. There was always some tension between those who wanted to reduplicate what we experienced within the SBC and those who realized that CBF was "new wine" needing "new wineskins" (Matt 9:17). With this mission statement, we were declaring that we were not just a dissident and disgruntled collection of moderate Southern Baptists or a support group to help us heal from our collective wounds. We were not just a protest or resistance movement against fundamentalism, nor were we an alternative denomination identical to the one from which we had separated. We saw ourselves as a fresh work of grace and a new community of Christians. We viewed ourselves primarily through a relational lens. We were a "fellowship."

Our inclusion of male and female, laity and clergy as equals in ministry was evidence of how much we sought renewal. The decision to "network" without being a "convention of churches" requiring doctrinal conformity was dramatically different from where we had come. The decision to "empower" without producing endless programs that were marketed and sold for a profit was innovative. The decision to "mobilize" without owning and operating institutions was a dramatic, if not radical, step of creativity.

Within the mission statement there were a number of biblical references and theological confessions that affirmed our collective convictions: "We believe in the priesthood of all believers," "We believe in the authority of Scripture," "We believe in the autonomy of every local church," "We support the separation of church and state." Other explicit confessions of faith were equally clear: "As Christians, the tie that binds us is our common faith in Jesus Christ," "We believe the call of Christ extends to every area and relationship of life, both private and public, personal and social," "We will find ways to help churches and individuals explore the moral and ethical imperatives of the Gospel and to apply them to every dimension of life."

These confessional statements were important because they countered the relentless criticism from fundamentalists that CBF did not believe the Bible or that we were heretical. There was also one brief but clear confessional statement of what we believed about the gospel:

We believe the Bible teaches God is the one triune God, Creator of all people in God's own image. All people are separated from God by sin. Christ is the Savior and Redeemer for all peoples. The Holy Spirit convicts and converts all who believe in Christ, teaches the Church in the voice of the Living Christ, and empowers the Church and all believers for the mission of Christ in the world. Christ calls us to minister redemptively to the spiritual, physical, and social needs of individuals and communities. Every believer and every church is responsible for sharing the Gospel with all people.

From this confessional center, Keith Parks led CBF's global mission efforts with a compelling vision. Keith came to CBF in 1993 after resigning as president of the Foreign Mission Board of the SBC. He was a Baptist leader with stature and worldwide recognition and respect. Keith was passionate about the Christian witness to those who had the least access to the gospel and those whom society had marginalized. Under his guidance, and that of the global missions coordinators who followed him, we made major paradigm shifts in cooperative missions. We shifted from a denominational approach to a partnering approach. We recognized the reality that cooperative missions will no longer be one-dimensional within a single denominational framework, but local churches will participate in God's mission in multiple ways with many partners. We moved away from a "program-based" model, where we sought to transplant our denominational programs around the world, to a partnering model working with indigenous ministries.

We shifted from a clergy-led missiology to one that affirms the gifts and calling of the whole body of Christ. We shifted from a fragmented understanding of the gospel to a holistic one, viewing the gospel as both social justice and evangelism. We shifted from a geopolitical approach to an ethnolinguistic approach, viewing the world not so much in term of nations and countries but as groupings of people. We shifted from a "mono-logical" to a "dialogical" approach where we listened to people of other faiths and learned from them, and in that relationship of mutual respect we offered witness of our faith in Jesus Christ.

The early mantra for CBF was "doing missions in a world without borders," and it captured my imagination. All of us knew that we were increasingly interwoven and interrelated as a planet. The world is indeed a global village. And what we do in New York impacts the West Bank. What happens in Nairobi and Calcutta impacts what happens in Atlanta and Los Angeles. Email and the internet bind us together as never before. Like it or not, in everything from banking and trade to the use of the English language for commerce and business, we are living in an interconnected world. And it is a world where troubles transcend borders. What happens to one people group affects another. When one part of the world hurts, we all hurt.

Therefore, what is done locally has an effect globally, and what is done globally has an effect locally. When we begin to live in this kind of world, then every act of compassion, every word of witness, every prayer of intercession has a global impact. It becomes part of a worldwide redemptive plan, even a cosmic plan. What missionaries do in ministry is similar to what we do where we live. Our prayers and their prayers, as well as the prayers of people all over the world, rise together as sweet incense before God. We give money and time, not only to send and support them but also to participate in what God is doing throughout the world.

Even before becoming coordinator, I was compelled by the distinctiveness and scope of CBF's mission efforts and by Keith Parks's leadership. I could see the groundswell of support, and I was excited about it. Already we were becoming a significant participant in the world missionary enterprise. Already we were commissioning/sending missionaries, adopting unreached people groups, sending funds for disaster relief, and partnering with the global church. God was at work among us.

Another evidence of renewal within CBF was the birth of new Baptist seminaries across the country and new affiliations of established seminaries with us. None of the new seminaries were started by CBF, but we provided significant financial support both with institutional funding and student scholarships. We did not own and operate any seminary but partnered with them to provide theological education for future ministers. Without selecting their trustees or participating in their governance, we became a part of their mission, and they in turn became a part of the mission of CBF. This resulted in an amazing burst of energy for theological, spiritual, and congregational renewal within the Baptist family.

First Gary Parker and then Terry Hamrick were the CBF staff members who served as liaisons with the seminaries, creating a consortium where the deans and presidents met regularly for conversation and planning. There was collegiality between the leaders and collaboration between the seminaries, but there was also some tension within the fellowship as to how many schools we should support and which ones we should support. Cecil Sherman advocated for a concentrated financial commitment to two or three schools, recognizing that we had limited resources. I disagreed and felt that each of them had value to CBF and that together we created an expansive Baptist community for theological education and leadership formation.

Terry Hamrick developed the idea of an "ecosystem" that included all the seminaries related to CBF. He requested major grants from the Lilly Foundation to fund a number of bold initiatives that fostered ministerial excellence and leadership development. This ecosystem also included the Center for Congregational Health, Passport, Inc., the Shiloh Network, and a number of local churches. Under Terry's leadership and with our partners, we developed and administered scores of peer learning groups, ministry resident programs, sabbaticals, internships, and lay leadership conferences. Together we created a youth ministry network, a collegiate ministry network, a doctoral student network, a supervised ministry network, and a pastors/scholars studio. Together we sponsored retreats for pastors, an annual Leadership Institute, and a number of theological education events for seminary faculty, administrators, and students. Together we developed resources for congregations to use in encouraging youth in discerning God's call to ministry. God was at work among us.

Still another evidence of renewal among us was the creation of a new pension board to provide retirement benefits for ordained ministers. The Church Benefits Board of CBF resulted from the tireless efforts of Gary Skeen and a cadre of courageous leaders who worked with him. From the beginning of his tenure, Gary began responding to requests that we provide retirement, life insurance, and disability benefits for ministers. It was increasingly clear that the SBC would soon prohibit any church participating with CBF to continue receiving benefits through their Annuity Board. In 2001, CBF formed the Church Benefits Board (CBB) and signed an agreement with the Ministers and Missionary Benefits Board (MMBB) of American Baptist Churches, USA, to become their marketing and servicing extension to provide retirement benefits for staff at churches that associated with CBF. This agreement continued until 2009, when CBB became independent of MMBB.

From the beginning, CBF did not declare itself as a "convention of churches" but as a "fellowship of churches and individuals." Because we welcomed individuals as members of CBF, even though their churches might not be a member, the IRS would not grant us a "church group exemption" status, which was necessary to offer retirement benefits. This meant that in order for CBF to have correct status and provide retirement benefits, the IRS would need to change its code of regulations, allowing an association of churches like CBF to include individual members. The only way to get this done was for Congress to pass legislation that would mandate the change.

We employed an accounting firm in Washington, DC, to represent us and asked their tax lawyers to seek a legislative solution. It was a daunting task. Gary Skeen met with our Georgia senators who then introduced us to Senator Charles Grassley of Iowa. Grassley was a member of the Senate Ways and Means committee and a Baptist. He understood our dilemma. He also had a person on staff who was a member of a church affiliated with CBF. Along with Brent Walker, director of the Baptist Joint Committee on Public Affairs, he helped our request move forward.

In 2007, the Pension Reform Act was passed by both houses of Congress and signed by President George W. Bush. In that bill was an amendment, introduced by Grassley, that included language stating that having individuals as members of an association of churches would not preclude it from being recognized as such. This changed our status, and within a few months the IRS ruled in our favor.

This was one of those times when few people knew that something momentous was happening. But for those of us who did know, it was a joyous moment. I never hear the phrase "It takes an act of Congress to get something done" without thinking of this experience, the result of which is that CBF's Church Benefits Board has become a premier provider for clergy retirement. It was a work of grace.

Bill Bruster was living in Dallas when I arrived as coordinator because his primary focus was on churches west of the Mississippi. I asked him to move to Atlanta because he was a masterful networker, an encourager to younger ministers, and an important advisor to me. I valued his counsel and enjoyed his company. I also asked him to work with the state/regional CBF organizations, each of which began autonomous and independent of the national organization. The CBF movement encompassed both the national organization and state/regional organizations, but we were each independent of one another while sharing similar values and viewing ourselves as integral to one another. The beginning and development of the state/regional organizations was strategic, and their coordinators joined with the national staff from Atlanta in regular meetings to form the Movement Leadership Team (MLT).

The friendships with these coordinators were deep and meaningful: Marion Aldridge (South Carolina, 1991); Harold Phillips (Missouri, 1991); John Lepper (Kentucky, 1991); Pat and Carolyn Anderson, Ray Johnson (Florida, 1991); Frank Broome (Georgia, 1992); T. Thomas, Steve Graham (Oklahoma, 1992); Ircel Harrison, Terry Maples (Tennessee, 1992); Bob Patterson, Larry Hovis (North Carolina, 1993); Rick McClure, Rob Fox (Virginia, 1993); Lynn Hawkins (Louisiana, 1993); Bradley Pope (Mississippi, 1993); Ken and Sandy Hale (Northeast, 1993); Dub Poole (Mid-Atlantic, 1994); Mart Gray, Ronnie Brewer, Terri Byrd (Alabama, 1994); Gilbert Sanders (North Central, 1994); Tom Logue, Ray Higgins (Arkansas, 1994); Rick McClatchey (Texas, 1996); and Glenn Foster (CBF West, 1997).

We spent a lot of time together in team building, conversation, and prayer. There were organizational tensions at times between us, most of which were caused by lack of clarity on how we were to relate to each other and how we were to fund our efforts. Our personal relationships, however, were too important to let organizational tensions distract. I never experienced any serious conflict within the MLT, which is quite remarkable considering the strength and diversity of its composition. We genuinely cared for each other and for the whole fellowship. My own vision was that the key to our organizational relationship was "convergence" between national and states/regions, not merger or subservience of one to the other. We each should maintain our identity and autonomy but work hard toward collaboration and customization of services to congregations.

It is impossible to pay proper tribute to all of the staff colleagues with whom I worked through the years at CBF. But five colleagues were especially significant in making it possible for me to function in my role as coordinator. Three of them were personal administrative assistants: Michelle Darrah, Charlotte Taylor, and Christa Sfameni. I simply could not have done what I did without their help. Two other colleagues were in senior leadership roles. Allison Tennyson was director of Human Resources. She combined a remarkable mixture of professional competence and personal Christian character in her work and personal life. Connie McNeil was my chief of staff and administrative coordinator in my later years as coordinator. Her leadership and continued friendship have been God's gifts to me.

I learned a lot about organizational leadership from other colleagues while at CBF. I learned about strategic planning, communication, visioning, fundraising, and teamwork. My experience as a pastor in multi-staff congregations proved invaluable, but being a pastor is different than being CEO in a denominational system administering a large staff and working under the authority of a governing board. On numerous occasions, someone would offer advice, usually well intentioned but unsolicited, about how to lead a staff, work with a board, deal with conflict, or practice good time management. I was frequently greeted with the suggestion, "You should read this book on team building," or "Here's a tape series on conflict resolution," or "This seminar would help you in understanding the business culture of today."

I did pay attention to many of the suggestions, and I did read a lot of literature about leadership. But what I found most helpful was that nothing is more important in organizational leadership than relationships. Every person working in a system is a person created in God's image, worthy of respect. And in an organization that identifies itself as Christian, every person is part of a community with Christ at the center. My goal in working with staff colleagues was to relate to each one with this in mind. Some members of the staff became close friends, and others did not. Some required close supervision and strong boundaries. Others did not. Some were regularly recognized and rewarded. Others were corrected and even terminated. But always my desire was to relate to each colleague with integrity, fairness, and charity.

The book that influenced my own philosophy of leadership more than any other was Parker Palmer's *Let Your Life Speak: Listening for the Voice of Vocation*. Palmer calls for a "leadership from within" in which there is a convergence between one's "role" and one's "soul." He suggests that a good leader is one who "casts light" and a bad leader is one who "casts darkness."[13] All of us have influence on others and therefore have the opportunity to lead. Some of us are placed in positions where our decisions and demeanor have influence not only on an organization but also on the people who work in it.

My own understanding of good organizational leadership evolved over the years. Good organizational leadership is helping people work together for a common good and for the good of one another. Leadership is a practice more than a position of authority. Leading doesn't always come from the top of a hierarchical system or from those in positions of authority. Leading is about influencing attitudes and behavior, empowering and encouraging, awakening awareness, creating energy, releasing potential, clarifying, and unifying. Leading can come from anyone and anywhere within an organization. A person can lead at one time and follow at another.

Organizational leadership is service because it is helping people. Leading is not about imposing a leader's will on those who follow, or having all the answers, or being able to solve all the problems. Its aim is directed outward, extending benefit to as many as possible.

Organizational leadership is dynamic because it requires acting, interacting, and reacting with people. Leading is not primarily about ideas, theories, or philosophy. It is about people working with one another and for one another and for a bigger and broader good. Rules and regulations can be important, but they cannot always define leadership. Organizational leadership is contextual because changing circumstances require innovation, adaptation, and experimentation. What constitutes leading in one situation may not be the same in another situation. Understanding the context is as important as understanding people.

Partners

CBF's decision to serve churches by networking and partnering with independent organizations and ministries, rather than owning and operating them, was a strategic one. It required that we take the concept of partnership seriously and invest in the relationships necessary for the partnerships to work effectively. One of my rich rewards was getting to know the leadership of various ministry partners, working alongside them and spending enough time with them to call them friends. It is hard for me to say whether it was more meaningful to participate in our shared ministry together or to experience these life-enriching relationships. I once heard someone remark that it is amazing what God will do through us if we don't care who gets the credit. One of the temptations in ministry partnerships is to seek the credit for our own organization above the common good. Partnerships are not always easy, but when they happen, nothing is quite so beautiful and meaningful.

Because of my recent renewal and awakening to contemplative prayer, I came to CBF with a desire to focus on spiritual formation. My own discovery of resources beyond my Baptist tradition and my efforts at Tallowood to introduce those resources to laity convinced me that others in the CBF family needed a similar introduction. One of the first decisions I made as coordinator was to appoint a task force to pray and discern how best to introduce the concepts and practices of spiritual formation to Baptist churches.

The task force compiled and then published a resource book that listed a wide range of resources in spiritual formation. It included resource people, workshops and training programs, networks and professional organizations, publications, links, and personal retreat sites. It was received with enthusiasm. It was later expanded and published as *Light for the Path: A Guide for Spiritual Formation Resources*. Each of the new seminaries being formed were including classes on spiritual formation. Baptists were awakening to the rich and varied approaches to Christian spirituality, realizing how much they needed to learn. It was also a time when the wider culture was experiencing an intense interest in spirituality.

At the Houston General Assembly in 1998, I issued a brief analysis of our need for spiritual formation and then issued an appeal to the CBF family:

> As I look at myself and other Baptists, I find a lot of performance-based religion. We have "a zeal for God but not according to knowledge." There is among us a competitiveness and compulsiveness. We are pressured, pulled and pushed in all directions, desperately needing to know the love of God at a deeper level.
>
> So I call us to spiritual formation that we might receive the grace of our Lord Jesus Christ, the love of God, and the fellowship of the Holy Spirit.
>
> A call to spiritual formation requires that we befriend silence and solitude and discover the abiding presence of God within us. The call requires that we nurture our interior life, the hidden life, so as to make our home in the triune God. The call to spiritual formation requires us to rediscover the disciplines that create a space for God and explore the literature of the ages that can instruct us as well as inspire us. Finally, a call to spiritual formation requires that we embrace the complexities of our time, the ambiguities of life, and the frailty of our humanness as means of grace and instruments of the Spirit. I call us to learn the life and practice of prayer so that we might be formed into the image of Christ.

In order to meet the challenges of the interest in spiritual formation, we formed partnerships that could serve as resources for individuals and congregations. One partner was Renovare, a newly formed interdenominational organization that was fostering learning opportunities across America. Founded by the well-known author Richard Foster, Renovare was helping Christians pursue renewal through relationships, retreats, and print and online resources. Richard spoke at our gathering in Houston and became an advisor, friend, and encourager. Margaret Campbell, who was a member of Tallowood, became chair of Renovare's board and offered her support and encouragement to CBF. Richard's books, especially *Celebration of Discipline*, introduced many practices that foster spiritual growth into Baptist congregations.

Another valuable partner in spiritual formation was Upper Room, a ministry of the United Methodist Church. Stephen Bryant, its world editor and publisher, made himself available to our leadership team as a consultant and coach. Upper Room published a number of workbooks and guides that the CBF family used: *Companions in Christ: The Way of Transforming Discipleship*, *Exploring the Way: An Introduction to Spiritual Formation*, and *The Way of a Child: Helping Children Experience God*. It also sponsored numerous "academies" for spiritual formation that were made available to pastors and lay leaders. These resources, along with the relationships of Upper Room's leadership, were transformative for many.

A number of teachers, authors, and spiritual guides offered their time and gifting to lead workshops, retreats, and conferences. E. Glenn Hinson, respected church historian, was a pioneer in introducing Baptists to spiritual formation, as was Bill Clemmons, another professor and author. Marjorie Thompson from Upper Room was a frequent speaker. Jeannie Miley, a popular author, led numerous retreats and breakout sessions. Trevor Hudson, a Methodist pastor from South Africa, had significant influence on us, both in his writing and teaching. Other effective teachers who helped us in the spiritual journey were Roberta Bondi from Candler School of Theology, Betty Talbert from Truett Seminary, President Molly Marshall of Central Baptist Theological Seminary, Loyd Allen from McAfee School of Theology, and Ruth Haley Barton, author and spiritual director.

Daniel Vestal with David and Colleen Burroughs

Another valuable partner with CBF in spiritual formation was "Passport," a Christian camping program for teens, founded by David and Colleen Burroughs in 1993. Combining worship, discipleship instruction, and mission and service opportunities with an inclusive and progressive theological voice for justice, the camps have attracted youth and children from across the country. Passport camps have provided an ecumenical, interdenominational experience that has not only nurtured spiritual growth and authentic community but has also given opportunities for young people to engage in community service and contribute to global causes.

In addition to providing formational experiences for youth, Passport has provided spiritual and leadership formation for hundreds of young adults who have served as camp staff. These former staffers now serve as clergy and lay Christian leaders in churches, nonprofits, and missionary organizations around the world as well as community leaders in their various locations.

The ministry of David and Colleen has been significant for CBF beyond their providing spiritual formation opportunities for youth. And their friendship has been significant for me personally. They are exemplars of how CBF has been a work of renewal among Baptists, and they have been instruments of that renewal. They have also lovingly challenged CBF to fulfill its global mission and live up to its core values.

Colleen wrote me a letter in August 1996, after the search committee voted to recommend me as coordinator, urging me to more intentional inclusiveness in my leadership.

> When our committee asked you why you had no women deacons in your church you said that it was not your issue. I am listening to Bob Dole struggle as he tries to relearn his native tongue so that he includes everyone in his dream for the future. I appreciate his effort. Bill Clinton has learned the language and action of inclusion and uses it to his advantage well. I believe he means it. Dr. Vestal, many will be listening to see if they are included in your future.
>
> Many people, men and women alike who will never darken the door of a Women in Ministry luncheon, left the SBC due to their stance on women. I encourage you to make it an issue for yourself. You are my new leader, set apart by God. I will support you. I will follow you and I will pray for you as you try not to put new wine in old skins.

Twelve years later, in 2008, David wrote me a passionate letter urging CBF's endorsement of the Millennium Development Goals (MDGs) in ways that would include church and youth involvement. I don't think we implemented many of the observations he set forth, but his urging was incisive and visionary. Here is an excerpt of that letter.

> I have felt for a while that our Christian participation in the MDGs is beyond the political arena—but more daily, more practical, more about the changes I can make that will further one or more of these goals in simple and real ways.
>
> Daniel, I am very interested in helping in any way that you feel would be appropriate to find new and "out of the box" ways for our missional churches to find deep and meaningful connections to both our field personnel and our Christian brothers and sisters around the world, who are struggling and in need of support. I send this letter with deep respect for all the amazing things that are

happening in the life of CBF, and an excitement about our potential future as a relevant resource for the local church.

Related to but separate from spiritual formation is moral and
ethical formation. How should Christians behave, and how does love
of God and neighbor inform their behavior? What does spiritual
formation have to do with character formation? Are Christian virtues
and values important not only within the Christian community but
also for society? If so, what are those virtues and values? How are we
to live out our faith in the family, in the community, in the world?
How do we as Christians answer and respond to the multiple moral
dilemmas in our world?

These are moral and ethical questions, and they are ones that
CBF addressed in partnership with a number of organizations:
Baptist Joint Committee on Public Affairs, Baptist Center for Ethics,
Christian Ethics Today, T. B. Maston Foundation, Baylor's Center
for Christian Ethics, Baylor's School of Social Work, and Mercer's
Center for Theology and Public Life.

The "ethics tradition" in Southern Baptist life was not a long one,
but it was rich and real to moderate Southern Baptists. The influence of Southern Baptist professors in Christian ethics, like Henlee
Barnette and T. B. Maston, had profound impact on many who were
influential in beginning CBF. This is especially true for students of
T. B. Maston. He taught thousands of students at Southwestern Seminary for forty-one years and personally supervised forty-nine ethics
majors. Foy Valentine, the longtime executive of Southern Baptists'
Christian Life Commission, made a bold statement in 1979:

> No Christian ethicist in Southern Baptist history comes close to
> having exerted the influence for good that he has exerted. Chris-
> tian ethics, both as an academic discipline and as a major emphasis
> in Southern Baptist life and work, bears the mark of T. B. Maston's
> genius.[14]

Because Earlene grew up in the Maston home, many of Maston's
students became early friends of mine, and all of them became kindred
spirits in the resistance to fundamentalism and in the birth of CBF.

It was not uncommon for me to see several of them in the Maston home when I was younger. They formed and informed many of my own ethical perspectives after the awakening of my social conscience in 1968.

These friends and colleagues were bold and courageous long before CBF began, but during the decade of controversy they were especially vocal, and then in the early years of CBF their voices were among the strongest in calling us to a faith that was relevant to the moral and social issues of our day. And all of them were profoundly influenced by Maston: Foy Valentine, James Dunn, Phil Strickland, Jimmy Allen, David Currie, Welton Gaddy, Randall Lolley, Carolyn Dipboye, Suzii Paynter, David Sapp, Larry Baker, Bill Tillman, Leta Tillman, Tom Logue, Ray Higgins, Pat Anderson, Robert Parham, Bob Adams, Sherry Adams, and many others. Each of them contributed to an "ethics tradition" that influenced CBF and me.

From its beginning, CBF had an awakened social consciousness and a kinship of conscience with Christians from other traditions who were committed to seeking social justice. Much of that can be attributed to these Baptist "ethicists." After the beginning of CBF, other Baptist professors and activists would articulate an ethical and moral vision compelling us to social awareness and action: James McClendon (Fuller Seminary), Ron Sider (Eastern Seminary), Curtis Freeman (Duke Divinity), Glen Stassen (Fuller Seminary), David Gushee (Mercer University), Robert Kruschwitz (Baylor), Ken Sehested (Baptist Peace Fellowship), and many others.

One ethicist in particular had a profound influence on me and on CBF: James Dunn. James was also a native of Fort Worth and a graduate from the same high school Earlene and I attended. While he was a Maston student at Southwestern Seminary, Earlene was a senior in high school. He asked her to type his note cards as he was completing his dissertation. Through the years he lovingly referred to Earlene as his "first secretary." He became a mentor to me and to one of my closest friends at Baylor, Ben Loring, who would later become pastor of FBC, Amarillo, Texas. By the time James was executive of the Texas Baptist Christian Life Commission, he had gained a reputation as a convictional and charismatic leader. He became executive

Earlene and Daniel Vestal with James and Marilyn Dunn

director of the Baptist Joint Committee on Religious Liberty in 1980, where he served for twenty years.

Small in stature and size (Oliver Thomas titled him "a Chihuahua who thinks he is a German shepherd"[15]), James Dunn was a fierce and fiery champion for religious liberty. As much as anyone else, he was the target of fury from fundamentalists in the SBC because he argued for separation of church and state, freedom of the press, and religious liberty for all, including those who didn't want to have anything to do with religion. He was a vocal critic of any and all efforts to align the power of government to aid the advancement of religion. He resisted government-sponsored prayer in public schools and government vouchers for church schools. He also advocated for equal access for religious organizations in public education, allowing faculty to be present in their meetings. He led the BJC in interfaith dialogues, interracial cooperation, and citizenship education, and he effectively represented religious liberty and church/state separation before the Supreme Court of the United States. But perhaps most important of all, he protected and preserved the Baptist Joint Committee after the SBC discontinued its funding and made every effort to destroy it. He rallied the support of CBF and other Baptist denominations to guarantee their future.

James Dunn was responsible for my one visit to the White House. At the close of the Clinton Administration, I was invited to a breakfast along with three hundred other religious leaders. I was assigned to sit at the table with President Clinton. After the breakfast and program, I had my "fifteen seconds of fame" when I shook hands with Clinton and said to him, "Mr. President, you are always welcome at CBF. Thank you for the opportunity to be here today." A few days later I received a phone call from the White House telling me that the president appreciated the invitation to attend our annual meeting and was seriously considering it. My first response was, "I didn't invite him to our General Assembly, and I didn't have the authority to invite him." My second response was, "How did he remember my few sentences spoken to him amid the hundreds of people that were greeting him?" In a couple of weeks I received a gracious letter from his appointment secretary telling me that he would be unable to schedule a visit to our gathering. I don't know whether I was relieved or disappointed. Perhaps both.

In theological education, CBF made a strategic decision not to own or operate seminaries but rather to partner with new schools that were emerging. The birth of these new seminaries resulted in some amazing relationships that I would not have known otherwise, especially with their deans and presidents. I considered it another gift of grace to know these scholars, educators, and administrators as friends. I learned from them both in informal conversations as well as in formal dialogues, and I accepted invitations from all of them to preach or teach to their students. They each had immeasurable influence on CBF and on me: Tom Graves at Baptist Theological Seminary of Richmond, Richmond, Virginia (1991); Nancy Ammerman, Scott Hudgins, and David Key at the Baptist Studies Program, Candler School of Theology, Emory University (1991); Wayne Stacy at Gardner-Webb Divinity School, Gardner-Webb University, Boiling Springs, North Carolina (1992); David Garland at George W. Truett Theological Seminary, Baylor University, Waco, Texas (1994); Alan Culpepper at McAfee School of Theology, Mercer University,

Atlanta, Georgia (1996); Mike Cogdill at Campbell University Divinity School, Campbell University, Buies Creek, North Carolina (1996); Vernon Davis and Don Williford at Logsdon School of Theology, Hardin Simmons University, Abilene, Texas; Tom Clifton and Molly Marshall at Central Baptist Theological Seminary, Kansas City, Missouri; Bill Leonard at Wake Forest Divinity School, Wake Forest University, Winston Salem, North Carolina (1999); Furman Hewitt and Curtis Freeman at the Baptist House of Study, Duke Divinity School, Duke University, Durham, North Carolina (1988); and William Hendricks at Baptist Studies Program, Brite Divinity School, Texas Christian University, Fort Worth, Texas.

Two of the deans, along with their wives, were especially close to Earlene and me. Bill Leonard and I both grew up in Fort Worth and had known each other since junior high school. Our mothers were friends and members of the same church. When we renewed our friendship during the SBC controversy, no one was more encouraging and supportive of me. When he became dean at the newly formed Wake Forest Divinity School, he became a leader in theological education among Baptists. As a church historian and keen observer of religious life in America, Bill became a "thought leader" among us and an interpreter of the times. As a popular teacher, preacher, and writer he influenced both clergy and laity and often offered me counsel and advice.

Alan Culpepper and I were students together at Baylor, but our friendship did not flourish until he became dean of Mercer University's McAfee School of Theology. Before my arrival as coordinator, CBF negotiated a $2.5 million lease agreement with Mercer for office space on the second floor of the theology building. This meant I saw Alan often, and we bonded both as colleagues and friends. Alan is one of the finest biblical scholars in the world, and he is also an astute and effective leader. After my retirement from CBF I became a part of the Mercer community, and Alan asked me to teach at McAfee.

Other ministry partners were strategic for CBF, and the relationships with their leaders were meaningful for me. After his retirement from the BJC, James Dunn was succeeded by Brent Walker, an articulate and persuasive spokesperson for religious liberty and church/

state separation. A number of independent religious news organizations not only provided a flow of objective reporting on what was happening in CBF but also provided resources for local congregations. Associated Baptist Press was led by Greg Warner and then David Wilkinson. *Baptists Today* was led by Jack Harwell, Bob Balance, and then Johnny Pierce. Robert Parham established the Baptist Center for Ethics. I had profound respect for each of these journalists and deep appreciation for their influence in moderate Baptist life.

Dave Odom served as director of the Center for Congregational Health and became a sought-after consultant and coach for churches, organizations, and individuals. I sought Dave's counsel and appreciated his friendship. Bill Wilson also served as director for the Center for Congregational Health and then for the Center for Healthy Churches. Bill's leadership and influence was enormous, and he was a great encouragement. Diana Garland was dean of Baylor's School of Social Work and a beloved presence among us. Pam Durso was the effective executive for Baptist Women in Ministry and a frequent speaker at CBF events.

Influencers

During my tenure I enjoyed some significant relationships with individuals whose scope and sphere of influence was well beyond mine and well beyond that of CBF. These relationships had profound influence on me personally, as well as on many others. Even though they were not engaged with CBF in governance or administration, they cared deeply about us and invested time, energy, and money. They were a source of encouragement, and their influence has had a lasting impact.

James Earl Carter

Jimmy Carter, the thirty-ninth president of the United States, is perhaps the most famous Baptist in the world and has been a friend and supporter of CBF from its beginning. Within days after my selection as coordinator, I received a handwritten note that said, ". . . we are fully committed to this movement of moderate Baptists. . . . I am able and willing to give you my full support. You can call on me. In

**Rosalynn and President Jimmy Carter with
Earlene and Daniel Vestal**

Christ, Jimmy Carter." Through the years, President Carter lived up
to that promise. I was privileged to participate in a number of his
initiatives and also witness his personal ministry to individuals, some
of whom were in positions of power and some of whom were little
known. In my travels, I also had opportunities to visit with government, business, or religious leaders who were curious about CBF's
identity and mission. It was always helpful to say, "President Carter
is a member of CBF," or "I am a Jimmy Carter kind of Baptist." His
character and compassion gave instant credibility and opened count-
less doors.

President Carter has a passion for reconciliation and resolving
conflict. He is always looking for ways to bring people together
in common causes, even when they disagree with one another. He
brought that passion to his Baptist family by convening multiple
meetings aimed at creating Baptist unity. He convened two such
meetings in 1997 and in 1998, bringing Baptist leaders together. I
helped him compose the list and set the agenda for the first of these
in November 1997. The following February he convened another
gathering of invited guests representing the Baptist family. The result

was a "Declaration of Cooperation" signed by a wide range of Baptist leaders, including leaders from the SBC, the CBF, and the Baptist World Alliance. It pledged joint efforts for racial reconciliation and efforts against religious persecution. The document received widespread notice and created some energy, but little else came of it.

In 2000, the SBC changed its doctrinal statement to become more rigid and narrow, which led President Carter to distance himself from the SBC and call for a smaller group of "traditional" Baptists to come to the Carter Center to find ways to counter fundamentalism. He crafted a statement that affirmed belief in Scripture and rejected "human statements of faith as official creeds carrying mandatory authority or as instruments of doctrinal accountability." I signed the statement along with a number of Baptist leaders from Texas and Virginia.

In 2001, President Carter addressed more than 8,000 participants at CBF's anniversary General Assembly in Atlanta. He offered a passionate and personal challenge to what was a historic milestone for CBF and for me a memorable moment. In 2002 and 2003, CBF was making application for membership in the Baptist World Alliance, and President Carter wrote letters of support. In 2004, I accompanied Buddy Shurden, Hardy Clemmons, and Bob Setzer on a trip to Plains, Georgia, with a request that President and Mrs. Carter allow CBF to begin the "Jimmy and Rosalynn Carter Offering for Religious Liberty." They graciously hosted us in their home and agreed to our request.

In 2005, President Carter, at my request, welcomed a delegation from the China Christian Council and agreed to address the Atlanta ceremony of the Bible Exhibition of the Church in China. The exhibition, which featured the story of Bibles in China, traveled to three locations: the Crystal Cathedral in Los Angeles, the Church of St. John the Divine in New York, and Second Ponce de Leon Baptist Church in Atlanta. In his opening address, Carter recounted the remarkable story of his private conversations in 1979 with then premier of China, Deng Xiaoping, when he requested that the Chinese government allow churches to be reopened, Bibles to be published, and missionaries to be allowed to return. He recounted to an amazed crowd of how the first two of his requests were granted, and how in 1980, the first Christian church was allowed to gather for public worship and Amity Press began publishing and distributing Bibles in China.

Ye Xiaowen, director of the State Administration for Religious Affairs (SARA), accompanied the delegation responsible for the exhibition. In one of my earlier visits to China I had visited with Ye Xiaowen, and he had informed me that he was a great admirer of President Carter and requested a private visit. Carter agreed to the visit. The day before the exhibition, I accompanied Ye Xiaowen to the Carter Center and listened as the two conversed on a wide range of topics. It was clear that Ye Xiaowen respected Carter and wanted to engage in serious conversation. He gave both of us a beautifully bound book commemorating the First World Buddhist Forum convened by the Chinese government only a few months earlier. Carter listened intently and then asked with his familiar smile, "Did the Dalai Lama attend? Was Tibet represented? Did you invite him?" The conversation then turned to a cordial but candid exchange that was fascinating for me to hear. Days after the exhibition I received a letter from Ye Xiaowen expressing appreciation and interest in continued dialogue and greater understanding between our countries.

A few years later I received a request from Tony Peck, general secretary of the European Baptist Federation, asking if President Carter would write a personal letter to the president of the Republic of Azerbaijan. A Baptist pastor, Zaur Balaev, had been imprisoned, and Azerbaijani Baptists needed support and help. Carter did write the letter appealing for intervention and release. On another occasion I received requests from Korean Baptist leaders appealing for President Carter to assist them in efforts for peace on the Korean peninsula. Other requests came from Baptists in Italy, the Republic of Georgia, and elsewhere asking for his help. Even when he had to decline invitations, he always responded with grace and thoughtfulness.

In 2006, President Carter decided to convene another gathering of Baptists that was more ambitious and expansive than any of his previous efforts. The result was the New Baptist Covenant Celebration in Atlanta, January 30–February 1, 2008. It was one of the most remarkable events I have ever experienced. Jimmy Carter's leadership and influence in our world has been inestimable. I value his friendship as one of God's greatest gifts. In 2012, I wrote him the following letter.

Dear Mr. President

The words of the Apostle Paul express the deepest feelings of my heart. "I thank my God upon every remembrance of you. I always pray with joy because of your partnership in the gospel from the first day until now." (Philippians 1:3)

Thank you for your example of Christ-likeness through the years. Thank you for your courage and conviction, for your compassion and care. Thank you for the way you have lived in public and political life, in church and denominational life, in family and home life. You have been an inspiration to so many, and to me personally in ways I can never adequately express.

I'm deeply grateful for your friendship and the times of fellowship we have shared in years past. I have such fond memories of your support and involvement in the formation and growth of Cooperative Baptist Fellowship. The times you welcomed Baptist leaders from Korea to your office and other private meetings made lasting impressions. Your testimony to leaders of the China Christian Council and Chinese government was profound and significant. Your consent and allowing us to use your name for a CBF offering designated for human rights resulted in much good being done with those funds. And how can I forget the gracious hospitality that you and Rosalynn gave me in a visit to Plains? You have always been accessible and supportive, as well as honest and straightforward. Please know that you are loved deeply by Christians around the world.

Your efforts to bring Baptists together in greater unity have been a source of inspiration and challenge to others. Thank you for all the time you have given to efforts of reconciliation, especially within the "New Baptist Covenant." Except for the initial gathering of CBF, no Baptist event has meant more to me than the New Baptist Covenant Celebration in 2008. What a moment. And it continues to have influence and impact. The seeds you have helped plant will continue to bear fruit.

May God continue to strengthen you with the Holy Spirit. May you continue to experience a fullness of joy and peace that passes all understanding. May God's grace sustain you and God's great love surround you.

Earlene joins me in wishing you a happy birthday with every assurance of our prayers for you and Rosalynn.

In friendship, Daniel Vestal

Walter B. (Buddy) Shurden

More than any other Baptist scholar, Walter Shurden shaped CBF in its formation and interpreted the reason for its very existence. Through his writing and speaking he articulated "four fragile freedoms" that Baptists cherish: Bible freedom, soul freedom, church freedom, and religious freedom. He traced how these freedoms have captured and conveyed the essence of Baptist identity from our beginning in the early seventeenth century. Then, as an incisive interpreter of secular and ecclesiastical politics as well as popular culture, he was a vocal critic of the fundamentalist takeover and a thought leader in the moderate resistance to it.

> BIBLE FREEDOM is the historic Baptist affirmation that the Bible, under the Lordship of Christ, must be central in the life of the individual and church and that Christians, with the best and most scholarly tools of inquiry, are both free and obligated to study and obey the Scripture.
>
> SOUL FREEDOM is the historic Baptist affirmation of the inalienable right and responsibility of every person to deal with God without the imposition of creed, the interference of clergy, or the intervention of civil government.
>
> CHURCH FREEDOM is the historic Baptist affirmation that local churches are free, under the Lordship of Christ, to determine their membership and leadership, to order their worship and work, to ordain whom they perceive as gifted for ministry, male or female, and to participate in the large Body of Christ, of whose unity and mission Baptists are proudly a part.
>
> RELIGIOUS FREEDOM is the historic Baptist affirmation of freedom OF religion, freedom FOR religion, and freedom

Dr. Walter (Buddy) Shurden

FROM religion, insisting that Caesar is not Christ and Christ is not Caesar.[16]

One reason Shurden's influence was so profound is because this articulation of Baptist principles gave clarity and definition to why so many Southern Baptists resisted the takeover. It violated Baptist principles of faith and practice. The fundamentalist takeover violated Bible freedom by insisting that documents other than the Bible ("The Baptist Faith and Message" or "The Chicago Statement on Biblical Inerrancy") become more authoritative than the Bible itself.

> Historically, Baptists have resisted any and all creeds. And they have for two very good reasons. First, no one doctrinal statement can summarize adequately the biblical mandate for behavior and belief. It is better, therefore, to stay with the Bible alone. Second, Baptists have feared creeds because of the seemingly inevitable tendency to make the creed the norm and then to force compliance to the creed. This is precisely what happened in the recent controversy over the Bible in the SBC. When creeds replace the Bible, we lose both the Bible and the freedom of approach to the Bible.[17]

The fundamentalist takeover violated soul freedom by pressuring and intimidating individuals to conform to only one interpretation on the inspiration and nature of Scripture (inerrancy).

> Soul freedom means the right to choose. Faith is voluntary. No one is forced to believe because no one can be forced to believe. Some words cannot be put together. "Forced love!" There is no such thing. You can force labor. You can force slavery. But you cannot "force" someone to love God. The voluntary nature of faith is crucial to the Baptist identity. To try to make someone believe what they honestly cannot believe exploits both the individual and the biblical meaning of faith.[18]

The fundamentalist takeover violated church freedom by excluding churches from meaningful involvement in the SBC if they differed with the SBC's interpretations on certain issues (like women as pastors) and demanding that they alter their practices to conform to the SBC's interpretation.

> For Baptists, church freedom means that a local Baptist Church has the right and responsibility to run its own affairs under the Lordship of Jesus Christ. No bishop or pastor, no civil leader or magistrate, no religious body or convention of churches can dictate to the local church. To permit such dictation is to abdicate freedom and obligation. Idealistically, Baptists want the local church to be a Christocracy.[19]

Finally, the fundamentalist takeover violated religious freedom by identifying Christian discipleship too closely with political partisanship and advocating the use of government power to advance religion (such as state-sponsored school prayer).

> Sometimes referred to as "Civil Religion," this attitude calls for, among other things, prayer in public schools, the channeling of public tax dollars into the support of private religious programs, and the presence of religious symbols in civil contexts. Christians have to work hard at distinguishing between pietism and patriotism, assessing critically where one begins and the other ends.

When the cross of Jesus is wrapped in the flag of any nation, danger, if not downright heresy, is close by.[20]

Shurden was a valued and validating member of the Interim Committee that drafted our founding documents in 1990 to 1991 and assisted Cecil Sherman in crafting "An Address to the Public." He was a frequent speaker at CBF events and a member of the search committee that called me as executive coordinator. On the occasion of my receiving the "Courage Award" by the Whitsett Baptist Heritage Society at the General Assembly in 2011, it was Shurden who presented it and spoke some kind words. At the same assembly, he delivered an address reflecting on the first twenty years of CBF titled, "I Remember. I Hope." It was one of the finest messages I had ever heard. After reflecting on what he remembered, he offered three hopes for the future. His third hope had a special meaning for me, partly because of my heritage from an evangelist father.

> Third, I hope . . . that we CBFers will find new ways to think of what it means to be "lost" in our society. Eschatological fears no longer fuel a theology of outreach in American churches, moderate, conservative or liberal. Scaring hell out of people no longer works for churches, so a redefinition of "lost" is in order if our churches are to have authentic growth. Loneliness and the need for community, alienation and the need for reconnecting, meaninglessness and the need for purpose, the inability to find a sanctuary for shame and guilt, and the deep, deep sense that one is not loved— these are the marks of "lostness" in our time. All of this is as real today as that first century garbage dump that they called Gehenna, located on the southwest corner of Jerusalem. If we do not believe that people live hellish lives today in homes that surround our churches, we will have little success in developing any passion and urgency for the gospel at any level, local or national.[21]

John Franklin Baugh

John Baugh was a larger-than-life figure and one of the most remarkable people I have known. Following his graduation from high school in Waco, Texas, he worked at the local A&P grocery to help his family during the Depression. Because of hard economic times, he dropped out of Baylor and hitchhiked to Houston, where he met Eula Mae Tharpe, a pastor's daughter. They married in 1936, and he joined Second Baptist Church, Houston, where she was already a member. He was again hired by A&P and advanced to become a store manager.

As the war ended, John and Eula Mae started a frozen food business in their garage; Zero Foods Company, a wholesale distributorship, was "designed to supply frozen foods in institutional-sized containers to hotels, hospitals, school districts, fast food stores and large grocery chains like the A&P."[22] An early crisis occurred when a business partner who had committed by "gentleman's agreement" to finance 50 percent of a large container of frozen foods decided on a Saturday afternoon to withdraw his capital. John and Eula Mae had some money, but not enough to pay the $30,000 due by Monday. His company and integrity were in serious jeopardy.

He went to Sunday school and worship the following morning, where he and Eula Mae accidentally met his mentor and friend, Earl Hankamer, a wealthy and respected Houston oilman. Hankamer could see that John Baugh was worried, so he asked him what was wrong.

The two stepped outside the church and John related to the wealthy deacon what had happened the day before. He did not need to detail what his failure to meet the payment on Monday would do to his credit rating and his general business reputation. The deacon was himself a businessman who understood such things.

The conversation took no more than two minutes. Those one-hundred and twenty seconds would change John Baugh's life forever.

He said he had chosen his partner unwisely and was facing a $30,000 debt he could not pay. He said he had little hope of getting a line of credit because he had always paid his debts with cash not credit. Ironically, he needed credit now more than ever before.

"Is that all," his friend the deacon inquired in the sincere tone of voice for which he was known far and wide . . . . He wanted to

John Franklin Baugh and Daniel Vestal

help John as he himself had been helped by an unselfish mentor while in similar business circumstances some twenty years before.

"Johnny," he said, "I'll tell you what. Can you please be in my office at 10 a.m. tomorrow?" The office was in a downtown bank.[23]

Monday morning, Earl Hankamer, one of the bank's directors, assured John Baugh that the bank believed in his business and was glad to extend him a $50,000 line of credit. This event was a turning point in John's life, and in the years ahead he would extend similar confidence to countless others. Zero Foods flourished, having a branch in San Antonio and servicing most of south Texas. John became active in industry organizations and met other food distributors from across the country in the National Frozen Food Association (FFAA), where he became a director and then president.

He proposed the idea to create a nationwide food service company by having a simultaneous merger of nine privately owned companies. These nine pioneers of the food industry agreed unanimously to accept the ownership structure recommended by John, affirming their respect for his fairness and integrity. Sysco Corporation was founded May 1, 1970, and became a public company on the same day. It has since grown to become the largest food services company in North America. John Baugh served with distinction as chairman, CEO, and senior chairman.

Because of his experience in the corporate world and his keen insight into human nature, he saw the dangers and consequences of a fundamentalist takeover of the SBC. As a non-clergy Christian, he saw the deception being used to achieve a takeover. He also saw the connection of a fundamentalist takeover to partisan politics. He predicted early that the SBC, as the largest Protestant denomination in America, would become an institutional platform for a broader agenda: a takeover of a national political party by the "religious right" and then an imposition of its agenda on the US government. Few listened and even fewer heeded his warnings. Many dismissed and scorned him. He correctly discerned that much more was at stake in this struggle than the soul of the SBC. This was the beginning of a struggle for the soul of America.

After the fundamentalist takeover was complete, no one was more committed to moving forward than was John Baugh. When I became pastor of Tallowood in Houston, John and Eula Mae decided to join. They did so in a quiet and unpretentious way without telling me or anyone else of their intentions. They left the church where they had been members for more than fifty years and where both had served in strategic leadership roles. To the day they died, they were committed to helping Baptists build for the future. That commitment included financial generosity to a number of Christian causes.

On one of my several visits to their San Marcos ranch, John dismissed himself one morning after breakfast and said he would return before lunch. He said he had a meeting. Upon returning, he informed Eula Mae, Earlene, and me that he had just visited with Bruce Babbitt, the US secretary of the interior, about environmental issues related to Aquarena Springs, a water park in San Marcos that he owned. He was casual about the meeting, although I was more than a bit curious, wanting to know all the details. Then he said, "I've decided to sell it for $10 million and give the money to Baylor

University as an endowment for the George W. Truett Theological Seminary." I was overwhelmed and speechless.

John Baugh was an active church leader, a respected civic leader, an honorable business executive, and a generous philanthropist. To me he was a beloved friend, and although there was a thirty-year age difference between us, we shared a bond of mutual trust and respect. I became pastor to John and Eula Mae and conducted both of their funerals. At John's memorial service, I compared him to John the Baptist, the last of the Hebrew prophets and the forerunner to the Messiah: "There was a man sent from God whose name was John" (John 1:6). Like his biblical predecessor, John Baugh was a witness.

He was a witness to the value of hard work. I've never known anybody who had more devotion and dedication to work than John Baugh. He was a witness to honesty, truthfulness, and integrity. This man's word was his bond, even in the commanding heights of corporate America. He didn't cheat. He didn't lie. He didn't steal.

He was a witness to faithfulness and fidelity in marriage. And what a witness that has been, especially in a day when promiscuity and unfaithfulness are so commonplace. John and Eula Mae's marriage was an inspiration and a testament to devotion.

He was a witness to the truth that "it's more blessed to give than to receive." I once heard some say, "If I had as much money as John Baugh, I would give it away." But John and Eula Mae were generous before they were wealthy. They cared for people in need when they had little as well as when they had much.

John Baugh was a witness to the biblical struggle for justice and righteousness. His resistance to the fundamentalist takeover of the SBC and its marriage to the political and religious right caused some to be uncomfortable. They would say, "John, why be so concerned about Baptist politics?" Why? Because he was passionate about justice and righteousness.

John was a witness to so much more during his ninety-one years: a witness to love and care for family, a witness to loyalty and devotion to friends, a witness to the importance of Christian education and institutions of benevolence, a witness to faithfulness to the church and all its ministries.

But before and beyond all this, from first to last, John Baugh was a witness to Jesus Christ. What motivated and sustained his life was his allegiance to Christ. What guided his behavior and formed his character was faith in his Savior and Lord. He was like his biblical counterpart—always pointing people away from himself to "the Lamb of God that takes away the sins of the world" (John 1:29).

Barbara Nell "Babs" Baugh

Barbara was the daughter of John and Eula Mae Baugh. Their love for her and her love for them formed and shaped her life more than anything else. She was nurtured and supported from birth to childhood to adolescence to adulthood by her remarkable parents. And she would, in turn, love and honor them until the days they died. She would also become, in her own right, a remarkable person. It is impossible to think or speak about Babs without thinking and speaking of her parents and then speaking of her two daughters, Jackie Baugh Moore and Julie Baugh Cloud. She was the center link in a community of three generations that have had enormous influence, especially in the Baptist family.

After the deaths of her parents in 2007, she became president of the Eula Mae and John Baugh Foundation established by her parents in 1994. Together with her parents, and then with her daughters, Babs has led the Baugh Foundation to distribute more than $95 million to all kinds of religious, educational, and humanitarian causes, and especially to Baptist causes. More than any other individual I know, Babs has influenced the CBF network of institutions, organizations, and ministries through her generosity. But her generosity and influence were never with the intention of control but only encouragement and collaboration.

Her experience of love and grace with her own family helped her practice love and grace to others. She loved all kinds of people like they were family, which meant she was always working to bring them together in unity and collaboration. She had an infectious smile and delightful wit that could disarm almost anyone. She enjoyed music, food, art, and all kinds of whimsy, which made her a delightful host. And host she did. Over and over again, she hosted dinner parties,

Barbara "Babs" Baugh

trips, concerts, receptions, and soirees, often with noble purposes and often just for fun.

A couple of years before I retired from CBF, she and I decided to host a visioning retreat at Callaway Gardens, Pine Mountain, Georgia, and invite the organizational leadership that was representative of the CBF network. She funded the expenses for every participant and spouse. Her humor and fierce commitment to moderate Baptist causes was a glue that helped us have honest and hopeful conversations. It was a great gift.

Babs died on June 14, 2020, after a long battle with Parkinson's disease. At her graveside memorial, Molly Marshall, a longtime friend and respected theologian, offered these final words: "Saints are those who refract the light of God. In her compassion, warmth, humor, generosity, and service, Babs Baugh has allowed us to see a joyful life. While I cannot imagine the world without Babs in it, her joy is now complete, and we give thanks."

Othniel (Oti) Bunaciu

Othniel is a Romanian pastor whose life and ministry has had profound influence on Earlene and me. I first met Oti when, in 1980, I led a delegation from FBC Midland, on a weeklong mission to the church where his father, Dr. John Bunaciu, was pastor of the Ferranti Baptist church in Bucharest. It was at the time when Nikolai Ceausescu, a communist official, was leader of Romania, and all Christian churches were under strict regulations of what they could and could not do. It was a difficult period in Romanian history, but in spite of government oppression churches were flourishing and growing.

As the week came to an end, I asked John Bunaciu how he could explain this growth in his country, where severe restrictions were placed on churches and so many challenges were present. How were their churches growing with new believers? In America we have so much freedom and so great an access to the public with radio, television, and publications, and yet we were not experiencing such results. John Bunaciu responded, "In our country we recognize that there is a great struggle between good and evil. And we have discovered that the greatest weapons we have in this warfare are the weapons of God's word and prayer."

As I returned home, I decided to reach out to our government and register concerns about religious freedom and human rights for Baptist churches in Romania. I called a friend, Foy Valentine, who connected me with Bob Maddox, President Carter's liaison with denominations. Maddox arranged appointments with representatives of the national security council and state department. I flew to Washington, where I met with Dr. Philip Becker, a career diplomat and the chief Romanian desk officer in the state department.

It was a cordial conversation, and Becker listened to my concerns attentively. It soon became clear that he was a Christian and had more than a professional interest in what we were discussing. As we talked, the conversation shifted from a private citizen giving information to a government representative and became a personal conversation between two Christian believers. When Becker felt comfortable, he said to me, "Rev. Vestal, many of us in diplomacy, who are also Christians, believe that there is a spiritual struggle going on in our world

**Othniel Bunaciu, T. Thomas, Peter Wallace, Daniel Vestal,
Tony Twist, John Bunaciu**

between good and evil. Although our government offers economic, educational, and even military help to many countries, the most important thing we as Christians can do in this struggle is to offer the word of God and prayer."

This was not the preacher talking to the diplomat but the diplomat talking to the preacher, and it mirrored almost exactly what John Bunaciu had said to me only a few days earlier. These words have stayed with me through the years and been a reminder of the universal spiritual realities that lie at the center of everything we do as Christians to influence and impact our world.

Oti Bunaciu, like his father, is a person whose considerable influence emerges from a foundational commitment to the word of God and prayer. During that first visit to Romania, he interpreted my sermons and engaged in serious conversation about his future. He went on to receive his theological education, including a degree from Regent's Park College, Oxford University. His scholarship is equaled by his compassion for people. Oti succeeded his father as pastor and is in great demand throughout Europe as a preacher and teacher. His influence in church and society is inspiring.

What I have seen in Oti Bunaciu is a model of Christian ministry that I have seen in few others anywhere in the world. In a cultural and political context very different from my own, he has been an example of faithfulness and fortitude. Oti's friendship for the past forty years has provided me a living link to the global church and a partnership that has taught me so much about the gospel. Located in a poorer neighborhood of Bucharest, the church found itself surrounded by a despised minority in Romania, the Roma people. Under his leadership the church began providing educational opportunities for Roma children and multiple other ministries to their families. The "Ruth School" evolved into the "Ruth Project" and has become a successful and respected educational and social service institution in Romania and a model of collaboration attracting scores of international partnerships, including CBF.

In addition to all this, Oti Bunaciu is professor and dean of the faculty of Baptist Theology at the University of Bucharest, the largest and most prestigious university in Romania. He travels and teaches extensively and has completed a tenure as president of the Romanian Baptist Convention. He is widely respected as a preacher, a theologian, and a contributor to the cultural, social, and spiritual consolidation of Romanian society. Oti is a catalyst for transformation in so many ways, and he is my friend.

Philanthropists

One of my key roles and responsibilities as coordinator of CBF was fundraising. As an ecclesial body, we had a budget that was funded primarily by churches sending undesignated gifts or special offerings. However, we also received money from individuals who gave directly to us, and their gifts sustained our mission and ministry. Some of the individuals who contributed directly to CBF made transformational gifts, and that introduced me to some personal relationships that were also transformational.

There is a vast body of literature about fundraising in nonprofit and non-governmental organizations. Some of it is good, and some of it is bad. I made an early commitment to read and learn as much as possible about the best practices in "resource development," only to discover that most of the literature didn't resonate with me. As a pastor I had preached and taught about Christian stewardship, tithing, and giving to the church as well as the importance of generosity in one's lifestyle. But I was unacquainted with the task of building relationships with philanthropists who might give large sums of money.

I didn't want to be manipulative or show favoritism to individuals because they had wealth. Yet I also recognized that philanthropy was both a privilege and a responsibility given to some. I had a certain amount of anxiety and insecurity when it came to asking someone to give a large amount of money. What I lacked more than anything else was motivation other than the financial success of the organization I was leading. All of this changed when I read Henri Nouwen's little book, *The Spirituality of Fundraising*. In it he contends that when we ask individuals to give of their financial resources, we are not only inviting them to participate in a work of God but also providing an opportunity for them to grow spiritually. This gave me motivation for what would become an enjoyable ministry and also an opportunity to develop meaningful friendships and partnerships in ministry.

Early in my tenure, Bob and Norma Stephenson from Norman, Oklahoma, paid for an early printing and distribution of my book, *It's Time: An Urgent Call to Christian Mission*. The book became an effective resource for local churches, helping them to discern God's mission in the world and discover their participation in it. I still remember the exuberant joy that Bob and Norma expressed when they funded the book's publication. Nell Barret, the widow of an Atlanta dentist, was the first person I met who wanted to include CBF in her will, so she asked to meet with me along with Reuben Swint, CBF's Foundation president, to design an endowment fund that would be established at her death. Again, after she knew how her estate would be disbursed upon her death, she was so appreciative and grateful.

Ed and Laura Ann Vick from Raleigh, North Carolina, were blessed with financial resources, and they wanted to create an endowment fund for seminary scholarships. Susanne Morse of Pendleton, South Carolina, gave multiple gifts for medical missions. Linda Lewis of Farmville, North Carolina, was a philanthropist who gave to global missions. Jim and Juandelle Lacy, dear friends from Midland, Texas, used their wealth wisely and generously. Tom Nunnley and Roland Wilson, lay leaders at Dunwoody Baptist in Atlanta, were responsible for an endowment gift to fund church planting. For each of these friends, philanthropy was both a calling and a blessing.

Pat Ayers, CBF's third moderator, is one of the most gracious people I know. She is generous with her money, her time, and her energy. Her influence extends well beyond the Baptist community, as she served many years on the governing board of "Bread for the World" and also served as its chair. Her numerous financial contributions to CBF and other Christian causes are exceeded only by her public voice of conscience and significant participation in numerous nonprofit organizations.

Paul and Shirley Piper befriended CBF and gave transformative gifts to church planting, evangelism, missions, leadership development, and congregational resourcing. Earlene and I joined the Pipers on numerous occasions, one of which was a trip across the western US to learn about rural poverty. I will never forget the conversations with the residents of a Native American reservation and watching them weep as we discussed the plight of those in extreme poverty.

An anonymous donor approached me for the first time in 2002 to explore a partnership in the worldwide missionary enterprise of CBF. It proved to be one of the most remarkable partnerships I would experience and an example of Christian stewardship and generosity that continues to amaze. This philanthropist, who wanted their privacy protected, asked that I outline in detail how we would disburse their gift over a period of several years. After considerable work by the global missions and finance staff, I would submit the proposal with explanatory notes and exact figures. This would often be followed by alterations and changes through personal conversations and emails. The donor would then approve the plans and provide the funds.

This process occurred over a seven-year period in which the anonymous donor contributed transformative gifts to global missions. It was an amazing experience for me personally, and it was a great encouragement to CBF. These repeated acts of philanthropy not only empowered the mission efforts of CBF but also impacted the lives and living conditions of millions of people all around the world. Just as remarkable as the amount of money given is that the donor did not want any recognition or public congratulation. These were truly gifts offered unto the Lord.

With all these philanthropists, and many others, I felt that I was involved in sacred partnerships. I never felt that I was "raising funds" or "developing donors." Rather I felt that these were holy relationships where all of us were involved in something far bigger than ourselves. We were simply stewards of the resources of time and treasure that God had given us. What a privilege.

Chapter 8

Cooperative Baptist Fellowship: Issues and Concerns

Women as Pastors

At the first General Assembly after becoming CBF coordinator, I delivered the keynote address, "A Vision of Hope." Toward the end of the message, I acknowledged a change of mind and heart in my view of women as pastors. My acknowledgment was a public confession and a request for grace and forgiveness.

My change began before being called as coordinator, but it crystalized during my first few months of leadership. There was not one particular moment that I can identify as a turning point where I could say, "The light dawned, and I repented." Rather there was a series of steps that altered not only my perspective but also my attitude. It was a spiritual process that at the time was difficult to interpret. I can look back and see some factors that helped me get to a place where I could affirm women as pastors.

First, I experienced a deconstruction and reconstruction of my biblical hermeneutic. Historically, Baptists have held to a male-dominated clergy because we believed that is what the Bible taught. Like our Orthodox and Catholic ancestors, we thought it seemed clear from Scripture that only men should be bishops (overseers) in the church, since only men can "be the husband of one wife" (1 Tim 3:2). Although we didn't base that conviction on apostolic succession, which is part of the justification for an all-male priesthood, we did base it on what we believed was apostolic precedent, i.e., all of the twelve apostles were male. This influenced how we interpreted Scripture, especially the Pauline letters.

All of us interpret Scripture with certain presuppositions that influence our hermeneutical perspective. What is important, I believe, is that we at least examine those presuppositions and perspectives and not just accept them uncritically. What happened to me was that I faced my own interpretations about women as pastors in ways that allowed my assumptions to be challenged. I admitted that I had interpreted Scripture from a patriarchal, masculine, and hierarchical perspective without realizing it. I had not viewed myself as sexist or chauvinistic, but in fact I had imposed on Scripture some presuppositions that were more from my Texas, Baptist, revivalist culture than I had realized.

I also examined the presuppositions imposed on me from an American, business, corporate culture where men are CEOs far more than women. Men make up the majority of governing bodies, boards of directors, and corporate institutional leadership than do women. It was easy to transfer that perspective to my interpretation of Scripture and apply it to the functioning of the church.

As I began to examine my presuppositions in light of the life, ministry, and teachings of Jesus rather than a Texas Baptist culture or corporate business culture, I began to change. Scripture was and is still central to my theology and authoritative in my life, but I became more intentional about interpreting Scripture with Jesus as the interpretive principle. Jesus not only gathered men around him as disciples but also gathered women who then became central to his ministry. Women were the last to leave him at the cross and the first to proclaim the resurrection.

What happened to me, and I must say not without some pain, was a deconstruction and reconstruction of my hermeneutic. I came to believe that the example of Jesus presents a much more egalitarian vision of the church and its ministry. I came to believe that the kingdom of God, as embodied in the life and ministry of Jesus, looks very different than the kingdoms of this world when it comes to the relationship between women and men. In God's kingdom, which the church is to represent, the relationship between women and men is one of mutual submission and full equality. In those texts that seem to call for a masculine ministry, particularly in 1 Timothy where the writer calls for the bishop "to be the husband of one wife," I came to believe that these were not intended to be normative for all churches in the future. Rather they were instructions intended for a particular historical context, much like instructions mandating that women wear a veil or not speak in public.

I also came to believe that the mission of the church is to be fulfilled more from a gift-based ministry than a gender-based ministry. I concluded that organizational offices and church polity are not as fixed as I had interpreted them to be. The Holy Spirit bestows gifts to all in the body of Christ, male and female alike. The calling and equipping of God to ministry functions as an expression of the sovereignty of God. God freely and mysteriously chooses human beings for tasks, for roles, for positions, for places.

Another factor that influenced my change was my encounters with effective women pastors. In his television documentary, Moyers asked W. A. Criswell, pastor of First Baptist Church in Dallas, Texas, what he would say to a woman if she believed God had called her to be a pastor. He smiled and said, "Well, I would just say she is mistaken." The reason I can recall his answer so clearly is because that's pretty much what I had always felt. I distinctly remember the first time I met a woman who was serving a Baptist church as pastor. I asked her, "Please tell me about your call to ministry and your spiritual journey." As she recounted her story, I was shocked at how much of a disconnect there was between my rigid hermeneutic and the real person in front of me who clearly demonstrated evidence of a divine call.

I also remember the first time I met Julie Pennington Russell, then pastor of Nineteenth Avenue Baptist Church in San Francisco, California. She was a caring, competent pastor serving an inner-city congregation, preaching the gospel, equipping the saints, and leading effectively. It simply couldn't be called a mistake. The encounter was transformative.

It brought to mind the experience of Simon Peter with Cornelius. For Peter, the idea that the Holy Spirit could be given to the Gentiles did not fit with how he interpreted Scripture. However, when there was clear evidence that the Gentiles did indeed receive the Spirit, Peter was astonished. And he was changed. Later he would say, "Who was I that I could hinder God?" (Acts 11:17). What Simon Peter felt was what I felt when I encountered women who were demonstrating fruitfulness in ministry as pastors.

Another factor that influenced my change was exposure to the global church. Today in China, anywhere from 30 to 40 percent of the pastors are women. In many other parts of the world, women give much more leadership at every level of ministry than in America. They serve not only as lay leaders, missionaries, and educators but also as pastors, bishops, executive administrators of denominations, and seminary presidents. They are equally effective as men in senior ministry roles, fulfilling their calling to lead God's people.

All of these factors in combination with one another were used by the Spirit to overcome my fears about being untrue to Scripture. I experienced an inner release from many of my anxieties. I came to know, in a very gentle and quiet way, a confidence and assurance about God's presence and work in women's leadership in ways that I previously could not admit. My own change was subtle rather than spectacular and sudden. But it was a change that was both created by and resulted in a spiritual renewal.

On Thursday night, June 26, 1997, in Louisville, Kentucky, I offered the following conclusion to my message: "In a pastors meeting in Kansas City I was asked the question, 'Daniel, have you changed in your attitude and convictions about women in ministry, and particularly about women as pastors?' I answered, 'Yes, I've not only changed, but I've had to repent and ask God to forgive me. And I have not only been shown grace by God, but by so many of you, and I'm grateful.' The wind of the Spirit of God is blowing across the world, calling women, and they are responding. This fellowship will attract an increasing number of Baptists because we believe in that movement of the Spirit."

Responding to Critics

My first few years as executive coordinator were both exhilarating and exhausting. I was in a learning mode, adapting to a new way of life and a new ministry role. I was on the road most weekends, preaching in various churches, and working during the week to administer a staff.

My first few years were also marked by what seemed like an endless response to events beyond my control. I gave a great deal of energy in responding to the efforts by President Carter to create a broader consensus and collaboration among Baptists who had been excluded by the SBC. I had to respond to the transition in global missions leadership with the retirement of Keith Parks. I was responding to the convictional and vocal element within CBF who wanted us to affirm same-sex covenanted relationships (same-sex marriage was not legal at the time) and encourage churches to ordain gay and lesbian ministers. In my first years, CBF did engage in a strategic planning process that resulted in the adoption of a new vision and mission statement, but a great amount of time and energy was given to reacting and responding to external pressures and internal challenges.

I was forced to respond to a constant stream of criticism of CBF from several SBC leaders. I spent an inordinate amount of time answering untrue and unfair statements about CBF in the religious media and online articles, especially from a Southern Baptist layman in Missouri who seemed to make it his personal mission to discredit CBF. Pastors were urging me to publish and distribute some thoughtful and honest response to the criticisms that seemed to be everywhere. So in the spring of 1998 we published an eight-page brochure that addressed many of the prevalent questions about the fellowship. In a question-and-answer format I responded not only to the frequently asked questions about our mission but also to various accusations circulating in Baptist life. The following is a brief excerpt from that brochure.

Question: Is CBF a liberal, moderate, or conservative organization? Answer: Is there a choice for none of the above? We all know those words are often used more as political poison pills than as meaningful indicators of the faith stance. If you're asking me to wear a label, I'll gladly say I'm a Christian first, a Baptist second. Those are names with profound meaning. We in the Fellowship are frequently described by the media and others as moderates. In my own case, I have come to identify with the term in that it describes the mainstream of Christian faith and Baptist identity. A mainstream position will not be trivialized by nonessentials. For me, a mainstream Baptist stands firmly on the revealed truth of Holy Scripture. A mainstream Baptist is committed to the heart of the biblical faith—Jesus Christ is Lord—is not contentious with those who have the same commitment.

Question: What does CBF believe about the Bible? Answer: This is a fellowship of Bible-believing Christians. Our mission statement includes a clear, confessional statement about our love of Scripture, our confidence in Scripture, and our belief in and commitment to Scripture as the authority for our faith and practice. We try to honor the truths of Scripture in our life together. I don't say we are perfect, but I see in our partner churches and our cooperative ministries a deep love of God and neighbor. The evidence of our belief is not in pledges of allegiance to creedal statements about the Bible but in our obedience to the Bible.

Question: Critics have accused the Fellowship of being "silent" on volatile issues such as abortion, homosexuality, same-sex marriage, etc. Don't you need to define a position on these issues? Answer: Our approach to these issues is shared by well-known Christian groups like the Billy Graham Evangelistic Association, the American Bible Society, the Willow Creek Association, the Salvation Army, and many others. Neither we nor they make official pronouncements on these and many other issues. Doing so is outside CBF's stated mission. We are not a convention. We are a resource network for Baptist Christians and churches.

Question: Do you really think your focus on the CBF mission will satisfy some of your accusers? Some are circulating stories claiming that the members of the Fellowship secretly do have agendas on these issues. Answer: Well, I do sometimes wonder whether the real problem these critics have with our silence is that it frustrates their desire to define us for their own purposes. Voices at the extremes of these volatile issues can be shrill, judgmental, and divisive. That makes it easy for those with politically motivated agendas to sow suspicion. One of the saddest consequences is that Christians with sincere personal convictions, who could find a welcoming home in CBF, may be unfairly discouraged from getting to know us. It's no secret that this Fellowship is helping to do God's work. I see it here every day.

Question: If the accusations being made about CBF are untrue, why don't you simply refute them point by point? Answer: First, that kind of counterattack does not help the cause of Christ. We have what I think is a healthier approach. We try to communicate clearly who we are and what our mission is. We welcome questions and invite feedback. We try to foster conversation and cooperation among churches and individuals with diverse viewpoints. Second, the attacks have been coming in a steady stream for years. Were they not so hurtful, the sheer volume of them would be comical. Even if the Fellowship had the resources to research and correct every misleading statement, we would not stoop to do so. That is not our mission.

The publication of the brochure did not stop the attacks from some of the SBC leadership, but eventually they did subside and lessen in their intensity. Other issues became more important to the SBC, and we became less and less relevant to their agenda. We also gained recognition among other Christian denominations and respect within the broader Christian community for our cooperative spirit and shared ministry efforts.

Interacting with the Media

My introduction to religious journalism was in 1977 while I was pastor in Midland, when I was elected to the board of directors for the *Baptist Standard*, an official publication for the Baptist General Convention of Texas (BGCT). It was a weekly publication with a circulation of almost 400,000 readers. The editor, Presnall Wood, once boasted to me that more people in Texas read the *Baptist Standard* than *Time* magazine. It was a free press receiving no funds from the BGCT, which meant it could both commend and criticize the convention as well as provide coverage on social and political issues. When Lyndon Johnson was president, he summoned the editor at the time, E. S. James, to the White House to ask for his counsel and appeal for his help. The influence of the *Baptist Standard* and other Baptist news publications across America was significant in the latter half of the twentieth century.

During my years on the board (1977–1986), the fundamentalist takeover of the SBC was gaining momentum. The origin of the takeover efforts was in Texas with Paige Patterson and Paul Pressler, both members of Texas Baptist churches. Their names and activities were often in the *Baptist Standard*. I witnessed enormous pressure exerted on the editor and reporters, especially from fundamentalists who didn't want their political activities reported and surely didn't want any editorial that was critical of their efforts. Paul Pressler vigorously objected to the news articles and editorials questioning motives and methods. He asked for a "face to face" meeting with the editor, and since I was chair of the board, I participated in the conversation. It was my first experience with such anger toward a free press. The phrase "fake news" wasn't in use at the time, but the accusations and hostilities were fierce.

As the fundamentalist takeover neared its completion, the anger toward the *Baptist Standard* and other similar press organizations, especially the *Baptist Press*, intensified. Editors Dan Martin and Al Shackleford were fired, and others resigned because they were considered dangerous to the takeover. New press organizations were formed independent of one another to assure the free flow of information: SBC Today (later named Baptists Today), Associated Baptist Press (later named Baptist News Global), Center for Christian Ethics (later named Ethics Daily and Good Faith Media). Considerable time, energy, and money were expended in the furor over the role and responsibility of a free press in a free society.

When I decided to seek the SBC presidency, I became the subject of news myself, which was an unfamiliar experience for me as a pastor.

Seeing one's picture and name in a publication, sometimes favorably and other times unfavorably, can be disconcerting. Before, during, and after the Las Vegas and New Orleans conventions, I was "in the news" more than any time before or since. It reinforced my understanding of how influential the media is and my conviction of how important a "free press" is. The forming of CBF in 1990 and 1991 was "news," not only to Baptists and other people of faith but also to many in the broader culture. I was surprised by the different ways journalists understood and interpreted what had happened. Some saw it only as a denominational battle, while others rightly saw it as part of a much greater struggle within America.

No one understood this better than the television journalist Bill Moyers, who is both theologically and journalistically educated. He truly understood both worlds. More than anyone I knew, Moyers discerned the connection between religious movements, popular culture, and politics. His interview with me was part of a documentary that clearly showed the connection between the fundamentalist takeover of the SBC and the marriage of fundamentalism to Republican political power. His documentary also demonstrated the power and influence of the media, which I would discover in an even greater way as I came to CBF.

Ministry in a local church is different from ministry in an ecclesial organization where decisions about budget, personnel, and programs are reported in the media, both secular and religious. As a pastor I had lived in a "fishbowl" kind of existence where church members watched me and my family, but there was a measure of privacy and protection from the broader community. In coming to CBF, I discovered the challenges of ministry where the media were always monitoring and often editorializing.

I was unaccustomed to working in an environment where newspaper and online articles reported on actions taken or statements made. I learned to measure my words more carefully and pay attention to how I would speak in a public setting because a reporter might quote me incorrectly. I have deep commitment to a free press and great appreciation for its value. I have also recognized that journalists, even religious journalists, sometimes have their own biases, so I learned to conduct interviews and engage in news conferences with care and caution. David Wilkinson, Ben McDade, and Lance Wallace were experienced journalists on CBF staff, and they helped me navigate my interaction with the public media. I relied heavily on their counsel.

Human Sexuality

Through all my years as coordinator, I spent a lot of time responding to what was described then as "the issue of homosexuality." From its beginning, CBF was different from the Alliance of Baptists, another network of churches that separated from the SBC. The alliance was much more united in advocating for what was then defined as "welcoming and affirming" of LBGTQ+ people (an abbreviation that was not used at the time). Churches in CBF were overwhelmingly negative toward performing same-sex marriages or ordaining a gay or lesbian staff minister. The pressure was intense from a few pastors, several seminary professors, and young Baptist leaders to move CBF in a more progressive direction. On the other hand, there was intense pressure from a larger number of CBF pastors who, for varying reasons, did not want us to pursue an advocacy role on LBGTQ+ issues.

I sought to balance these pressures by leading CBF to focus on what united us rather than what divided us. We published videos and brochures designed to answer our critics and emphasize the freedom of conscience and the autonomy of every local church in this and other social, ethical issues. Yet the intensity of the rhetoric increased. Because of our hostile and external critics from the "right" and the public pronouncements from our friends on the "left," we continued to be defined by others. After much self-examination, I came to believe that it was time for CBF to bring some clarity and self-definition on the issue.

During my first four years as coordinator, more than 250 churches were related to CBF. It became clear to me that the vast majority of our partner churches had already reached their own consensus on the issue of homosexual practice as it relates to congregational leadership. Stated simply, these churches would not ordain or call a practicing homosexual to serve as their pastor or other ministry staff roles. Neither would the leadership of these churches perform same-sex unions. There were a handful of churches that believed differently, but the vast majority of our partner churches had reached their consensus.

In many ways, the conflict within the CBF constituency was also a conflict I felt within my own conscience. I found myself unable to accept same-sex marriage as compatible with the teachings of Scripture, yet I felt empathy and solidarity with those who wanted us to be more welcoming and inclusive. That internal struggle caused me to explore in a more intentional way the wide spectrum of literature regarding human sexuality and Scripture.

I read the biblical interpretations and cogent arguments from varying viewpoints. I had numerous conversations with scholars and friends. I prayed and sought new clarity in my own understanding. I worked my way through the congregational resource by the Alliance of Baptists and the Baptist Peace Fellowship of North America titled "Rightly Dividing the Word of Truth." It is an excellent document with incisive articles from biblical scholars, theologians, and scientists. It also offers personal stories, denominational statements, and an extensive bibliography. I studied the work of Richard Hayes, professor of New Testament at Duke Divinity School, who wrote *The Moral Vision of the New Testament.* I studied Stanley Grenz's book, *Welcoming but Not Affirming: An Evangelical Response to Homosexuality,* and Catholic scholarship, including James Hannigan's *Homosexuality: A Test Case for a Christian Sexual Ethic.*

After this soul searching, I retained the conviction that displeased many of my friends and colleagues in CBF. I could not in good conscience perform a same-sex marriage ceremony or ordain someone to ministry who was in a same-sex marriage, though I fully recognized that others could. I also became convinced that in our secular society, "civil unions" between same-sex couples should be made available to those who choose them. Same-sex marriage was not legal at the time, but now that it is legal, I believe that same-sex marriage should be available to anyone who desires it. I also believe that civil and human rights should be guaranteed to everyone and that genuine love and respect should be offered, regardless of one's sexual orientation or gender identity.

Finally, the differences within CBF reached a crisis point. On the drive to the Orlando General Assembly in June 2000, I received a telephone call from a prominent and respected pastor in Virginia telling me that he would bring a motion to the floor of the business session to withdraw funding from Wake Forest Divinity School because of its open admissions policy with regard to sexual orientation. I asked him to wait at least a year with the promise that the elected leadership would address his concerns as a larger policy and funding issue. He agreed. I spent most of my time in Orlando huddled with the officers in conversation, and in its fall meeting the Coordinating Council approved a "Statement of Organizational Value" on the issue of homosexual behavior and CBF's funding arrangements with its eleven partner seminaries.

I personally drafted the statement and first showed it to the senior staff for their suggestions and critiques. I met with the deans and presidents of all the schools that related to CBF. There was a thorough discussion over a two-day period. Some liked the statement and some did not. They all appreciated the struggle and opportunity for involvement in the decision process. Several recommendations were made by them and included in the statement that was then taken to the Advisory Council. The Advisory Council discussed the issue thoroughly and made some additional changes before unanimously approving the statement. It was then presented to the Coordinating Council, who debated for two days and then voted, 38-25, to adopt the following statement:

> As Baptist Christians, we believe that the foundation of a Christian sexual ethic is faithfulness in marriage between a man and a woman and celibacy in singleness. We also believe in the love and grace of God for all people, both for those who live by this understanding of the biblical standard and those who do not. We treasure the freedom of individual conscience and the autonomy of the local church. We also believe that congregational leaders should be persons of moral integrity whose lives exemplify the highest standards of Christian conduct and character.

Because of this organizational value, the Cooperative Baptist Fellowship does not allow for the expenditure of funds for organizations or causes that condone, advocate, or affirm homosexual practice. Neither does this CBF organizational value allow for the purposeful hiring of a staff person or the sending of the missionary who is a practicing homosexual.

At the next General Assembly in Atlanta in 2001, a motion was made that instructed the Coordinating Council to review and rescind the policy statement. The motion failed by approximately a 60–40 percent vote. This was the tenth anniversary of CBF, larger than any previous General Assembly. More than 8,000 participants had gathered to hear President Jimmy Carter. The attendance at the business session was sizable, and the debate was cordial but intense. Both before and after the vote, emotions and sentiments were strong, because this decision would inform the budgeting and hiring process in the future. The statement was never intended as a mandate for congregations as to what they should practice or to individuals as to what they should believe.

The adoption of a hiring and funding policy did not end the disagreements within CBF over human sexuality, nor did it silence our external critics. But it did set a direction, for better or for worse, for the agenda of the fellowship for the remainder of my tenure. We turned our attention and focus to conversations about the missional church, HIV/AIDS, global poverty, ecumenical relationships, and interfaith dialogue. We accepted the challenge of disaster response and resourcing congregations. I continued to spend a lot of energy in the following years in private conversations and personal dialogues with a number of folks who were displeased with the policy and my leadership. They were principled in their convictions and cordial in their demeanor, but the conversations were exhausting.

In my last year as coordinator I decided, along with CBF leadership, to convene a public and open conversation on human sexuality. Along with my friend David Gushee, who is director of Mercer University's Center for Theology and Public Life, we co-sponsored "A Baptist Conference on Sexuality and Covenant." It was planned and led by David, alongside Rick Bennett on our staff, with plenary speakers and small-group discussion in a context of worship. The conference was respectful, honest, and noncoercive in nature, and I felt it was one of the best events CBF ever sponsored.

So is there a way forward, both for the church and society, on issues of sexuality? Can we find a way to bridge the gap between those who are very different in their convictions on human sexuality? Is it even possible to look for some common ground that would allow individuals, churches, organizations, and civil society itself to disagree strongly on these issues and still move forward in some kind of authentic community? I would like to respond with a tentative yes.

Let me suggest that we accept the tension caused by the differences between us as a kind of "checks and balances" that would be an instrument of Providence to forge a new and different kind of consensus and community. Could it be that we need each other, gay and straight, conservative and progressive, to gain a truer understanding of human sexuality? Could it be that no one theological or hermeneutical perspective contains all the truth? Could it be that we hold the tension between the wonder and beauty of human sexuality as far more complex than we have assumed, and on the other hand affirm that revelation from Scripture offers norms and boundaries that we need, even though we will disagree as to what they shall be?

Could it be that the real tension between us is a gift of God intended to form us into a more holistic society? I don't know. But I do know that I am a far more informed person and a far better person than I was because of the tension that still exists within me concerning human sexuality. I cannot say I like the tension or enjoy living in it. But in all honesty, I don't see the tension going away in the foreseeable future, at least not in my lifetime. I have also learned that my own growth, formation, and transformation comes as a result of such tensions, and I surely want to keep learning when it comes to issues such as human sexuality.

Joe Phelps is a colleague and fellow pastor in CBF whose convictions on human sexuality are different than mine. A few years ago he greeted me at an event with a warm embrace and said something that struck a real cord within me: "Daniel, I love and appreciate you.

You're wrong on the gay issue, but I'm grateful for you." I didn't say anything in response, but I felt the same way. There was a kinship and community between us that transcended our differences. That kinship helps me live with tension. Perhaps neither one of us will change each other's minds, but perhaps both of us will change each other's hearts.

One of the consequences I see in the fierce debate about human sexuality is not the debate itself but the animosity and anger in the debate that creates such fear and even violence. All of this makes it impossible for us to work together on other concerns that desperately need addressing. Can the person who has or supports same-sex marriage live beside and love unconditionally the person who holds the traditional view of marriage and not be attacked as abominable or as something even worse? Can the person who holds to a traditional view of marriage live beside and love unconditionally the LGBTQ+ person or the person who supports same-sex marriage and not be attacked as a bigot or homophobe?

Is it possible for us to suspend our antagonism of each other without sacrificing the integrity of our individual consciences? Is it possible for us to determine that we will love one another? Period. Full stop. Without ambivalence. I hope so. Debate will continue. Differences will not go away, but my deepest desire is to see the realization of authentic community without coercion and violence.

Cultural consensus in American society has shifted dramatically on issues of human sexuality in the past twenty-five years, with many variants within that consensus. I predict that there will be further clashes between the American consensus and that of other societies in the world, not only in societies shaped by Christianity but also in those shaped by other religions and other ethical, moral norms. I also believe that global concerns will become so intense and the desperate need for human community will be so great that our tensions over human sexuality will be minimized, though not erased, so we can live together more harmoniously.

Regardless of what the future may bring, the example and teachings of Jesus mandate that we who are his followers work hard to create communities of mutual trust and respect. We may even differ on how to do that, but we can and should not differ on making it our priority.

Chapter 9

Cooperative Baptist Fellowship: Passions and Priorities

The Missional Church

In 1999, I read Darrell Guder's book, *Missional Church: A Vision for the Sending of the Church in North America*, and it brought new clarity and conviction about the worldwide missionary enterprise in which I had always fervently believed. The book was a turning point for me because it refocused my attention to "the mission of God" ("Missio Dei") as the foundation and motivation for engaging the world with the message and ministry of Christ.

I had, from childhood, felt an urgency for missions based primarily on the Great Commission with its global mandate. I saw missions as crossing all barriers primarily as an obligation, a duty, an act of obedience to the command of Jesus. We were sent "to make disciples of all nations," to "go into all the world to bring good news." Later as I discovered the enormity of human suffering and spiritual struggles of people around the world, I felt even more urgency. I was also convinced that a spiritual and moral darkness engulfed humanity, and the greatest need of all people was "the knowledge of the glory of God that shines in the face of Jesus Christ." The words of the familiar song, "Send the Light," captured and conveyed my motivation for missions: "There's a call comes ringing o'er the restless wave / Send the light / Send the light / There are souls to rescue / There are souls to save / Send the light / Send the light."

Guder's book articulated the mission of the church in a different way. It emphasized the mission of the church as an extension of the mission of God. God is on a mission to reconcile the world through Jesus Christ. God is on a mission to redeem and restore a sinful and broken world to God's own self. What is most urgent is that we discern God's mission and then discover our participation in it.

This perspective gave me a more robust theological conviction as to why and how Christians should proclaim the good news of Christ, both by word and deed. It did not negate my earlier motivations, but it gave me a greater confidence and urgency. It also introduced me to new conversation partners who brought greater clarity about the difference between mission, missions, and missionaries.

The mission of God is rooted in the character and nature of God. God the Father sends God the Son. The Father and Son send the Spirit. The Father, Son, and Spirit send the church. These movements within the holy Trinity form a missional view of God, a community of "persons" within God's own being that is on a mission. God is always sending, going, giving, blessing, revealing, and redeeming. Mission is the result of God's initiative rooted in God's purpose to restore and heal creation.

God's mission then creates the church to participate in God's mission. The church exists for mission. The church is not a vendor of religious goods and services giving the gospel to lessen the felt needs of its customers. This means that there is something fundamentally wrong with a popular notion that we should "market the gospel" or "brand the church." Neither is the church a chaplain to society, which means that there is something fundamentally wrong with a popular notion that we should simply be about "human flourishing" or "the health, wealth, and prosperity" of society. Neither is the church a voluntary association of individuals much like a fraternity, a social club, a political party, or a nonprofit organization. The church is surely more than a place where we "go" on Sunday mornings.

The church is the mystical body of Christ in the world. The church is the living temple in which the Holy Spirit lives and works. The church is a people, a community that is sent into the world much like Christ was sent into the world. The church is a fellowship that discerns God's redeeming mission and participates in that mission by incarnating the living presence of Christ. Mission is not about an activity of the church. Mission is the result of God's initiative rooted in God's purpose to renew and remake all things. Mission flows from the mission of God rather than the church's effort to extend itself. Mission is not what a church does as part of its total program. Rather, the church's essence is missional. Mission forms the church's identity.

A missional church continues to affirm the calling of career missionaries and engage in efforts of congregational missions but is characterized by many other markers. First, a missional church is one that makes disciples of Jesus Christ, baptizes them, and then teaches them the way of Christ. This means that the church must always seek to understand what it means to be a disciple. The church must immerse itself in the words and spirit of Christ and engage in the practices or disciplines that will enable it to hear and follow the call of Christ. As we do all of this, we lovingly invite others to join us in the journey of discipleship. And our invitation will always be relational.

Second, a missional church is passionate about the kingdom of God on earth. Its agenda is not to build up its own institution or expand its own influence or feed its own ego. Its purpose is not to preserve a tradition, protect its programs, prevent conflict, or even focus on its own survival and growth. Rather, the missional church is passionate about the rule and reign of God in people's lives, in culture, and in the world. First of all, it receives the kingdom, and then it serves, proclaims, represents, and prays for the kingdom. Everything the church does should conform to the character and culture of God's kingdom as it is revealed and embodied in Jesus.

Also, a missional church embraces suffering, beginning with its own suffering. It will endure and embrace whatever inconvenience, discomfort, or hardship comes to us in following Christ. It will rejoice in testing and challenges. It will celebrate difficulties and discipline because it knows that this is the way to growth. It will not whimper or whine when, for whatever reason, it finds itself limited or misunderstood. These become the occasions to demonstrate the power and grace of God. Then, because the missional church embraces its own suffering, it will embrace the suffering of the world. Wherever there is pain or hardship, you will find the missional church partaking of it, seeking to understand it, to alleviate it, to address its root causes, and simply to identify with it. Like Christ, we embrace and enter into the sufferings of humanity.

Also, missional churches require missional living by individual members, which means we live cross-culturally. We are "in" this world but not "of" it. There is an alien and foreign quality to our existence when it comes to the values that surround us. This means Christians cannot succumb to the commercialism, competitiveness, and crass materialism that surround us. We refuse the militarism and triumphalism of our culture. We are cross-cultural, rejecting the violence and racism in our cultural ethos. We seek lives that are shaped by Jesus and his kingdom. We willingly embrace the ethic of a crucified and resurrected Jesus and not one of civil religion or consumer church.

Missional living requires that we become incarnational, immersing ourselves in personal relationships with people, especially with people who are different from us. We don't stand apart or aloof from others to judge or condemn. Rather we identify with them, learn from them, and listen to them, even when we disagree with them. And most of all, we love them unconditionally and sacrificially. Missional living is also linked to the idea of servanthood. Like Jesus, we will not aspire to power or position, to fame or fortune, but to a simple life of self-giving. We will defer to one another, seek ways to meet one another's needs, and look for practical ways to promote the welfare and well-being of others.

Missional churches also require missional praying. We do not inform God in our praying, nor do we instruct God in our intercession. But we do join God when out of love we pray for the mission of God in the world and all those who participate in it. God has ordained that our praying is a way to participate in the healing of the world. Communion and communication with God is one of the greatest joys in participating in God's mission. As breathing is necessary to life, so prayer is necessary to mission.

Missional praying means interceding for the homeless and the hungry, the lost and the lonely. Missional praying means petitioning for ministers and missionaries who serve Christ in difficult and dangerous places. Missional praying means holding those before God who have no access to the gospel as well as those who do but whose hearts have been hardened to the gospel. Missional praying means wrestling with principalities and powers and resisting evil in the name of Christ. Missional praying means seeking the face of God and not just the hand of God, for others as well as for myself. Missional praying means dispelling darkness with the glorious light of God's love.

Missional praying, like all praying, is born out of an awareness of desperate need. I recall someone saying, "I don't pray except when I am in trouble or when someone I love is in trouble. But the fact is that I am always in trouble, or someone I love is always in trouble. So I pray all the time." When we are faced with overwhelming and crushing challenges, we don't need to be told to pray. We do it instinctively and intuitively. In times of crisis, we call out to God for help. In a similar manner, as we observe the crises and sufferings of others, we call out to God for help, for justice, for mercy.

Missional praying is born out of desperate and overwhelming human need that is beyond human remedy. We simply must have divine help. Therefore, we pray. Perhaps one reason many of us don't pray for the world is because we are insulated and isolated from the sufferings of the world. Perhaps we are apathetic, indifferent, lukewarm. But when we come into contact on a personal, firsthand basis with real suffering, we feel the crushing need to pray. We ask God to do what we cannot do, and we ask God to help us do what we must do. We pray both with our lips and with our lives. We ask for help, and then we do what we can to help. It has been my experience that those most in touch with human suffering and spiritual struggles are the ones who pray the most and also accomplish the most.

Missional praying is born out of struggle with spiritual powers, forces, and realities that are external to us. The presence and power of evil is evident in systems and structures that trap individuals in vicious cycles of violence and cruelty. Sin is not only personal but also corporate and collective. Social evils are real. So we pray, both for ourselves and for others, "Lead us not into temptation, and deliver us from the evil one." Without a conviction of sin and evil, and God's triumph over sin and evil, we will have little effectiveness in prayer.

Missional praying, most of all, is born out of love. It is God's love for us that creates a response of love to God and love to neighbor. For me, prayer is receiving God's love and then responding by offering love back to God that includes love to neighbor. In prayer, we do not force God to act contrary to God's own nature, because that very nature is love. But in a mysterious way, we enter into and become participants of that love. The more we experience God's love, the more we pray. Prayer itself is an act of love, an attitude of love, an expression of love. Love is itself a way of prayer.

Missionaries

Less than two years after its beginning, CBF assumed the responsibility of supporting career missionaries. In January 1993, ten couples resigned from the International Mission Board of Southern Baptists to become CBF-supported missionaries. All of them were living and serving in Europe. Later that year, CBF invited Keith Parks, who had recently resigned the presidency of the IMB to become our first global missions coordinator.

From the beginning of his tenure, Keith Parks led CBF to send and support an ever-expanding number of mission personnel. Some were appointed from the ranks of Southern Baptists, some from other Christian ministries, and some from secular organizations. A stellar global missions staff was put into place, and they were paid the same salaries as the field missionaries: Tom Prevost, Grace Powell Freeman, Betty Law, and Harlan Spurgeon. The missionaries were organized into semi self-governed teams with little hierarchical administrative structure. There was no distinction between home missions and foreign missions. Our mantra was "a world without borders," and our focus was on those who had the least access to the gospel or were the most marginalized in society.

Our missionary teams grew in numbers, and our influence in the world missionary enterprise also grew far beyond our numbers.

For me to step into a burgeoning missionary movement was both exciting and challenging. I knew I had a lot to learn, so I set myself on a trajectory of study and apprenticeship. I decided early to visit as many of the field missionaries as possible, both to learn from them and to get to know them. I felt that in order to be an advocate for their ministries and to pray effectively, I needed to see them in their context. This would require travel and time. During my fifteen years as coordinator, I took twenty-nine international trips (see page 218).

Some view travel as pleasurable and even luxurious. For me it was laborious and demanding. Although I loved being with people when I reached my destination, I found the journeys both physically and emotionally exhausting. I learned some practices that minimized the stress of travel and sought to "redeem the time" by using it for writing, reading, prayer, and meditation. But it was still difficult.

On average, I preached in twenty to thirty different churches each year, nearly always on a Sunday. I averaged three to four international trips a year to visit missionaries or attend a meeting of the Baptist World Alliance. I often joked with friends by telling them that when I die, if Saint Peter greets me and says, "There is a trip you must take to participate in a meeting," then I'll know I have ended up in the wrong place. Travel was hard, but the results were rewarding, especially when it involved missionaries.

In my travels to Asia, I was overwhelmed with the vast numbers of people who knew little or nothing of the Jesus story. I was also overwhelmed by the courageous efforts of those whose passion was to tell that story. Ericka and Kent Parks, Beth and Tom Ogburn, Tina and Jonathan Bailey, Mary and Hunter Huff, and Kay and Stan Parks inspired me with their ministries of discipleship and church planting among ethno-linguistic groups of people who often transcended the borders of their residency. Suzy and Kirk Persons translated the New Testament into the language of a little-known people group scattered across Asia. Ellen and Tom Burnette also lived in Asia and worked in ministries of agriculture, water sufficiency, and community development. Ben and Leonora Newell served in Asia as well, introducing the concept of "business as mission" to those who were marginalized in society.

CBF International Travel

1998   Prague, Czech Republic; Jordan and West Bank, Jerusalem
1999   Sao Paulo, Brazil
2000   Sumatra and Java, Indonesia
2002   Shanghai, Nanjing, and Beijing, China
       Seville, Spain (BWA)
       Skopje, Macedonia
2003   Rio de Janeiro, Brazil (BWA)
       Hyderabad, Delhi, and Nagpur, India
2004   Toronto, Canada
       Seoul, Korea (BWA)
       Accra, Ghana; Nairobi, Kenya; Johannesburg, South Africa;
       Harare, Zimbabwe; Prague, Czech Republic
       Nairobi, Kenya
2005   Seoul, Korea
       Istanbul, Turkey
       Birmingham, England (BWA)
2006   Seoul, Korea
       Bangkok and Chiang Mai, Thailand
       Bucharest, Romania
2007   Accra, Ghana (BWA)
       Hyderabad, Vizag, Srikakulam, Sethhampet, Bay of Bengal,
       and Delhi, India
2008   Prague, Czech Republic (BWA)
       Zagreb, Croatia
       Cairo, Egypt
2009   Shanghai, Nanjing, and Beijing, China
       Amsterdam, Holland (BWA)
2010   Addis Ababa, Ethiopia
       Port au Prince and Grand Guave, Haiti
       Seoul, Korea
2011   Port au Prince and Grand Guave, Haiti
2012   Bucharest, Romania
       Santiago, Chile (BWA)

On one occasion, Earlene and I were privileged to stay in the home of Melin and Ron Green, who lived in a small Indonesian city. They insisted that we sleep in their bedroom, and during the night I was awakened by the sound of insects being captured in a fluorescent light and the Muslim call to prayer. They homeschooled their children and worked as agricultural consultants in a very difficult context. When we left their home I told Earlene, "I feel unworthy to serve in the same organization with people who sacrifice and give so much of themselves to the cause of Christ."

Before becoming coordinator of CBF, I had traveled to India with my son Joel, whose ministry in the northern state of Bihar had taken him there more than fifteen times. In that first visit, I felt overwhelmed, both physically and emotionally, by the cultural differences between India and America. I had culture shock. The sights, sounds, and smells in urban centers, especially Calcutta, assaulted my senses and psyche. The heat was oppressive, and watching animals roam everywhere was almost more than I could handle. Even in the more rural areas, I found the population density to be suffocating. I had studied Hinduism and found it difficult to comprehend, but being personally confronted by its pervasive influence in the culture was disorienting.

A decade later when I traveled to India with Sam Bandela, a CBF field missionary, I was more mentally and emotionally prepared. Sam, who was born in Hyderabad, has a deep love for the people of India and an understanding of its culture that can come only from being indigenous. In Vizak, Andhra Pradesh, I preached twice at St. Paul's Church, established in 1838 as an Anglican congregation but now affiliated with the Church of South India (CSI). When the British left India in 1948, the CSI was formed as an effort to create a united church across denominational lines with a shared liturgy and connection. Afterwards we visited an HIV/AIDS clinic established to serve a growing population infected with the disease.

We then drove three hours to a region northeast of Vizak, where a sainted pastor, Narayana Paul, lived and served for thirty-five years among several tribal peoples. Narayana Paul was a Christian convert from high-caste Hinduism who had a beautiful laugh and a contagious smile. After his conversion, he felt a calling to the tribal peoples of Vizak, where he preached for eleven years before his first convert. Together with his wife, Grace, he lived a humble and simple life among the poor. He trained hundreds of church planters and established a Bible school, an orphanage, and a hospital. At his death, more than 30,000 Christians walked in his funeral processional.

When we arrived at his compound, we were greeted by children singing and dancing as we made our way to a beautiful buffet that was prepared in our honor. They placed flower garlands around my neck, seated me in a circle of five hundred villagers, and then proceeded to wash my feet as a token of friendship. I have never felt more humbled in my life. After lunch we went into a simple "brush arbor," where I preached and taught for several hours. Sam had purchased bicycles for some of the evangelists and church planters to use as they traveled from village to village. We had a prayer of dedication and thanksgiving for each bicycle.

From there we went toward the Bay of Bengal, at Narsapur, for a "sewing center" graduation ceremony. More than sixty young women who lived in the neighboring coastal villages had been enlisted for classes that would teach them to use a sewing machine. This protected them from being recruited by prostitution rings and provided them a sustainable income. At the ceremony, each was awarded a "Certificate of Completion." Sam had purchased sewing machines and enrolled them in a multi-week course where they could learn how to earn a living as a seamstress. The ceremony was a joyous occasion with family members and friends attending. Each young woman was presented with a certificate, a Bible, and a sewing machine. I will never forget watching them leave the ceremony carrying these items with pride for their accomplishment and greater hope for their future.

From there we went to the Bay of Bengal, where the tsunami of 2004 had devastated the region only a few months earlier. I made my way to the beach and imagined the trauma. Several fishermen approached us in boats that had been purchased by World Vision and wanted to engage us in conversation. Seeing that I was not Indian, the first thing they did was speak the name "Jesus" and point to their hearts. I smiled and answered, "Yes, Jesus." CBF's financial response to the tsunami had been overwhelming, as had been the response of so many others around the world. We received and distributed more than $2 million. But as I stood on that beach, I wished that it had been much more.

Also in Asia, I discovered the vibrancy and influence of the Christian community in China and Korea. Both countries have experienced an indigenization and contextualization of the gospel since World War II that has resulted in remarkable growth. In China the China Christian Council (CCC), Three Self Patriotic Movement (TSPM), and Amity Press represent a post-denominational ecclesiastical system that has cooperated with the Communist government to allow thousands of churches to reopen and millions of Bibles to be printed. In Korea, the planting of churches, many of them mega churches with frequent and fervent prayer gatherings, has resulted in remarkable growth. In my travels to both countries, I found favor with Christian leaders who welcomed international friendships.

In China, our CBF field missionaries had already begun substantive conversations with the CCC, TSPM, and Amity Press. Ina and Ron Winstead, Brenda Lisenby, Anita and Jack Snell, and Helen and Don McNeely were mature missionaries who nurtured good will both with government and recognized church leaders. Their ministries opened many doors for collaboration and shared ministry. In 2005, when the CCC wanted to "showcase" a Bible exhibit in the US, they chose Atlanta as one of the three venues (Los Angeles, New York, and Atlanta). Along with the Crystal Cathedral in Los Angeles and the Cathedral Church of St. John the Divine in New York, "The Bible Ministry Exhibition of the Church in China" was hosted at Second Ponce de Leon Baptist Church in Atlanta. It was an electrifying event with President Jimmy Carter bringing the keynote message and recounting his diplomatic experiences with the Chinese government.

The story of the Christian church in China is one of most amazing sagas of the twentieth century. Its survival under intense persecution, its emergence as non-Western and post-denominational, and its explosive growth is a witness to the power of the gospel and the reality of a truly global church. As many as 40 percent of all pastors in China are women. In addition to the churches that register with the CCC, there are untold numbers that do not, and the relationship between the two is much better than many in the press would lead one to believe. I preached in one Shanghai church where the pastor told me that she had to preach the same sermon at each of the three morning worship services, because if she didn't the congregants would attend all three services. I learned a lot from the churches in China.

Likewise, in Korea the growth and development of Christian churches is amazing. From a sectarian minority of less than 5 percent of the population after WWII, the Christian population increased to more than 50 or 60 percent, and its influence in society is impressive. My introduction to the Korean Christian community came through a Korean American pastor, Yoo Jong Yoon, who was CBF's coordinator for our Asian network. Rev. Yoon, who was instrumental in delivering relief to North Korea, was also instrumental in facilitating numerous visits with South Korean Baptist, Presbyterian, and Pentecostal leaders. They opened their hearts, their pulpits, and their churches in ways that still amaze me.

I experienced a spiritual fervor and passion in South Korea that is unique and unmatched in America. While they understand the personal spiritual disciplines, their corporate practices of prayer and worship are what distinguish and define them. Their churches are organized into small cell groups that meet in homes through the week for prayer and encouragement. Early every morning, they gather for corporate worship experiences. They sing together, pray together, and weep together, and they do it with an intensity that is difficult to explain. Their worship is emotional, visceral, and physical as well as liturgical. But most of all it is communal. In addition to daily and weekly worship, they take frequent prayer retreats where they spend time together in extended fellowship.

I learned a lot from the churches in Korea and particularly from pastors who welcomed me into their circles of friendship. Pastor Seok-jeon Yoon of Yonsei Central Baptist in Seoul invited me to participate in a sanctuary dedication. Pastor Kim Jong Eh of Sunglim

Baptist in Gwangiu invited me to conduct revival services. Pastor Park Se-Ok of Spring of Heaven Baptist invited me to participate in the dedication of a tract of land. Pastor Shin Chul Mo of Korean Baptist Press helped organize the Cooperative Baptist AMEN Fellowship (CBAF) to support Korean missionaries in Asia. Pastor Sung Hyun Kim, president of Christian World Mission Center and overseer of Seoul's Sungrack Church (the largest Baptist church in the world), became a dear friend.

In my travels to the continent of Africa, I discovered a richness and diversity in the Christian community that both surprised and challenged me. In contrast to the Chinese and Korean expressions of congregational life, which seem to manifest greater uniformity, the African expressions are widely divergent and diverse. These differences are especially true between churches in Sub-Saharan African nations and northern African nations. The differences result from European colonization, tribalism, the slave trade, and Islam's powerful influence. In visiting African churches, I experienced an emotional immersion in the global church and realized how much Christians in the West have to learn from it. I also experienced an intellectual deconstruction in awakening to the realization that so much of my Christian formation is European centered.

Ethiopia and Egypt have Christian roots going back to the New Testament. The evangelical Christian presence is relatively recent, but it is vibrant. David Harding, a CBF field missionary, is a "missionary kid" born in Ethiopia who introduced me to various evangelical denominations, including Baptists. In Adidis Ababa I spent several days at the MCM hospital, which was founded and funded by the Korean mega church, MyungSung Presbyterian Church. Pastor Kim Sham-Hwan had invited me to preach a few years earlier in Seoul, so I was familiar with their remarkable medical ministry in Ethiopia.

David also introduced me to "self-help" groups that use micro-enterprise lending as a way out of extreme poverty. We attended a meeting of one "cooperative" composed of fifteen to twenty small business owners whose initial capital came from loans given them by the cooperative. Each week the members put aside a few pennies to form their own "bank." They decided together who would receive loans, the rate of interest, and the time allowed for repayment. After our "coffee ceremony" (coffee was first grown in Ethiopia), each member recounted their stories. One said, "I received a loan to purchase a sewing machine." Another said, "I received a loan to start a fruit/vegetable stand." Still another said, "I received a loan to become a barber." There was mutual approval and affirmation after they shared their stories. Each week the members meet together, repay a portion of their loans, and decide who else might join.

After hearing their testimonies, I asked for permission to ask some questions. "How do you decide who can join and receive a loan?" The answer: "Each person must fill out an application, and we decide together." "What do you do if someone doesn't repay their loan?" The answer: "Everyone repays their loan. We know each other and hold ourselves accountable." "Is this a religious group?" The answer: "We have Muslims, Orthodox, Catholic, and Evangelicals." What is amazing is that there are thousands of these "self-help" groups across Ethiopia, many of them sponsored by Christian churches and denominations.

When the terrible earthquake and tsunami hit Haiti in 2010, I traveled to Port-au-Prince with a delegation of Christian leaders to explore how we might offer immediate and long-term relief. One suggestion was that CBF fund the expenses for a number of Haitians to travel to Ethiopia and learn about "self-help" groups for implementation in their country. This concept was not new; the 2006 Nobel Peace Prize winner Muhammad Yunus began the Grameen Bank project offering micro-credit to millions of poor people. In 2007, Phil Smith and Eric Thurman wrote a book that impacted me and reinforced what I had seen in Ethiopia: *A Billion Bootstraps: Microcredit, Barefoot Banking, and the Business Solution for Ending Poverty*.

Of all the places in the world where I have visited, none was more disturbing than Haiti after the earthquake. It was already the poorest nation in the western hemisphere, with indescribable human suffering. The earthquake's devastation disrupted what little societal infrastructure was in place, created chaos, and killed hundreds of thousands. In spite of the fact that 3,000 NGOs work in Haiti, the entire country seemed paralyzed.

After arriving and touring the carnage in the capital city, our delegation made its way to Grand Guoave, the epicenter of the earthquake. We traveled on paved roads, then on to gravel roads, on to dirt roads, and on to foot paths in the open countryside. The evidences of a brutal disaster were everywhere: collapsed houses, dead animals, wreckage, open sewage. The sights and smells of death were all around us. I thought to myself, "I don't know what hell is like, but this seems to be as close to it as I can imagine."

We rode in total silence. And then from a distance I could hear singing. At first, the melodies were faint but then grew clearer as we drove through the debris and arrived in a small village. A group of twenty-five women were sitting in a circle singing hymns with broad smiles as they awaited our arrival. I was overcome with emotion. My mind went to Psalm 139: "Where can I go from your spirit? Or where can I flee from your presence? If I ascend to heaven, you are there; if I make my bed in Sheol, you are there" (vv. 7-8).

In Egypt I experienced a different kind of poverty and a unique ministry that seeks to counter it. Chaoui and Maha Boulos are CBF field missionaries living in Beirut, Lebanon, where both of them were born. In addition to their relief efforts among refugees, they plan and conduct contemporary Arabic worship services that celebrate the gospel and address the spiritual hunger of citizens in Jordan, Egypt, Syria, and Lebanon. They invited me to Cairo, where for four nights we gathered in an open-air space outside the walls of a Catholic monastery. I preached each evening to more than 1,000 attendees and then spent at least an hour in prayer and conversation with those seeking spiritual nourishment.

Small evangelical churches in Cairo sponsored these "Celebrations" by renting buses for church members and invited neighbors to attend. Coptic Christians and Muslims, as well as evangelical Christians, rode the buses together and then sat together for two hours of singing, praying, and listening. What inspired me most was the intensity and fervor of Egyptian Christians amid the despair and desperation of so many. Being the recipient of so much spiritual and material privilege, I felt unworthy to preach, but I also felt honored to preach. I wept with those who wept, and I rejoiced with those who rejoiced. I prayed with and for many who needed help, hope, and healing. I also prayed for myself.

At the end of each celebration service, I was exhausted but exhilarated. On return to our hotel, I listened to Chaoui and Maha talk about spiritual needs in the Arab world and the hopelessness that so many feel in the Middle East. They reflected on the seeming intractable problems and complexities of Middle Eastern politics, but always with a conviction that spiritual appetites must be satisfied. I also experienced an immense capacity for hospitality in the Arab world. Years earlier, I had been in Jordan and sat in tents with Bedouins as a recipient of hospitality. Tamara Tillman, another CBF field missionary, introduced me to my first but not last experience of Arab hospitality. My time in Egypt fed my own spiritual hungers because the Egyptians offered me their smiles, their love, and their warm hospitality. I felt that I had been among saints, sinners, and seekers, and that all of us were nourished.

In the sub-Saharan countries of Africa, I encountered an explosive and expanding Christianity that was profoundly simple and simply profound. Rooted in Western missionary efforts and European colonialism, sub-Saharan African Christianity has flourished and matured while still struggling with political independence, extreme poverty, and widespread corruption. I found a resolve and resiliency in African Christians and churches that shamed me for my often petty and pretentious behavior.

Melody and Sam Harrell were both born on the continent of Africa and lived in Nairobi as CBF field missionaries. They gave me a copy of Vincent Donovan's book, *Christianity Rediscovered: An Epistle from the Masai*, and gifted me with an introduction to Masai Christians. Both were gifts that expanded my horizons and deepened my faith. Sam, more than anyone else, helped me understand the richness of African Christianity and the enormous challenges facing both church and society.

Fran and Lonnie Turner, CBF field missionaries living in South Africa, took Earlene and me to a poor township outside of Harare,

Zimbabwe, where we visited in the home of a man dying of AIDS. We were greeted in a tiny living room by his brother and two sisters. We talked, wept, and prayed together. After our visit we went into the yard, where neighbors gave each of us an ear of roasted corn as expressions of hospitality. We ate it quietly and said our goodbyes. Fran and Lonnie educated us in the AIDS pandemic ravaging Africa not only with staggering statistical information but also with personal human encounters. Lonnie couldn't talk about AIDS without welling up in tears.

In Kumasi, Ghana, Barbara Baldridge, CBF's global missions coordinator at the time, accompanied Earlene and me on a visit to Dr. Frank Adams, the general secretary of the All Africa Baptist Fellowship (AABF). A humble man with a keen intellect, Adams had a vision and passion for the African church to join in God's global mission of liberation and justice. Although he was a Ghanaian, his passion extended to all the nations of his native continent. In a letter he sent me after our meeting he described his vision:

> The movement of the Spirit is taking place at what we might call a new missionary frontier, through the popular movements in the developing world. Those who have been the most exploited and oppressed are becoming the protagonists of history. The rediscovery of the biblical story as the story of liberation, of the God of the Bible as the God who appears in history as the liberator of slaves, and Jesus of Nazareth as the Messiah of the poor who inaugurates a new kingdom of justice belonging to the poor, provides the basis for a dynamic Christian presence on this frontier. A new church is emerging, a church born out of the suffering and struggle of people and those who stand with them. The church in Africa has come of age and is not lacking in any gift. It is a continent of spiritual dynamism and fervency. The Holy Spirit is certainly awakening the slumbering African giant to take up its God-given place in the world.

Frank Adams was one of the most visionary and courageous Christian leaders I have ever met. It was a privilege to sign a partnership covenant between CBF and the AABF to enter into a cooperative relationship for peacemaking, holistic development, and theological education.

My travels to Europe were less frequent than to anywhere else in the world, partly because CBF's mission presence was smaller. What presence we did have was primarily among refugees and those marginalized by society. I did visit Skkopie and Gostivar, Macedonia, where several CBF missionaries had been relocated from Albania: Rick and Martha Shaw, Bert and Debbie Ayers, Tony and Dusty Buesing, and Arville and Shelia Earle. Not long after the Bosnian war and the displacement that it caused for thousands of Serbian and Kosovar Muslims, the United Nations established Cegrane, a refugee camp. The Earles took Earlene and me, along with Jordan England (who would later become our son-in-law), to visit the camp. It was a life-changing experience. To sit in the tent of a displaced family, along with 30,000 other families displaced because of war, and hear their story of loss was heartbreaking. I tried to put myself in their conditions and could not even begin to imagine the trauma and suffering.

The family were victims of hatred and violence; simply because they were Kosovar Muslims, they had lost their home and possessions. But they had not lost their dignity or self-respect. We talked and exchanged pleasantries before listening to their story of hardship. They asked if we could keep in touch after leaving, which we did for several years following. I will never think of refugees and immigrants in the same way after visiting Macedonia.

In Bucharest, Romania, I visited my friend Oti Bunaciu, pastor of Providence Baptist, on several occasions, as well as our CBF field missionaries, Kathy and T. Thomas, and Tammy and Ralph Stocks, who worked among the Roma people. The Romany are a despised minority not only in Romania but throughout Europe. The established churches of all denominations have had little to do with them, as they live in isolated enclaves often characterized by crime and poverty. T. Thomas challenged Oti and the church where he was pastor to pay attention to the Roma children and open their hearts to them. The church responded and started the Ruth School, using their building to house an educational experience for the Roma children. It has since grown into a sizeable and significant presence in Bucharest: the Ruth Project.

On a visit in 2006 to celebrate the dedication of a new building, I was accompanied by Juandelle Lacy and her daughter Rhonda from FBC Midland, Texas, who have been generous donors and good friends to Oti. Jim and Juandelle Lacy had accompanied me to Bucharest twenty-five years earlier and had nurtured their friendship with Oti and his family throughout that time. Their generosity and support, along with many others, has helped establish the Ruth Project as a shining example of Christian love for the marginalized and poor.

Global Poverty

After the General Assembly in 2001, the focus of my leadership centered on two themes: "missional church" and global poverty. Darrell Guder's book *Missional Church: A Vision for the Sending of the Church in North America* captured my imagination. It was the clearest work I had read on a theology and program for local churches to participate in "the mission dei" (the mission of God). Global poverty, I believed, was the single greatest moral and social issue of our time. It was an issue where an emerging convergence was taking place between people from different faith traditions. We may have significant differences between us and great divides on many issues, human sexuality being one of them. But when it came to the misery and suffering of poor people, we were experiencing a growing unity. I felt that the human family was increasingly being seen as just that, the human family.

Poverty is a global problem. Statistics may not always tell all the truth, but we simply cannot ignore the fact that 1 billion people in the world live on less than $1 a day. We cannot close our eyes to the fact that 8 million people around the world die each year simply because they are too poor to stay alive. That means that 20,000 people die each day because of poverty and poverty-related problems. What became clear to me was that while prosperity is on the rise for many people, a growing disparity between the "haves" and the "have nots" is also on the rise. The gulf between rich and poor and between rich nations and poor nations is increasing at an alarming rate. This requires action.

Poverty is a moral problem that an awakened conscience cannot ignore. The prophets of Israel were stinging in their rebuke to those in power who failed to seek justice for the poor. They were equally stinging in their rebuke of religious leaders who condoned such behavior. The moral test of a society is how it treats the poor and powerless. When taxation takes money from the poor and gives it to the rich, that's a moral issue. When trade policies protect the rich and hurt the poor, that's a moral issue. When corporations make excessive profits at the expense of the poor, that's a moral issue. When budgets give preference to the rich and ignore the poor, that's a moral issue.

Poverty is a complex social problem. All kinds of factors contribute: government corruption, natural disasters, trade policies, the environment, corporate greed, and much more. If we want to point fingers at those most responsible, there is plenty of guilt to go around. Elected leaders, business leaders, and religious leaders have failed. Institutions in our civil society must accept their share of culpability, including the media, the academy, and the church. As individuals, each of us have shut our eyes and closed our hearts to the poor. None is without sin.

Poverty is a spiritual problem. Poverty is rooted in a failure within the human spirit. Greed and apathy are spiritual vices. Compassion and justice are spiritual virtues. When Jesus was asked to define the greatest commandment he answered, "Thou shalt love the Lord thy God . . . and thou shalt love thy neighbor as thyself." Then when asked, "Who is my neighbor?" he told the parable of the good Samaritan. Love of neighbor, anyone in need, is inextricably tied to love of God. The Bible is clear. Worship, devotion, and piety are worthless if they are not accompanied by care for the poor.

Poverty is a global, national, local, personal problem. This requires action at all levels and by all of us. Alleviation of poverty requires both prayer and work, compassionate service and political will, engagement with poor people and advocacy for poor people, private action and public action, substantive change and symbolic change. Alleviation of poverty requires effort by church and state, by for profit organizations and not-for-profit organizations. It requires creative partnerships between business and government, church and state, individuals and families.

The response of CBF to the problem of global poverty was remarkable. In 2001, CBF made one of the most important decisions in its ten-year history. We decided to make a twenty-year commitment of presence and ministry in the twenty poorest counties of America. We titled the commitment "Together for Hope." We surprisingly discovered that these counties were located in distinctly different locales among different racial groupings. The Appalachian counties were predominately White. The Mississippi Delta and Cotton Belt counties were predominately African American. The Rio Grande Valley counties were predominately Hispanic/Latino. The South Dakota counties were Native American reservations. These counties had some of the worst poverty in America, and it was complex and devastating.

Together for Hope focused on long-term partnerships with a commitment to listen to the poor and those already working among the poor in order to learn what methods were culturally appropriate with the goal of transformation. It was not about sending people for short-term projects or "throwing money" at problems; it was about building relationships of trust in which time and money were invested. Our concern for the poor and powerless was not a matter of partisan politics or an effort to accomplish a denominational program or a trend or a fad. Rather it was central and integral to the gospel of Jesus. As he cared for the poor and powerless during his incarnate life, he now cares for the poor and powerless through us in his glorified life.

Also, the risen Jesus becomes present to us in the poor and powerless. He is not only present within us, or when two or three of us gather in his name, or when we celebrate Communion and proclaim the word. In mysterious and unexplainable ways, the risen Jesus is also present in the poor and powerless among us. On one occasion, Jesus took a child into his arms and said, "Whoever welcomes one of these little children in my name welcomes me" (Mark 9:36-37). A child is vulnerable and powerless, and Jesus identified himself with such a one. In his parable of the sheep and goats, he spoke of himself as embodied among the poor and powerless: "Inasmuch as you did it to the least of these, you did it unto me" (Matt 25:40).

The poor and powerless are not saints. They are like the rest of us: they are sinners. But if we want to see the face of the Lord, we must go to the margins of society, to those who suffer. And as we represent Christ among them, we will find that Christ is already there. We will meet him there among the people to whom we are sent to minister.

Christ is hidden among the poor and powerless. Christ's presence is not spectacular, nor does it confound and convince us. In fact, in the final judgment, neither believers nor unbelievers will have seen him in those who suffer. They will say, "When did we see you among the poor and powerless?" And he will answer, "I was there; they were me and I was them." Whether one interprets these words symbolically or sacramentally, the imperative and urgency are clear.

The poor and powerless among us are not to be seen as an inconvenience, as less fortunate, or as an underclass. They are not statistics of government research or numbers for a foundation grant. They are not units in a housing project, inmates in a prison, victims of violence, or clients or patients. The poor and powerless are Christ to us; Christ with us; Christ among us. If we ignore them or refuse them, we are ignoring and refusing Christ.

In addition to Together for Hope, CBF's mission field personnel around the world engaged in transformative ministries to the poor and powerless. Many of them lived in difficult and dangerous places, and all of them were experiencing the presence of Christ through their solidarity with the poor and powerless. I felt humbled to serve alongside them and had many opportunities to see what they were doing. Their ministries were inspiring: agriculture and literacy projects in Thailand, water wells in Ethiopia, mobile medical clinics in India, HIV/AIDS drugs in Zimbabwe, relief efforts in Gaza, medical services in Jordan, agricultural development in Indonesia, microenterprise in Moldova, relief in Kenya, and community development in various cities of the world.

CBF responded to the issues of global poverty in multiple organizational partnerships. In 2001, we signed a memorandum of understanding (MOU) with World Vision and made a $100,000 commitment to relief and transformational development in Afghanistan. A letter from Richard Stearns, president of World Vision, expressed appreciation: "In this time of national grief and uncertainty, it is heartwarming to witness your support of the people in Afghanistan who lack such basic necessities as food, shelter, clean water, and access to medical care."

In 2004, we signed another MOU with Bucker International to provide $60,000 in relief and aid to the poorest counties along the Lower Rio Grande Valley in Texas. A letter from Ken Hall, president of Buckner, expressed appreciation: "Buckner is honored and privileged to be your partner."

In 2005, we signed an MOU with Bread for the World as part of the One Campaign, an advocacy initiative with the rock star Bono as its public spokesperson. A letter from David Beckman, president of Bread for the World, expressed appreciation: "We'll continue to work with you to create opportunities to deepen your churches' involvement in the movement to end poverty and hunger."

In 2005, we signed an MOU with Habitat for Humanity to participate in a "group build" in New Orleans after Hurricane Katrina. I joined in that build, although I have little carpentry or construction ability.

In 2007, we voted to adopt the United Nation's Millennium Development Goals (MDGs) as a framework for addressing global poverty. All 191 member states of the UN had pledged to work toward eight goals: eradicate extreme poverty and hunger, achieve universal primary education, promote gender equality and empower women, reduce child mortality, improve maternal health, combat HIV/AIDS and other diseases, ensure environmental sustainability, and create a global partnership for development. Our adoption of these goals was a clear message to other organizations, Christian and non-Christian, that CBF was making a corporate commitment to live out our love for the poor in specific ways.

We also addressed issues of global poverty by responding to natural disasters. On December 26, 2004, a massive earthquake and tsunami occurred in the Indian Ocean, causing the deaths of more than 227,000 inhabitants of India, Thailand, Indonesia, and Sri Lanka. It was one of the deadliest natural disasters in recorded history. In August 2005, a category 5 hurricane hit New Orleans, causing massive death and destruction. On January 12, 2010, a 7.0 earthquake struck Haiti, affecting more than 3 million people and killing more than 160,000 people. After all of these natural disasters, CBF responded with compassion and commitment. Individuals and churches gave more than $5 million for immediate relief, and thousands of volunteers gave of their time in rebuilding efforts.

Because of CBF's financial and programmatic response to the issues around global poverty, I was privileged to participate in a number of public events and coalitions, the purpose of which was advocacy and awareness. In 2004, I joined with forty other leaders in a faith-based movement to overcome poverty, Call to Renewal. I also participated in a Service of Unity at the National Cathedral in Washington, DC.

On June 6, 2005, the eve of Hunger Awareness Day, I joined a coalition of thirty-five faith leaders to urge President Bush and the nation to do more to reduce hunger in our country and around the world. The coalition was "One Table, Many Voices: A Mobilization to Overcome Poverty and Hunger." We urged the president to protect the national nutrition programs from funding cuts and damaging structural changes, to use the G8 Summit to increase development assistance and debt relief, and to forge trade policies that would help reduce hunger, poverty, and disease in Africa.

Also in 2005, I spoke at an event outside the United Nations in support of the MDGs in an ecumenical prayer vigil. I also joined a delegation of interfaith leaders to meet with the secretary of state, Dr. Condoleezza Rice, to advocate for a greater commitment to global poverty issues. What I remember most about this particular event was what happened a few minutes before I went into her conference room at the State Department. My cell phone rang, and I quickly turned it off. After the conversation with Secretary Rice, I listened to my voicemail. It was from Henry, a man in Atlanta who lives on a disability check in a one-room apartment. We had shared several meals together and had become friends. For me this phone call was more than serendipitous. It was providential. It was a reminder that the problem of poverty is so vast as to require the energy and resources of the US government. At the same time, it is so personal as to require my attention and friendship with one person.

In February 2008, I joined thirteen evangelical leaders in crafting a letter to President Bush as part of the Micah Challenge, USA. Bush's policies towards Africa had been impressive, particularly in his fight against HIV/AIDS and malaria, education efforts, and medical services for girls and young women. Our letter urged him to use his influence for debt cancellation and relief in impoverished nations.

In the final judgment, the risen, reigning Christ will pronounce words of reward or rebuke on the basis of how we acted in relation to the poor and powerless. Even if we did not see him, did we serve them? It is not enough to empathize with the poor, to feel bad about their problems, or simply to study and analyze them. The question that will ultimately be asked is, "What did we do to serve them and thereby serve Christ?" These words haunt me still.

Ecumenism

The ecumenical movement was not much on my radar as a pastor. I made precious few efforts to promote Christian unity beyond my Baptist family. The Arthur Blessitt revival in Midland was an exception, but even that experience had evangelism as its focus more than ecumenicity. I wasn't hostile to other Christian denominations but more indifferent than anything else.

What changed my perspective were the five years at Tallowood where I was introduced to contemplative prayer and the practices of Christian spirituality from faith traditions other than my own. During that time, I found spiritual sustenance and nourishment from the broader Christian community. I discovered experientially that I truly did belong to one household of faith that was apostolic and universal. I became friends, and even family, to those both past and present with whom I had theological differences but with whom I shared an even deeper kinship. They became family because we shared the divine life that was within us.

This discovery fueled a passion within me to nurture Christian unity in whatever ways were possible. In coming to CBF as coordinator I saw part of my role as being a "bridge builder" within the Baptist denomination and between all denominations. I became convicted that the Christian community as the body of Christ on earth was essentially one. Yet anyone with eyes to see can discern brokenness within the body of Christ on earth. The church in all its geographical, denominational, and local expressions suffers division.

I found the metaphor of a bridge, both as a noun and a verb, helpful in imagining and working for Christian community. As a noun, the metaphor is easy to imagine. Bridges reach across a gulf, a chasm. People are on different sides of an issue. People are separated from one another by misunderstanding or hostility. Bridges connect people and make it possible for them to leave one side and either cross over to the opposite side or meet somewhere on the bridge. This means we can find community on the bridge instead of being separated from one another.

However, if this is to happen it requires some action. We must traverse the bridge, choose to live on it instead of on only one side. Here is where the bridge metaphor changes from a noun to a verb. We choose to leave one side and live on the bridge instead. We "bridge" the divide by creating a new place where we are no longer separated because of our differences. We choose to live somewhere on the bridge because we desire to be together.

Differences between us are many, and the causes are many. First, we differ from one another in matters of conscience. We don't understand and interpret Scripture in the same way. We don't see Christian history in the same way. We place greater or lesser emphasis on one set of values than on another set of values. We differ in theological systems, ethical judgments, and spiritual practices.

Also, we are differentiated from one another in many ways: social location, age, gender, sexual orientation, race, ethnicity. Each of our temperaments and personalities are unique. I have lived a life of privilege compared to many, and no matter how much empathy I have for the poor, I have never really been poor. I also have my own worldview, theological convictions, and moral judgments that differentiate me from others.

Also, our differences are exacerbated by the fact that all of us at times are difficult to live with. Given our sinful human nature, we act out of fear, anger, and pride. We behave badly even when we don't want to behave badly or when we wish we didn't behave badly. Our "difficultness" surely doesn't help create or nurture unity.

All of these differences create chasms and gulfs between us. We cluster together around them and then shout at one another. We all experience this kind of separation, even alienation, and then feel guilt and shame, and at other times anger and resentment. What shall we do? Is there any hope for unity and community amid our multitude of differences?

I believe the bridge metaphor can help us. The bridge is an "in between" space, a "suspended space," a "liminal space." It may feel uncertain, insecure, and frightening, but I want to suggest that as a spiritual practice we learn to live in this space in order to bridge our differences. This does not mean we abandon or deny our convictions, identity, and uniqueness, but we acknowledge that these alone do not define us. We are equally defined by our love and relationships with those on the other side of the divide. We choose to admit that our convictions, though real and important, cannot and do not exhaust the truth. We choose to relinquish our hold on our defining differences from one another as the most important reality in our lives. We choose to venture, as an act of love and faith, onto a bridge where perhaps we will meet those from the other side who have also chosen to venture. We choose to value something greater and grander than our defining differences and value it so highly that we are willing to live on this "in between" bridge space.

And just what is this "in between" bridge space? Perhaps there are a number of ways to name it. Some would name it as a common humanity, a shared faith, a mutual respect. Others would name it as love itself—compassion, grace, or mercy. For me, the "in between" bridge space that brings us together is Christ—the crucified/living Christ who not only reconciles us to God but reconciles us to one another and lives within each one of us who confesses Christ as Lord.

To live in Christ—the "in between" One—means I live in a liminal space, an already but not yet kind of existence. To live in Christ means I value my oneness in Christ and my oneness with others more than I value my differences with others.

In choosing to live in our oneness in Christ, we will find that our differences are bridged. This does not mean that our differences are ignored or denied. It doesn't even mean that our differences are resolved or removed. We still will differ with one another. We still will be differentiated from one another. And we still, at times, will be difficult. But Christ, both symbolically and literally, transcends these differences and enables us to live out of a new reality and participate in a new kind of community.

This community is both a gift and an achievement. It is received as a divine act that has been created through the reconciling life, death, and resurrection of Christ. This community is also a gift in that it is guaranteed by the indwelling spirit, which is itself a "down payment" of a completed unity promised in the future. But if we are to participate in this unity, it requires from us an intentional and fervent action on a daily basis. It means that "Christ's love compels us, because we are convinced that one died for all, and therefore all died" (2 Cor 5:14). To live in Christ means that "from now on we regard no one from a worldly point of view" (2 Cor 5:16). To live in Christ means that "if anyone is in Christ, the new creation has come. The old is gone, the new is here" (2 Cor 5:17). Here we are able to let go of everything else that separates and divides us and live in a "bridge" kind of relationship with those who are different from us.

In the literature of Celtic spirituality, much is made of "thin places." These are places where the line between temporal and eternal, physical and spiritual, heavenly and earthly is blurred and permeable. One experiences both sides at the same time. Thin places are something of an intersection or a meeting point of two different but complementary realities. Thin places are sacred and holy while being ordinary and common.

Using this symbolic language of a bridge, I believe that living in Christ creates a thin place where our differences are transcended and we are transformed. A sacred community is created. Differences are not necessarily dissolved or dismantled, but in mysterious ways Christ causes us to cohere and creates something new and beautiful.

The bridge community is fragile and may feel tentative because we must suspend some final judgments and permanent conclusions. We must leave some questions unanswered and some conversation open-ended. This can be disconcerting and even frightening. But again, this provides opportunity for the Spirit of Christ within us, which is both strong and sweet, to create something transcendent.

Baptist Ecumenicity: Baptist World Alliance

In 2003, CBF was admitted into the Baptist World Alliance (BWA) as a member body. It was a significant moment for both organizations and also a revelation of just how difficult it is to nurture Christian unity. What is seen as an inclusive act by some can also be seen as a divisive act by others. Schism and separation from the SBC created CBF as a new association of Baptist churches. As such, we made application to the BWA for formal recognition and membership. We did so to demonstrate our desire to be a part of the worldwide Baptist community as a contributing and cooperating member body.

The BWA at the time was composed of more than 200 Baptist conventions, unions, and associations representing almost 50 million baptized believers. Founded in 1910, it was and is the only world-wide ecumenical body of Baptists. The preamble to its constitution states the following:

> The BWA extending over every part of the world, exists as an expression of the essential oneness of Baptist people in the Lord Jesus Christ, to impart inspiration to the fellowship, and to provide channels for sharing concerns and skills in witness and ministry. The Alliance recognizes the traditional autonomy and interdependence of Baptist churches and member bodies.

CBF had financially supported the BWA for the first ten years of our existence without applying for membership. We worked in close and collegial relationships with a number of Baptist conventions around the world in mission and educational efforts, and we participated in the BWA gatherings every five years. After I became coordinator, several of our field missions personnel, along with a number of global missions staff and a considerable number of pastors, urged me to pursue membership. I confess that I was hesitant at first because I anticipated the resistance that SBC leaders would present and the discord it would create within the BWA itself. Both of these fears were realized.

In 2001, I gave permission to proceed with membership application. The BWA membership committee met in July 2001 in Charlottetown, Prince Edward Island, Canada, and deferred our application on two grounds. They had questions about the separate identity of CBF from SBC, and they had concerns about the acrimonious relationship between SBC and CBF. The following year, I worked closely with our moderator, Jim Baucom, a Virginia pastor, along with Philip Wise, an Alabama pastor, both of whom were strong believers in CBF and in BWA. We arrived in Seville, Spain, in July 2002 to make our case again to the membership committee.

The committee was cordial and responsive to our position but wanted us to submit a clear statement of how CBF was organizationally separate and distinct from the SBC. These two gifted pastors sat with me, and together we listed twenty "indicators" of why and how we were not "an integral part" of any other BWA member body. We presented them to the committee. (These indicators were later adopted by the Coordinating Council. See appendix C.)

The following day, when the committee brought its report to the General Council of the BWA, it was a favorable one. The last few sentences of the report were as follows:

> The Membership Committee believes the application from the CBF can be recommended to the BWA General Council for acceptance in 2003. Given the years of serious differences, we consider it is necessary for the CBF to affirm publicly the statement in 6.2 of this document that they have separated themselves from the structures and organization of the SBC, and have a distinctly diverse understanding to the SBC of what it means to be an organized body of Baptist churches and individuals in covenant relationship. The Membership Committee also invites the President and

the General Secretary to work with others toward enabling better understanding and respect between the CBF and the SBC. The Committee believes there is goodwill from member bodies, toward acceptance of the CBF into membership of the BWA.

Billy Kim, a well-known Korean pastor, was president of the BWA and moderated the General Council. After the report of the membership committee, he allowed a time for discussion. I didn't say a word but was surprised by how much approval there was for CBF's application and how much anger there was toward the efforts of SBC leadership to block our membership. When the time came for a voice vote to accept the report of the committee, it was overwhelmingly favorable. But when the question was asked, "Is there any opposition?" there was a vocal "no" from the SBC delegation sitting together on one side of the room. I felt sadness because of the volume of their voice vote. I also felt sadness because the SBC delegation was clearly out of touch with representatives from the global Baptist community. There was no unity.

The following year (2003) in Rio de Janeiro, Brazil, the General Council of the BWA voted by secret ballot to admit CBF as a member body. The response from SBC leadership was immediate and intense. Chuck Kelley, president of the New Orleans Baptist Seminary, stated that the action by the BWA "might well be the last straw which finally breaks a severely strained relationship stretching back several years." Paige Patterson, president of Southwestern Baptist Seminary, unfairly accused the BWA of a "leftward drift" and threatened an exit. Paul Pressler stated openly, "If you want them and their theology, that's your decision, but it is not our decision to accept them."[24]

Within four months of CBF being admitted to the BWA, a Southern Baptist study committee issued a blistering critique of the BWA with a recommendation to leave and eliminate all funding. The committee, which was composed of Morris Chapman, Jimmy Draper, Tom Elliff, Paige Patterson, Paul Pressler, Jerry Rankin, Joe Reynolds, Gary Smith, and Bob Sorrell, never mentioned CBF by name but excoriated the BWA for liberalism and anti-Americanism and recommended defunding within nine months. Denton Lotz,

BWA's general secretary, immediately issued a lengthy and passionate statement, "The SBC Schism, A Sin against Love."

> We are extremely sorry at this tragic decision which alienates 16 million Southern Baptists from the rest of the 32 million Baptists of the world. . . . Of course the BWA rejects categorically this false accusation of liberalism. . . . In reflecting on this tragic decision, I have realized that this decision is really the triumph of ideology over doctrine. SBC doctrine is a call to unity among its churches. Why then separate from the world of Baptists? In the end, it became a question of power and control and the desire of forcing Baptists of the world to fit into one particular mode or mold of interpretation of thinking. This is contrary to all Baptist understanding of the competency of the individual and of soul liberty.

Although the SBC did not welcome CBF into the BWA, other Baptists did. I received congratulations and affirmations from a number of Baptist leaders. It was both heartening and sobering. Soon the Baptist General Convention of Texas, the Baptist General Association of Virginia, the Baptist General Convention of Missouri, and the District of Columbia Baptist Convention became members, as did numerous Baptist institutions, local churches, and even individuals. I wrote Denton Lotz pledging our love and loyalty:

> Denton, we take our membership in BWA very seriously. We are honored to be admitted and we hope to be worthy members that take our place alongside other Baptist bodies around the world. We have only been members for six months, so please give us time to "find our place" and share collaboratively in the mission of the noble institution called BWA. We see ourselves as new participants and partners in a 100-year-old alliance of Baptists. To use terms from elsewhere, we are "rookies" or "freshmen" in this enterprise. To be sure, many of our pastors and churches have been in BWA through SBC, but this is a new day with CBF as a member body. We will have to discern our role, involvement, and support like any other Baptist body. We will probably make mistakes in the discernment, but I can assure you that we will act prayerfully.

In the following years, CBF did discern our role and intensify our involvement. When BWA celebrated its centennial in 2005 in Birmingham, England, we were there in large numbers along with 10,000 other Baptists. When natural disasters came and Baptist World Aid responded with relief, we were there as a partner and contributor. When Denton Lotz retired as general secretary and Neville Callam was called as the next general secretary, we were there in support and affirmation. When strategic revisioning took place and difficult conversations were necessary, we were there in full participation.

I personally invested time and energy as a new member of BWA's General Council and worked with Neville to create a new network of denominational CEOs for fellowship and sharing of best practices. In 2009, Neville asked me to chair a special commission with the responsibility of drafting a document that would articulate principles and guidelines for intra-Baptist relationships. The commission worked for four years to produce the "Intra-Baptist Covenant" that was then translated into twenty-seven languages.[25] It is an excellent statement that sets the foundation and framework for Christian unity in the Baptist tradition.

On July 4, 2013, after I had retired from CBF, I brought the report of the commission to the General Council in Ocho Rios, Jamaica, where it was adopted unanimously. It was serendipitous, perhaps providential, that the adoption of the statement took place in Jamaica, the home of origin for Neville Callam, one of the finest Baptist leaders I have known. The following are my concluding remarks, which capture the challenge of all ecumenical efforts.

I would like to close with a personal word. My experience in the BWA has been a rich one, but also a challenging one. I have known moments of exhilaration, but I have also known moments of tension. And I confess it is difficult to say which have been more important for my spiritual formation.

I believe the time has come for us in the BWA to talk about how we talk. I also believe the time has come for us to learn to listen to one another in deeper ways. I don't know which is harder, to talk in a way that pleases God or to listen in a way that pleases God. But I know they are both hard. And we desperately need the

Holy Spirit to help us. My prayer is that this document will be an instrument of the Holy Spirit to do both.

Baptist Ecumenicity: The New Baptist Covenant

Being part of BWA meant that CBF was also part of one of its regional bodies, North American Baptist Fellowship (NABF), which includes twenty-two Baptist denominations in the US and Canada. In our NABF meetings, I got to know the leaders of these denominations, especially Roy Medley, general secretary of American Baptist Churches, USA. Roy and I nurtured a genuine friendship, and he became a "soul brother" to me. We were in similar ministry positions, and we began our ministries about the same time. I also became friends with the leaders of four of the historic African American Baptist conventions: William Shaw, president of the National Baptist Convention, Inc.; Stephen Thurston, president of the National Baptist Convention of America; Melvin Wade, president of the National Missionary Baptist Convention; and Tyrone Pitts, general secretary of the Progressive National Baptist Convention.

These friendships proved to be invaluable in making possible one of the most remarkable ecumenical experiences I have had: the New Baptist Covenant Celebration, January 30–February 1, 2008. Several important factors converged to bring about this event, the first of which was the enthusiasm of the Black Baptist leaders in endorsing and supporting it. Then there was the stature and influence of President Jimmy Carter, who made a commitment to host a number of planning sessions at the Carter Center in Atlanta and to be personally involved in those sessions. Then the leadership of William Underwood, president of Mercer University, was crucial. He not only gave personal time and energy to the effort but also put the financial and human resources of Mercer at the disposal of the planners. Then Jimmy Allen, a respected leader both in the SBC and CBF, devoted himself unselfishly for more than three years as moderator and convener.

Thirty racially, geographically, and theologically diverse Baptist organizations created the alliance and covenanted together to

- Create an authentic and prophetic Baptist voice for these complex times.
- Emphasize traditional Baptist values, including sharing the gospel of Jesus Christ and its implications for public and private morality.
- Promote peace with justice, feed the hungry, clothe the naked, shelter the homeless, care for the sick and marginalized, welcome the strangers among us, and promote religious liberty and respect for religious diversity.

Platform personalities at the celebration included a "who's who" of Baptist public figures: John Grisham, author; Marian Wright Edelman, activist and author; Grant Teaff, football coach; David Satchel, US surgeon general; Tony Campolo, preacher; Kate Campbell and Kyle Matthews, musicians; Julie Pennington-Russell and Charles Adams, pastors; and others. The event was nonpartisan, but numerous political leaders from both parties gave major addresses: Jimmy Carter, Bill Clinton, Al Gore, Charles Grassley. Lindsey Graham was scheduled but had to cancel at the last minute. In addition to plenary sessions, the celebration featured numerous breakouts dealing with topics such as racism, religious liberty, poverty, AIDS, faith and public policy, stewardship of the earth, evangelism, financial stewardship, and preaching.

More than 15,000 Baptists gathered at the Georgia World Congress Center in Atlanta for a three-day event that was, for me, nothing short of historic and exhilarating. The racial demographic was almost equal between members of Black and White congregations. But what was amazing about the NBC celebration was that no one person or organization could take credit. It was bigger than all of us and a shining example, though brief, of what can happen when unselfishness and unity are more important than anything else. What I experienced during those three days was a glimpse into what I believe the kingdom of God should look like on earth. It was a visible and tangible image of both diversity and unity. During every minute of the event, I felt like Simon Peter on the mountain of transfiguration, not knowing what to say except, "It is good for us to be here."

After Atlanta, President Carter and others continued the NBC by convening numerous gatherings and facilitating partnerships between Black and White churches. I was not significantly involved in NBC after Atlanta, but I did write an article in summer 2008 at the invitation of its editor, Bill Epps, for the *National Baptist Voice*, an official publication of the National Baptist Convention, USA, Inc. So much has happened since the Atlanta celebration—Barack Obama's presidency, Black Lives Matter, George Floyd's murder, and what seems to be a new awakening to racial injustice in America—but the pastoral prayer I offered then is one I still offer today.

One of my firm prayers is that in the providence of God the New Baptist Covenant Celebration will be a "Kairos" moment of illumination and transformation for all of us. But I'm especially praying that we Euro-American Baptists will learn, really learn, what the Spirit would say to us from our African American Baptist sisters and brothers. As I see it, Euro-American Christians, be they mainline, evangelical, nondenominational, or charismatic, rarely understand the incredible gospel power in Black churches and the spiritual impact of Black churches on culture. I don't know exactly why this is so, but the time for this to change is now.

I believe that the Black Baptist tradition offers one of the brightest rays of hope for renewal in the body of Christ in North America. Let me suggest four reasons I believe this is so.

First, this tradition loves the biblical story. In its theology, liturgy, and rhetoric, the emphasis is on the stories of the Bible and the grand narrative that they all comprise. In music, worship, preaching, and conversation, there is a remembering and retelling of the epic drama recorded in Scripture. And this is especially true when it comes to the drama of the life, death, resurrection, return of Jesus. I recently heard one African American pastor say, "The name of Jesus is sweet in our churches."

Second, this tradition has a passion for social justice. Having lived under the yoke of slavery, exploitation, segregation, and racism, the members of Black churches pray for justice and the pastors preach about justice. They do not shy away from addressing the social, political, or moral issues of the day or advocating with leaders in business and government for the welfare of the community and the nation.

Third, this tradition worships with freedom and joy in the spirit. Music is lively and expressive. Preaching is dialogical and interactive. Prayer and praise are emotional as well as cognitive. I believe that when many Euro-Americans worship in an African American church, they are empowered and set free to celebrate in ways they fear to do in their own churches.

Fourth, this tradition resists the demonic and endures pain with courage. Black Baptists know from experience that "we wrestle not with flesh and blood, but with principalities and powers and spiritual wickedness in high places." They have been radiant and resilient in overcoming institutional evil, systemic sin, and organized oppression. Their conviction that Jesus understands suffering, that he overcame suffering, and that he is preparing a place where there will be no more suffering has enabled them to bear suffering with dignity and courage.

These are some of the reasons I believe that the witness of Black Baptists desperately needs to be heard and received within the larger Baptist family. We will not realize Dr. King's vision of "the beloved community" with more demographic studies, sociological analysis, or strategic plans. We must have nothing less than a spiritual revolution that encompasses our thinking, our behaving, and our relating.

Please do not interpret my words as a romanticized or sanitized vision of the African American church or community. Anyone who has read Robert Franklin's book *Crisis in the Village* knows the daunting challenges it faces. Indeed, many of us believe that the American experiment itself is in peril because of rampant consumerism, unbridled greed, and the growing disparity between rich and poor. Families are disintegrating. Global violence increases because of mindless terror and mindless military exploits. And one billion people live on less than one dollar a day. Our world is terribly broken.

Yet the seeds for its healing are of the gospel of Jesus Christ. And it is to the church that the gospel has been entrusted. When the traditions of the church is a good steward of that gospel, healing and transformation take place. The African American church tradition, and particularly the Baptist stream of it, has stewarded the gospel not perfectly but profoundly. That stewardship needs to be studied, spread, and shared.

Here I am not referencing the mega-church preachers or televangelists, Black or White, who preach a prosperity gospel or market success as a substitute for the cross, but rather, I speak of those Black Baptist churches large, medium, and small who are both faithful to their tradition and relevant to their culture. They tell the Jesus story. They act and speak prophetically. They rejoice in the spirit. They embrace their own suffering as well as the suffering of the world with grace.

These churches may not seem significant to the power structures of the world, to the scholarly journals of academic institutions, or even to popular media personalities. But they have incredible lessons to teach the whole body of Christ. They may even be the divinely appointed instrument for a spiritual revolution and renewal that we so desperately need.

May God grant all of us the good sense to listen and learn.[26]

Christian Churches Together in the USA (CCT)

Forming a new ecumenical body whose stated purpose is "to enable churches and Christian organizations to grow closer together in Christ in order to strengthen our Christian witness in the world" is no small matter. It surely is not for the "faint of heart" or the impatient. On March 31, 2006, in Atlanta, thirty-four participants (thirty churches/denominations and four Christian organizations) adopted the by-laws to officially constitute Christian Churches Together in the USA. CBF was among those participants.

Our coordinating council had voted for CBF to become a participant and authorized me to represent us, so when the question was asked at the Atlanta CCT gathering if we could affirm the theological affirmation, I answered "we do." And when the question was asked if we agreed to the purposes of CCT, I answered "we agree." It was a moment of joy for me personally and all those present. I was then elected to serve on the Steering Committee and helped prepare for a public launch the following year.

The theological affirmations required of participants were as follows:

- Believe in the Lord Jesus Christ as God and Savior according to the Scriptures.
- Worship and serve the One God, Father, Son, and Holy Spirit.
- Seek ways to work together in order to present a more credible Christian witness in and to the world.

The Purposes of CCT required of participants were as follows:
- To celebrate a common confession of faith in the Triune God.
- To discern the guidance of the Holy Spirit through prayer and theological dialogue.
- To provide fellowship and mutual support.
- To seek better understanding of each other by affirming our commonalities and understanding our differences.
- To foster evangelism faithful to the proclamation of the gospel.
- To speak to society with a common voice whenever possible.
- To promote the common good of society and engage in other activities consistent with its purpose.

The formalizing denominations were American Baptist Churches, USA; American Orthodox Church in America; Christian Reformed Church in North America; Church of God (Anderson, Indiana); Church of God of Prophecy; Cooperative Baptist Fellowship; Coptic Orthodox Church; Disciples of Christ; Episcopal Church; Evangelical Lutheran Church in America; Free Methodist Church; Friends United Meeting; Greek Orthodox Archdiocese of America; International Council of Community Churches; International Pentecostal Holiness Church; Korean Presbyterian Church in America; National Association of Congregational Christian Churches; National Baptist Convention, USA; National Baptist Convention of America; Open Bible Churches; Orthodox Church in America; Polish National Catholic Church of America; Reformed Church in America; Syrian Orthodox Church; The Evangelical Covenant Church; The Salvation Army; United Church of Christ; United Methodist Church; and US Conference of Catholic Bishops. The formalizing Christian organizations were Bread for the World, Call to Renewal/Sojourners, Evangelicals for Social Action, and World Vision.

A press release announced the occasion:

Thirty-four churches and national Christian organizations, representing over 100 million Americans, have formed the broadest, most inclusive fellowship of Christian churches and traditions in the USA in a gathering at Simpsonwood Conference and Retreat Center near Atlanta Georgia, March 28–31, 2006. National leaders from five Christian families—Evangelical/Pentecostal, Historic Protestant, Historic Racial/Ethnic, Orthodox, and Catholic—made the historic decision to organize officially as Christian Churches Together in the USA. Its mission is "to enable churches and the Christian organizations to grow closer together in Christ in order to strengthen our Christian witness in the world."

From its beginning, CCT has given priority to prayer and worship, to building relationships of trust, and to discerning challenges that need to be addressed in society for more faithful Christian witness. In this meeting, the group focused on the issue of poverty in the United States, engaging in biblical reflection and in conversation with those who have experienced poverty as well as those with academic expertise. Affirming that overcoming poverty "is central to the mission of the church and essential to our unity in Christ," participants committed themselves to work together to address the causes of poverty in the United States.

The vision of CCT began with a diverse group of Christian leaders gathered in the fall of 2001 who expressed a longing for an expanded Christian conversation in our nation: "We lament that we are divided and that our divisions too often result in distrust, misunderstandings, fear and even hostility between us. We long for the broken body of Christ to be made whole, where unity can be celebrated in the midst of our diversity. We long for more common witness, vision, and mission."

Over these past years, a process of mutual engagement, agreement on purposes, and organizational planning has now resulted in an historic new expression of relationships among churches. "We finally found the courage to confront our obvious and long-standing divisions and to build a new expression of unity, rooted in the spirit, that will strengthen our mission in the world," affirmed the Rev. Wesley Granberg-Michaelson, General Secretary of the Reformed Church in America, who has served as interim moderator. "We are filled with excitement, hope, and expectation for how God will use this new expression of our fellowship together."

When I first heard about the 2001 meeting, I called Wes Granberg-Michaelson. I was attracted to the theological depth and demographic breadth of the participants, the focus on prayer and worship as a uniting factor, and the emphasis on spiritual discernment as a way to make decisions rather than debating and voting. I found the amazing diversity among participants fascinating, and I found an authentic humility and quiet patience among the participants even more fascinating. People spoke with passion and conviction, but they listened with equal passion. Wes gently moderated the conversations, and the worship leadership alternated between the "faith families." We really got to know one another as church/denominational and organizational leaders. Egos were not on display.

The meetings were hard work. We decided early to address poverty in the US, not just to learn statistics or about the amazing work that each group was doing to alleviate poverty. Rather the goal was to discern how we might foster a movement of transformation, an awakening of national conscience, and an understanding of the Christian gospel that motivates us to action. We listened to presentations from each "faith family" perspective. We broke into smaller conversation groups. We dreamed. We planned. We prayed.

We then decided to have the same kind of conversations about evangelism that we did about poverty, and this is where I probably learned more than I could have imagined. I listened as representatives from Catholic, Orthodox, Evangelical/Pentecostal, Protestant, and historic African American denominations talked about evangelism. I was amazed, surprised, humbled, and encouraged. The conversations were not about proselyting one another's members or methodology. Rather they were about the urgency and centrality of evangelism in an increasingly secular and consumer society. They were about the difference between the good news proclamation of Jesus and the proclamation of today's church, the real obstacles to gospel proclamation in totalitarian countries and the relationship of poverty to evangelism.

In 2007, a worship service celebrated CCT's public launch at the Lake Avenue Church in Pasadena, California. CBF was well represented with more than twenty representatives, primarily CBF's state and regional coordinators and Atlanta staff. Again, it was an experience of great joy. In January 2011, CCT's annual meeting was in Birmingham, Alabama, in spite of a severe ice storm. As I would retire from CBF in 2012, this would be the last annual meeting of CCT I would attend. It would also be one of the most prescient and predictive because its focus was on domestic poverty through the lens of racism. We offered the first ever clergy response to Martin Luther King Jr.'s "Letter from Birmingham Jail" and visited the Civil Rights Institute and the Sixteenth Street Baptist Church.

My involvement in CCT was probably the most personally transformative experience during my CBF tenure. I unlearned, and learned, so much that I simply would not have without the experiential and relational exposure to the richness of the body of Christ on earth. Praying with and talking with Christians from such different backgrounds made me realize our essential oneness and our spiritual unity as Christians.

My involvement in CCT was scholarly without being academic, spiritual without being sentimental, practical without being prosaic, and active without being activist. I don't know which was more satisfying, the incredible diversity or the shared unity. Above everything it was relational. For the few times we were together, either in a steering committee or in the annual meetings, we experienced an energy that I took with me into the rest of my work.

My involvement in CCT also opened a door for me to participate in an ecumenical service (along with 200 other invited clergy) at St. Joseph's Parish Church in New York, where Pope Benedict XVI was present. The occasion was on April 18, 2008, as part of his visit to the US. My assigned seat was center aisle east, row 4, seat 2, right behind all the Orthodox representatives. I arrived at the church early to make my way through the tight security, but I was so nervous that I left my cell phone in the taxi. I made my way through the streets, all of which were blocked off from traffic, and found my place in a beautiful but modest parish church building constructed by German Catholic immigrants.

When Pope John Paul II died, I issued a press release and posted my tribute on our website with suggested ways for Baptists to use it as a way to nurture ecumenical dialogue and build community.

> As Baptist Christians we give thanks to God for the life and legacy of Pope John Paul II. His devotion to Jesus Christ has inspired and challenged multitudes. In a world of war and violence, he was a voice for peace. In a world of greed and materialism, he was a voice for justice. In a world of oppression and tyranny, he was a voice for freedom. In a world of suffering, he was an example of courage and compassion. For many of us, his most memorable words were his constant reference to those of Scripture, "Be not afraid."
>
> In this hour of loss, those of us in Cooperative Baptist Fellowship offer our prayers for our sisters and brothers in the Catholic Church. We also offer our hand of Christian fellowship in serving Christ's Kingdom. And, we pledge solidarity with all Christians in being the presence of Christ to one another and to the world.

After Pope John Paul's death, I paid close attention to the news releases and analyses of Joseph Ratzinger's becoming Pope Benedict XVI. When the opportunity came to see him in person, I was excited. To my surprise, I was mesmerized by the pope's appearance and homily on Christian unity. Years earlier I had read the first volume of Hans Kung's memoirs and his account of Joseph Ratzinger's rise in the Curia. I had also read with appreciation Ratzinger's best-selling book, *Jesus of Nazareth*. He was a diminutive man with a faint smile and eyes that seemed to be darting in every direction. What I noticed most about his appearance were his red shoes. He spoke from a manuscript but was warm and even humorous. After his message he welcomed a few selected individuals to his chair on the platform for a brief greeting, and then processed down the center aisle less than three feet from me. We then dismissed to the church hall for a delicious meal, where I sat at a table with an executive of the National Association of Evangelicals, an archbishop of the Ethiopian Orthodox Church in America, a chaplain for Sing Sing prison, and a chaplain for Columbia University. It was an unforgettable experience and a reminder that the bishop of Rome does indeed have a "charism" of bringing together such a diverse group of Christian clergy. Who else in the world could have assembled such an audience?

Despite all contradictions to the contrary, I do believe the church of Jesus Christ is holy, apostolic, and universal. All of our transgressions, heresies, and divisions do not prevent me from making such theological affirmations or keep me from aspiring and working toward their fulfillment. The church is indeed global and expresses itself in every language, culture, and ethnicity on earth with an essential unity that both includes and transcends its diversity.

My involvement in CCT also led to some discoveries that required serious confession and repentance. I confess that for much of my life I have lived too small, too provincial, too sectarian. I failed to see that God's kingdom is so much greater than I understand. God's creation is so much grander than I have known. God's word is so far beyond what my small mind can comprehend. God's future is so much more glorious than I can imagine. I feel ashamed that I have too often worshiped my own images of God and replaced the wonder and amazement of divine worship with my own compulsiveness to control God and allow my culturally conditioned impulses to limit God.

When I consider the great commandment, "Thou shalt love the Lord your God with all your heart, mind, soul, and strength; and thou shalt love your neighbor as yourself," I realize that I have often neglected the weightier matters of faith and spent far too much energy on the lesser matters of faith. The prophet Micah summarizes true religion: "He has told you O mortal what is good; and what does the LORD require of you but to do justice, to love kindness, and to walk humbly with your God" (Mic 6:8). I confess that too much of my life has been given chasing after what, at the end of the day, is inconsequential. When I fix my attention on that noblest of all humans, Jesus Christ, who in his humanity incarnates and interprets

Deity, I feel like Simon Peter who said, "Depart from me, Lord, for I am a sinful man."

Interfaith Dialogue

Shortly after becoming coordinator I received a telephone call from Michael Miller, who worked with the Jewish Community Relations Council (JCRC) in New York City. He was distressed over some public remarks that Paige Patterson, then president of the SBC, had made at their recent meeting about "targeting Jews" for evangelism. He had contacted Patterson and asked if there were a place and time they could meet to discuss his statements, which were offensive to many in the Jewish community, especially in New York City. Patterson's requirement for any dialogue was that he be allowed to bring a large delegation, which Miller found even more offensive.

Miller's words to me were, "We simply want to talk to some Baptists and create better understanding between us." I asked how he got my name and decided to call me. He responded that they had followed the formation of CBF and were aware that we were moderate and might possibly be open to conversation. I agreed. A few days later I went to Washington, DC, and met with Gedale Horowitz, who was president of the New York City JCRC. He was considerably older than I was, an investment banker by profession and a deeply religious man. We met at a private club to which he had access and shared a delicious meal together. For reasons that are still unexplainable to me, we had an immediate chemistry of kinship with no pretension. There was a genuine warmth and kindness between us. After the meal he asked if we could talk openly and honestly about our faith differences and find ways to build understanding and community. He asked me to speak first.

I told him that I was at the very moment of our conversation experiencing an internal struggle. I felt deep emotion. I told him that part of the message of the Christian faith to which I had committed my life was a mission and mandate given by Jesus himself to "make disciples of all nations." I told him that I wanted everyone in the world to follow Jesus and love Jesus. I could not give that up. At the same time, I said I realized that after the tragedy of Christians'

persecution of Jews through the centuries, especially in the Holo-
caust, the relationship between Jews and Christians could never be
the same. What I believed is that I should give a witness of my faith
and then receive a witness he would give of his faith. I asked that we
both give to each other and receive from each other the truth that we
believed. As I spoke, tears came into his eyes, and our eyes met in a
moment of genuine understanding.

There was a long silence. Then Gedale Horowitz said, "Reverend
Vestal, you need to know that in interfaith dialogue I do not consider
you as an equal, but when you say that you cannot give up your
faith in Jesus and want to witness of him and also receive a witness
of my faith, then that makes you and me equals. Now we can have
dialogue." At this point tears came to my eyes, and again we shared a
moment of understanding.

The conversation that followed was both meaningful and fruitful.
We agreed that Michael Miller would come to the next General
Assembly of CBF and speak to us on interfaith dialogue. We also
agreed on other ways to lower tensions between Jews and Christians
and create opportunities to build relationships. I have never forgotten
what I experienced in Washington, DC, from Gedale Horowitz.

September 11, 2001, changed the world, and it changed my
world. The coordinated acts of terrorism on American soil resulted
in the tragic deaths of innocent Americans, and a political tsunami
swept over the world. The American response was a "war on terrorism"
and military invasions into Afghanistan and Iraq. One consequence
was heightened tensions between Muslims and Christians. Fear was
everywhere. Like everyone else, I realized how little I understood
Islam and how few Muslims I knew personally.

I set myself on an intentional course to study Islam in greater
depth by reading extended sections of Qur'an. I watched a PBS
documentary, *Islam: Empire of Faith*. I read Karen Armstrong's books,
Islam: A Short History and *Muhammed: A Biography of the Prophet*. I
worked my way through Hans Kung's *Christianity and World Religions: Pathways to Dialogue*, in which he argues that there can be no
peace among nations without peace among the religions. I studied
The Heart of Islam: Enduring Values for Humanity by Seyyed Hossein

Nasr, a leading Islamicist. Later I read the works of Fethullah Gulen and Irfan Ahmad Khan and explored the literature of Sufism and Islamic mysticism. I also made my way to some local mosques and Islamic centers to get acquainted.

In 2002, a former SBC president, Jerry Vines, made some critical and controversial remarks about Islam and about Mohammed in particular. They sparked widespread controversy and criticism in the press and serious concerns in the American Muslim community. The Muslim community was already under intense scrutiny because of 9/11, and his remarks only made them feel more vulnerable. I wrote a personal letter to the leadership of ten different Muslim organizations in the US expressing my dismay at his remarks and making clear that Jerry Vines did not speak for all Baptists.

One of the responses to my letter was from Dr. Sayyid M. Syeed, executive director of the Islamic Society of North America (ISNA), the largest Muslim organization in the country. He thanked me for my letter and asked if we could meet for conversation and dialogue. The result of the conversations was an invitation to speak at ISNA's annual gathering in Chicago and at their annual interfaith unity banquet. He offered me an eight-minute time frame to bring greetings to a convention that attracted more than 50,000 Muslims over a four-day period. I accepted his invitation gladly but also with some trepidation. This was to be an experience out of my comfort zone.

When I arrived in Chicago and checked into my hotel near the convention center, I realized I was a minority. I was a Christian among a large number of Muslims, and for a brief time I understood what it must feel like to be a religious minority. To my surprise, I felt comfortable in an event and space that was both different and the same as my own. I was familiar with large religious gatherings that offered plenary sessions, small-group breakouts, fellowship, and inspiration, but always in a Christian context. Here it was in a Muslim context.

I could easily identify with families, especially with families who had small children, as I walked the halls, the food court, and the bazaar, where hundreds of vendors were selling books, tapes, and all kinds of goods and services. My name was printed on the "Who's

Who List" of the eighty-page program. I felt welcomed. As I sat in an audience of several thousand and listened to clerics, jurists, and imams, I felt a kinship with those around me. When my time came to speak, I was ushered to a holding room and then to the stage, where I was assigned a chair and a reminder of my time limit. The introduction that preceded my remarks was gracious, with a clear statement that I had "reached out" to offer friendship when a prominent Baptist Christian in America had spoken disparaging words about Islam and its prophet. My words of greeting were brief but heartfelt.

> It is a great privilege for me to participate in this convention. I'm grateful to Dr. Syeed for the invitation to bring a brief greeting. Hans Kung, professor of ecumenical theology, wrote the following words in his classic work, *Christianity: Essence, History, and Future*: "No peace among the nations without peace among the religions, no peace among the religions without dialogue between the religions, no dialogue between the religions without investigation of the foundation of the religions."
>
> I have come to this convention to learn and listen. Most Christians have little knowledge of Islam, its history, its theology, or its practice. We are willfully ignorant of the faith that shapes the lives of more than one billion people on this planet. My desire today is to be a learner.
>
> I've also come to nurture friendship. Can Muslims and Christians be friends? I mean can they really be friends when there is mutual trust, open and transparent communication, and shared values? I believe they can, but it will take intentionality, patience, effort, and perhaps a sense of humor.
>
> Finally, I've come to this convention to let you know that there are many Christians who passionately yearn for justice, reconciliation, and peace within our human family. I'm from the faith tradition called Baptist, and I'm aware that in recent days there have been Baptist voices that have spoken words that are demeaning of Islam with a rhetoric of violence. Please know that there are other Baptist Christians, as well as Christians from other traditions, whose words and deeds are different than those often

reported in the media. It is desire for understanding, community, and common cause.

Islam and Christianity are both missionary faiths, i.e., we both feel compelled by a sacred mission. As we all know, there are profound differences between us, but I also believe that there are profound similarities. And one of them has to do with the human desire and divine mandate for justice and peace. Could we be at a point where citizens of this great nation, as people of faith, as members of a global village, might work together for peace? Could we be at a point where we all as children of God might pray together for peace? Might it be possible that instead of seeing ourselves in a struggle with each other, we see ourselves in a common struggle for the welfare and well-being of every person in the world? I believe that we are at such a point, and it is possible. To that end I offer you my hand, my heart, and my hope. God bless you.

A few years later, in 2005, Earlene and I were invited to an "experiment" in interfaith dialogue and friendship. It was transformative. We took part in a ten-day trip to Turkey with Christian, Jewish, and Muslim leaders. The immersion experience was sponsored and paid for by the Istanbul Cultural Center of Atlanta, a Muslim organization affiliated with and influenced by the Turkish Muslim scholar Fethullah Gulen. At the time I knew nothing of the Gulen movement and what would subsequently become a political conflict and controversy with the president of Turkey, Recep Tayyip Erdoğan. We accepted and enjoyed the hospitality of our hosts and relished the opportunity to learn. The experience of Christians, Jews, and Muslims spending time traveling together on a bus, eating together in restaurants, and visiting sites sacred and special to all three religions was remarkable. We spoke openly about our similarities and differences and the mutual respect and trust necessary for world peace. We stayed in hotels and in host homes. We listened to one another's stories and learned a lot about our respective faiths. It was, for me, life changing.

On return from Turkey, we continued our participation in this interfaith group of friends. I joined an Advisory Board for the Atlanta Istanbul Cultural Center and was invited to speak at a number of events, including a banquet at Auburn University sponsored by the Muslim campus organization. I offered three grounds for interfaith dialogue.

> First, we share a common humanity. All three of the Abrahamic faiths make distinctive and even exclusive claims for themselves. Jews claim to be God's chosen people. Christians claim to follow the Savior of the world. Muslims claim Mohammed as the last prophet. But before all these claims, we share a common humanity. We're part of one family, the human family. We are children of one parent. We share a common origin, nature, and bond.
>
> Second, we share a common brokenness. Martin Luther King Jr. had a metaphor in which he described his dream for America as a "beloved community." Perhaps we are at a place to begin to build that community with humility. All of us would do well to admit honestly and humbly that we have contributed to misunderstanding and confusion. All of us have had our share of fear and prejudice. All of us have acted foolishly and spoken foolishly. We are all broken, just in different ways and in different places.
>
> Finally, we share common suffering. Perhaps the acid test of anyone's faith, whether Jewish, Christian, Muslim, or whatever else, is what we do with our suffering. What do we do with our pain? And what do we do with the pain of the world? Do we enter into the suffering of others and act to alleviate their suffering? It seems to me that in a day of such great human suffering we have common ground, not only for dialogue but also for action. If ever we should care for one another, it is now. If ever we should find ways to work together to alleviate human suffering, it is now.
>
> So in thanksgiving to God for our shared humanity, in humility before God for a shared brokenness, and in love from God for a shared suffering, let us learn to live together and even work together for our common good.

In 2007, more than 300 world leaders of the Islamic religion issued an open letter addressed to world leaders of the Christian religion calling for peace between Muslims and Christians. It was titled "A Common Word Between Us and You," and it identified the double command of love to God and love to neighbor as the "common ground" between Muslims and Christians and the basis for peace and understanding.[27] It was a historic document that drew widespread attention and created numerous responses. The Baptist World Alliance (BWA), of which CBF was a member body, responded with a thoughtful theological document titled "From the Baptist World Alliance: To the Muslim Religious Leaders and Scholars Who Have Written or Signed 'A Common Word Between Us and You.'"

The BWA document was crafted by four Baptist leaders: David Coffee, president of the BWA; Neville Callam, general secretary of the BWA; Paul Fiddes, chair of the Commission on Doctrine and Inter-Church Cooperation of the BWA; and Regina Claas, chair of the Commission on Freedom and Justice of the BWA. Fiddes was the primary author. It was then presented to the annual meeting of the BWA gathered in Prague, July 21–28, 2008. I participated in that discussion and found in the BWA document a clear and compelling statement of essential doctrines that Christians confess and are unwilling to compromise while at the same time offering common understandings of love to God and love to neighbor that both Muslims and Christians can affirm. I distributed the BWA response to all of our CBF family, especially to field mission personnel who live and minister in predominately Muslim cultures.

The tension between interfaith dialogue and the Christian mission of evangelization is not an easy one to maintain. Both must be done without any coercion, intimidation, or violence. Both must be informed by the best possible knowledge of one's own faith and the faith of others with whom dialogue or evangelization is occurring. I personally believe that both are valid, but they should be seen as separate tasks of the church, with each task informed by the other. In both dialogue and evangelization, however, Christians give their own witness to truth and receive the witness of the other, always with the utmost respect and humility.

Chang Mai, Thailand

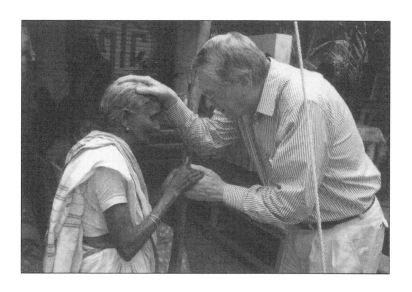

Bay of Bengal, India (after the tsunami)

HIV/AIDS clinic with Sam Bandela
Delhi, India

Seethammapeta, India
Evangelists and church planters receiving bicycles

Grand-Goâve, Haiti (2011)
Nurses Jenny Jenkins and Nancy James work with Dr. Steve James
to provide medical care to hundreds of villagers in remote Haiti.

Seoul, Korea (2005)
Yonsei Central Baptist (Pastor Yoo Jong Yoon is translating)

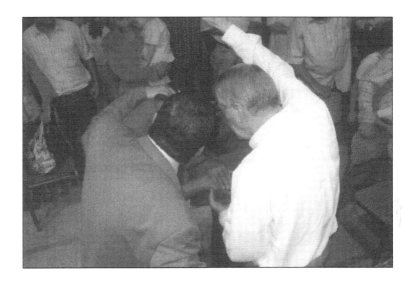

"Jesus Celebration" in Cairo, Egypt with Chauki Boulos (2008)

"Jesus Celebration" in Cairo, Egypt (2008)

Cegrane refugee camp, Macedonia

Cegrane

Han Wenzao, director of China Christian Council

Wang Ya Shi Church, Beijing, China

New Baptist Covenant (2008)

New Baptist Covenant, Bill Underwood with
denominational leadership (2008)

Habitat for Humanity home built in New Orleans
after Hurricane Katrina
Rev. Roy Medley, general secretary of
American Baptist Churches USA

Denton Lotz, general secretary, Baptist World Alliance

Roy Medley, American Baptist Churches, USA, and Tyronne Pitts, National Progressive Baptist Convention (Washington, DC, 2007)

Faith leaders meeting with Condoleezza Rice, secretary of state, on issues of world hunger

To Reverend Daniel Vestal
Best Wishes, Bill Clinton

The White House

Chapter 10

Retirement and Refocus

In 2009, several events transpired to cause me to think seriously about retiring from CBF. First, I turned sixty-five, the traditional age for retirement, and then I was diagnosed with prostate cancer that would require surgery. I was contacted, for the first time in a long time, by a pastor search committee in Texas asking if I would consider returning to my native state. Larry Baker, director of the Doctor of Ministry program at Logsdon School of Theology, Hardin Simmons University in Abilene, Texas, asked if I might be interested in assuming that role and possibly moving to San Antonio. And then in December, William Underwood, president of Mercer University, surprised me with an invitation to become director of the Baptist Studies Program at Mercer whenever I decided to retire from CBF.

In April 2010, Babs Baugh and I hosted a three-day retreat at Callaway Gardens in Pine Mountain, Georgia, for the leadership of twenty CBF partner organizations, state/regional CBF coordinators, CBF officers, and senior staff as well as some pastoral leaders. The retreat was born out of a conversation with Babs as we anticipated CBF's twentieth anniversary in 2011. She agreed to pay for all expenses, and we put the agenda in place for some extended conversations about our future.

The event was a good one and set in motion the transition for some needed organizational and structural changes. At the end of the retreat, I was transparent with those present and told them that Earlene and I were having conversations about our own transition and that I couldn't promise I would see the organizational changes through to completion. I assured them that I was committed to staying through the twentieth anniversary assembly in 2011. This was the first public reference I made about my personal plans.

On June 27, 2010, I had one of those unexplainable experiences that gave me great peace and assurance of God's providence and presence. CBF had received a generous gift of $1.5 million from the Piper Foundation to partner with Faith Comes by Hearing, a nonprofit organization that provides listening devices with Scripture recordings for churches to use in evangelism and formation. More than 500 churches were participating in the initiative. On this particular morning I happened to be listening to the recording of the David and Goliath story from 1 Samuel. It was in David's words that the inexplicable happened: "Know that the LORD does not save by sword and spear, for the battle is the LORD's" (1 Sam 17:47). For some strange reason, in hearing those words I realized I had been called to CBF and couldn't leave until I had received a "release" from that call. I didn't sense a release at the moment but rather a recognition of the need for it.

I shut off the device and drove to my office, pondering what it all meant. As I turned into the drive that led to my office building, there were four deer standing motionless in an open space within ten yards of my car. It was so unexpected that it took my breath away. I stopped, stared, and burst into tears. I was overcome with the wonder and beauty of what I was beholding. Then, without thinking about anything else, I felt a wave of peace and calm come over me, and I knew (I just *knew*) that all would be well.

On Thursday morning, September 9, 2011, I announced that I would be retiring from CBF effective June 30, 2012. I had indeed discerned a release from my call, and I wanted to give time for a search committee to be put into place for my replacement. It was time both for me and for CBF, and I felt grateful and relieved. The leadership and membership of CBF were gracious in their affirmations, and the General Assembly in June 2012 was serendipitously in Fort Worth, Texas, my hometown. Of all the words of commendation and beautiful gifts that were given, one of the most meaningful was an announcement of the "Daniel and Earlene Vestal Scholarship Endowment" to fund scholarships for future seminary students. All of our children were present for the final service and reception, as were my brother, sisters, and mother. It felt as if I had come full circle as I closed a satisfying chapter in ministry.

Mercer University

I did accept Bill Underwood's gracious invitation, and on July 1, 2012, I became distinguished professor of Baptist leadership at Mercer University. He decided, and I agreed, that my focus would be on nurturing Baptist leaders for church and society. Babs Baugh, through the Baugh Foundation, gave a generous gift to constitute the Eula Mae and John Baugh Center for Baptist Leadership in honor of her parents. I would also serve as its director. I would teach on the subject of leadership at Mercer's McAfee School of Theology, offer mentorship to young ministers, create resources for lay leadership development, network with global Baptist leaders, and preach and teach in Baptist congregations. It was a role that seemed to fit my gifting and experience, and I began with great enthusiasm.

In the years since, I have enjoyed every aspect of the role and have become increasingly convinced of the importance of the church, the academy, and the denomination working together to provide life-long learning for clergy and lay Christian leaders. Since the focus of seminaries is on leadership formation for clergy, I decided that the focus of the Baugh Center would be on lay leadership formation and that I would begin with deacons. Libby Allen, both a respected lay Christian leader and a deacon, joined me at the Baugh Center as administrative coordinator and soon became a trusted colleague and friend.

Deacon Leadership Development

Since every Baptist church has a diaconate, I decided that the Baugh Center would offer congregational resources for the spiritual and theological formation of deacons. My own pastoral experience with deacons was meaningful, although their functions varied considerably with each church. At Meadow Lane Baptist, there were twelve active deacons who met monthly in the pastor's office in an informal setting. They saw their task as giving of advice and consent to my leadership, even though I was only twenty-five years old. At

Southcliff Baptist, there were twenty-four active deacons who served three-year terms on a rotating basis. They were a more organized group who reviewed the church's financial statement each month and again offered counsel to the pastor and staff. At First Baptist Midland, there were thirty-six active deacons who functioned like a board of directors. They had enormous power and influence over the administration of the church.

At Dunwoody Baptist, there were forty-eight deacons who had almost nothing to do with administration except to review the annual budget and other major decisions that were to be presented to the church. Their primary role was ministering to families in the church who were assigned to them each year. At Tallowood Baptist, there were seventy deacons who divided themselves into ministry teams according to the gifting of each. The monthly meetings were times of worship and reports from each team as well as from the pastoral staff. The deacons' meetings were spiritual celebrations.

The configuration of diaconates still varies considerably from church to church, as does the matrix of lay leadership in congregations. But whatever the configuration and context, deacons are integral to a healthy and vibrant church. I value deacons and believe they should be servant and spiritual leaders just like pastors. Congregational and societal changes are indeed real, but the character and conduct of deacons as spiritually mature servants is as important as ever. And my experience is that deacons need help in becoming spiritually mature servants.

I asked seven Georgia deacons to form a leadership team for the purpose of creating a Baptist deacon network and developing resources that would help local congregations. They all agreed: Mike Hendley, FBC, St. Simons; Carol Palmer, Smoke Rise Baptist, Atlanta; Susan Broome, FBC, Macon; Mark Whitaker, Harlem Baptist, Harlem; Don Brewer, FBC, Gainesville; David Keel, FBC, Augusta; Connie Jones, FBC, Macon. I also asked my friend Frank Broome, coordinator of Georgia CBF, and Rachel Greco, who worked with Georgia CBF, for help. We convened deacon summits and retreats, distributed an online deacon newsletter called "Table and Towel," and provided other resources for deacons. Carol Younger, a gifted teacher, authored

God's Mission Requires Deacons, a theological and historical rationale for deacons. Dan Bagby, Philip Vestal, Greg DeLoach, Jack Glasgow, and Scott Dickison, all respected pastors, offered lectures and lessons for deacons on pastoral care, counseling, and spiritual formation.

And deacons themselves offered their own testimonies of best practices and public witness to one another. While I was preaching at Central Baptist in Bearden, Tennessee, I heard Bill Vinson, chair of the diaconate, offer a challenge in a Sunday morning worship where seventeen new deacons were being ordained. He gave the following statement:

> Our word "deacon" is a term which we transliterate from the Greek word *diakonos*. This Greek word is found in several forms, twenty-nine times in the New Testament. Only three of those times is the word translated "deacon" in most of our Bibles today. The predominant meaning of the word is "servant." For this reason, it seems appropriate that the role of deacon at Central Baptist Church is that of servant.
>
> At Central, you are not assigned to the "office" of deacon, and you are not part of a "board" of deacons. You are simply being set apart today as a servant of Jesus Christ for Central Baptist Church. And just as the term *diakonos* was applied to common slaves, it was also applied to Paul, Apollos, Timothy, Phoebe, Tychicus, Epaphras, Jesus, it now applies to you.
>
> Your job is not to vote on our administrative policy, police or judge members, establish protocol, or even cast the vision for the church. Those duties have already been assigned. Your job is to serve.
>
> This is not a position of prestige or self-importance. It is a role that requires a humble mindset to do whatever is required to glorify God and benefit the kingdom of God, even when those tasks are too menial for others to consider worth their efforts.
>
> And so my charge to you today is to fulfill your new role with service. Serve when every eye in the world is upon you, and when there is no one else to see: for the world is watching and God always sees.

Serve when there are no "thank-yous" and even when you are despised for service. For the world is watching and God always sees.

Serve when you are ignored by most and despised by the world. Serve when you are tired and you see no hope for success: for he will lift you up and all things are possible through him.

And serve when you don't want to and when others have long since quit: for you are now a deacon, a *diakonos*, a servant; and it is now, and forever will be, who you are.

A few years after beginning the deacon network, I wrote a reflection proposing that it is time to consider Baptist deacons as a "holy order."

The future of Baptist congregations will be shaped by the degree to which laity think and act with the mind of Christ. Those who sit in the pews every Sunday must take the demands of Christian discipleship as seriously as those who occupy the pulpits. The people (*laos* is the Greek word for it) of our congregations are called and commissioned by Christ to be the priests, ministers, prophets, and witnesses in their community and world.

And deacons are exemplars to other laity of what it means to be "full of the spirit and wisdom" (Acts 6:3). Deacons are not perfect, nor are they always the most gifted and visible members of a congregation. They do not call attention to themselves, but they are, by definition, servant and spiritual leaders. And as such, they have influence, profound influence, on the character and conduct of a congregation.

In searching for a historical model that might describe the kind of deacons that are needed in Baptist churches for our day, I want to be so bold to suggest that they become like a "holy order" of lay Christians. Their ordination sets them apart for a lifelong pursuit of Christ-likeness. Their special gift (*charism* is the Greek word for it) is service, both within the congregation and then to the wider community. Their lifestyle (1 Timothy 3:8-13) is founded on their "faith in Christ Jesus" (v. 13).

Deacons are accountable to the congregation that ordains them and then to one another since they meet regularly for prayer, conversation, and support. The diaconate is a smaller fellowship within the larger fellowship of the congregation, and deacons are accountable both to the diaconate and to the congregation. This kind of accountability is yet another similarity to the "holy orders" of other Christian faith traditions. Deacons are, and should be, held to a higher standard of belief and behavior. "They keep hold the deep truths of the faith in a clear conscience, and are worthy of respect" (1 Timothy 3:8, 9).

All this is not to suggest that deacons are super saints or separated from the trials and tribulations of daily life. But this understanding of deacons is suggesting that the role and office of deacon is a high and holy calling. Ordained deacons as lay leaders are as integral and necessary for the health and mission of the church as are ordained clergy. They function by divine design and are chosen by the congregation under the leadership of the Holy Spirit.

Unlike the "holy orders" of other traditions, deacons are not isolated from society. They live in the world like all other Christian laity. They are not celibate and do not give up ownership of property. They are not guided by a rulebook of the community. But they do occupy a place within the body of Christ that has scriptural precedent. They fulfill their calling in continuity with deacons going all the way back to the beginnings of the Christian movement: Stephen, Philip, Procorus, Timon, Nicanor, Parmenas, Nicolas, Phoebe (Acts 6:5; Romans 16:1).

These biblical roots should inspire humility and courage in individuals who service as deacons. They should remember that just as preaching (*kergygma* is the Greek word for it) and teaching (*didache* is the Greek word for it) are essential to the growth of the first Christian church, so service (*diakonos* is the Greek word for it) was of the essence of the early church's life and ministry. And for service the Holy Spirit led the earliest church to select deacons. This is like a "holy order."

Deacons are also part of a fellowship and fraternity that is global in nature. Baptist churches all around the world ordain deacons as servant leaders. The exact nature of their service differs according to cultural and congregational context, but in all of these different contexts, deacons serve. This is like a "holy order."

Can we even begin to dream of the difference it would make if churches envision deacons as members of a "holy order"? What if deacons themselves viewed their obligation as a calling to a lifetime of service and spiritual formation? Certainly, times change, culture shifts, and needs vary both within churches and society, but what might happen if deacons were Spirit-called to a lay vocation of thinking and acting with the mind of Christ?

Through the years I've seen different models of diaconates: board of directors (governance and administration), teams (according to gifts for ministry), lay pastors (organized for member care). All of these have had value and still may have value. But I believe our thinking must shift. Our horizons must broaden. Our imaginations must be challenged, especially as it has to do with leadership. What about deacons as a "holy order"?

In 2016, Libby Allen, administrative coordinator for the Baugh Center, and I co-edited a workbook for deacons designed to encourage robust conversations within diaconates as well as between deacons, clergy, and other laity. In addition to Carol Younger, two tenured pastors, Mike Smith and Guy Sayles, wrote the chapters. *Exemplars: Deacons as Servant and Spiritual Leaders* was published and made available to congregations. It addresses three basic questions: What do deacons need to be? What do deacons need to know? What do deacons need to do? And as the title suggests, the presupposition is that deacons are to be servant leaders and spiritual leaders.

Lay Leadership Development

In addition to deacons, other lay leaders in a congregation should also be both servant and spiritual leaders. I have struggled with the questions, "What does servant leadership mean? If Jesus identified himself as a servant, shouldn't we model leadership after Jesus?"

• Didn't Jesus connect servanthood to humility? The best example of this is when he spoke to his disciples after they were arguing about who would be the greatest. He rebukes their ambition, pride, and hubris and commends an attitude of gentleness and simplicity. He even uses a small child as a symbol of humility. He tells the disciples, "Humble yourself and become like a child" (Matt 18:3).

- Didn't Jesus connect servanthood to compassion for people, especially for people in need? Compassion is caring that then results in practical action. The greatest example of this is in his parable where the Samaritan shows mercy on a wounded stranger and gives his time, money, and energy to help him (Luke 17:22).
- Didn't Jesus connect servanthood to submission? A servant is not in control of their life but is under the authority of a master. A servant implies a master. In his parabolic act of washing his disciples' feet, Jesus speaks of his being the master and teacher and states that the disciples are under his authority (John 13:14).
- Didn't Jesus connect servanthood to action? Service is not just sentiment or good feelings. It is doing something that meets needs, solves problems, finds solutions, or responds to suffering. Service requires effort, energy, and intentionality (Matt 25:40).

I have also struggled with the questions, What does spiritual leadership mean?
- Isn't spiritual leadership empowered by the Holy Spirit? We are dependent on the Spirit above all. Our business experience may serve us as well as intellectual and other professional capacities. But unless the Holy Spirit is working in us and through us, all of our experience will have little lasting value (Zech 4:6).
- Isn't spiritual leadership guided by the Holy Spirit? We need divine wisdom and the unfolding of Providence in our decisions, small and large. Often there are no easy answers or simple solutions to entrenched problems. Only wisdom given by the Spirit is sufficient.
- Isn't spiritual leadership characterized by the fruit of the Spirit? Love, joy, peace, patience, kindness, generosity, faithfulness, gentleness, and self-control are qualities of character that the Spirit produces. If our leadership does not demonstrate these virtues, it is not spiritual leadership (Gal 5:22-25).
- Isn't spiritual leadership connected to the gifts of the Spirit? Each of us are given capacities and abilities that should find expression in congregational leadership. When we use those gifts, we find fulfillment and fruitfulness (1 Cor 12:4-6).

- Doesn't spiritual leadership foster and promote unity? The work of the Spirit creates unity that transcends differences and diversity. When the Spirit is working through us, we may not always agree with one another, but we will strive toward unity that is even more important than agreement.

Lay Theological Education

Early in my ministry I was introduced to Gordon Cosby, a Baptist minister who founded the Church of the Savior in Washington, DC. It was an innovative and covenanted Christian community in the nation's capital that had widespread influence across denominational lines. One of its innovations was the School of Christian Living, which offered scholarly yet practical theological education for laity. The courses, required of all members, not only included Bible, church history, and theology but also ethics, stewardship, and spiritual formation.[28]

Almost simultaneously, a well-known Southern Baptist educator, Findley Edge, was proposing that local churches become "miniature theological seminaries" with a core curriculum, specialized courses, and a functioning faculty within each congregation.[29] I was inspired by these notions but never able to implement them as a pastor. In coming to Mercer, I was convicted that in a time of constant turmoil and change, no greater need exists than developing Christ-like lay leaders for church and society.

Offering deacon leadership development was an entry point into a more robust offering of lay theological education. I asked McAfee professors and pastor-scholars to teach classes in local congregations on subjects in which they had expertise. Each class consisted of a cohort of laity who agreed to meet for six weeks in rigorous study and prayerful reflection. The purpose of Christian Leadership Formation (CLF) classes was for Christian laity to do the following:

- Learn the Scripture and listen to the Spirit in ways that transform their work into vocation.
- View their talents and position in society as an opportunity to serve Christ.

- Integrate biblical and theological truth into the complex realities of today's culture.
- Develop discernment that is informed by the truth of the Bible and the wisdom of the Christian faith tradition.
- Love deeply because the Holy Spirit is strong within them.

What I discovered in providing these classes were two competing narratives among Christian laity. One is that they deeply desire opportunities for learning and growth. The other is that they are extremely busy. What I also discovered was that many were willing to give their time and pay a modest tuition fee for learning that was unapologetically Christ centered and helped them develop practices that integrated faith into daily life, especially daily life in the world.

Teaching

When I arrived at Mercer at the invitation of Bill Underwood, I was also invited by Alan Culpepper, the dean of the McAfee School of Theology, to teach leadership for seminarians. This was new for me. I had been a leader in different contexts, but if I was to teach it, I knew I needed to become a student of leadership literature and theory myself. Leadership formation for clergy requires spiritual, theological, and vocational formation, but it also involves skill development in listening, speaking, and nurturing as well as character development in discernment, prudence, and courage. Leadership is difficult to define, and it is always contextual, but everyone knows it is important.

I plunged into the literature about leadership and soon discovered that it is vast and varied. I immersed myself in books, articles, tapes, and podcasts from the academy, business, government, and nonprofit organizations. I also read those who self-described themselves as champions of "Christian leadership" or "biblical leadership." I studied leadership theories and models offered by "experts," some who were famous and whose books were best-sellers. I read a number of biographies with the notion that there was much to learn from those identified as moral leaders or political leaders or corporate leaders or church leaders.

All of this was helpful, and I hope it was helpful to some of my students. But it all left me wondering, Can one teach leadership? Are leaders born or made? Is leadership simply a calling or gift, and if so, how does one know that they have it? Is everyone intended to be a leader? And what about bad leaders, whose influence did more damage than good? How did they learn leadership? I soon realized that I had more questions than I had answers. I also discovered that my students seemed to have more answers than they had questions. Everyone had strong opinions about leadership. Everyone had both bad and good experiences of leaders, and it was difficult to escape them.

One of the results of this soul searching was that I tried to teach practices of good leadership, examples of good leadership, stories of good leadership. I tried to teach about virtues and values that inform leaders in whatever time or place they live. I probed myself and my students to dig deep within themselves to discern and discover who they were at the center of themselves and then lead from that center. I taught about listening, first to God and then to others, and then about loving God and loving those whom one leads.

I did teach the various theories of leading and introduced subjects like organizational planning, time management, conflict resolution, team building, budgeting, and fundraising. I explored vision casting, core values, and tips on communication. But most importantly, I tried to instill in students the notion that leadership is a spiritual practice requiring resources. It's about influence more than power. As with any subject, some had "ears to hear" more than others.

In my teaching, I soon discovered that today's seminarians face congregational, denominational, and cultural challenges that I didn't face in earlier years. In many ways, the churches where I had been pastor represent an era that will not return. This realization would have been too much for me to bear had it not been for the fact that I myself was now a pastor again. And I was pastor of a very different kind of church than any of those I had known in my past.

"We are a People of faith, hope and love, as revealed in Christ, who seek to do justice, love mercy, and walk humbly with our God."

Peachtree Baptist Church, Atlanta

Peachtree Baptist Church

In the last year of my tenure at CBF, I was asked to preach at Peachtree Baptist Church in Atlanta (PBC). It is a historic congregation, founded in 1847, and had once been a much larger congregation. Because of changing demographics and internal conflict, it had diminished significantly in size and influence. The most recent pastor had resigned, so they asked if I could preach on occasion. I agreed. As I retired from CBF, they invited me to become their interim pastor and then their part-time permanent pastor. I agreed.

What unfolded was a surprise both to me and the church. We became a multicultural, multigenerational church. Located in an urban context, PBC had earlier been predominately a White, middle-class, program-based Southern Baptist church. Even though it was a loving, mission-minded congregation, it continued to dwindle. As I became its pastor, one of the gifts that PBC gave to me was the opportunity to explore mission and ministry with few members and limited financial resources but a willingness to explore and accept change.

Karen Zimmerman, a student at McAfee, agreed to become a student worker with a focus on developing relationships with the large international community that lived in the neighborhood. It wasn't long before many of her conversation partners, who were from all over the world, became her friends and then became friends of PBC. Our "little flock" began to grow, not only in numbers but also in racial and ethnic diversity. We became something of an experiment in congregational life; 40 percent of our attendees were people of color. It was not unusual to have ten to twelve different nationalities represented in a worship service with fewer than one hundred in attendance.

The older, long-term members showed hospitality and grace, while the newer members were discovering a diverse kind of Christian community where they were not a distinct minority. Our worship was somewhat formal and liturgical, but we sought to incorporate music from the various cultures that were now present. We sang the Doxology every Sunday. We prayed the Lord's Prayer every Sunday. We observed Communion every Sunday, and we did away with the conventional "invitation hymn" after the sermon that most Baptist churches practice. We also read Scripture, followed by the responsive litany, "This is the word of the Lord" and "Thanks be to God." For the most part, we sang traditional hymns with a few choruses. To my surprise, these formalized liturgies served as a uniting influence.

Karen Zimmerman became associate pastor, and her influence was enormous. Leslie Brogdon later became an associate pastor and provided effective leadership for children and families. Other seminarian interns joined the staff or did their field education with us. They represented a broad spectrum of racial/ethnic diversity, and each made great contribution: Taylor Johnson, Harris Gessner, Adam Gray, Ryan and Megan Hearst-Carter, Brian Kidd, Rene Pellom, Linda Abrams, Faith Richardson, Courtney Huggins, Byron Bell, Yungmin Lee, Teruco Tynes, and Deena Wingard.

In 2016, I wrote an article for Georgia CBF that describes the living experiment of PBC.

> Since stepping aside as executive coordinator of the Cooperative Baptist Fellowship, I have served a historic church in Atlanta as interim pastor. Like so many urban congregations, PBC has experienced a decline because of demographic changes in its neighborhood, denominational deconstruction, and internal struggles. What became clear is that the ministry methods designed for homogeneous, program-based churches had become inadequate in reaching people for Christ, particularly in a polarized and increasingly secular culture.
>
> In the past three years, Peachtree has set its heart on becoming an interracial, intercultural, and intergenerational church. We don't want to become a mega-church, a seeker church, or a contemporary church but rather a missional church that reflects the community in which God has placed us. We want to honor those parts of our Baptist tradition that are worth honoring and preserve the institutional structures that should be preserved, but we want to look and feel radically different when it comes to racial and cultural composition.
>
> This vision is rooted in the reconciling gospel of Christ and the ultimate goal of that gospel when people from every culture, nation, tribe, and language will gather before God's throne in

worship. We realize the mystical body of Christ transcends any one congregation, but we want our congregation to reflect the richness and diversity of Christ's present and coming kingdom.

So, how are we doing? First, the vision of an interracial and intergenerational church is compelling and life-giving to our "little flock" and those who participate with us. I repeatedly hear someone say, "I really like the diversity here," or "There is love in this place." Even though our numerical growth has been slow and the changes are incremental, we are experiencing spiritual vitality and genuine community. People are coming to Christ. People are coming back to Christ.

Ministry in a multicultural context is not easy, and it requires intentionality in worship planning, leadership development, and mission engagement. But most of all, it requires a great deal of humility and absolute dependence on God. We put a lot of emphasis on caring for one another across our differences and on the word of God and the Spirit of God that both unite us and empower us. We talk a lot about unity in diversity, and diversity in unity.

Relationships are important to us. Being together is central. We don't spend a lot of time fretting about the future or the cultural currents that swirl around us. We work hard at being attentive to the individuals who make up our fellowship, as well as those individuals who walk in our doors, live in our neighborhood, and struggle in our streets.

At our Thanksgiving dinner this past November, seventy-five people gathered in spite of a terrible rainstorm to eat turkey and dressing. There were fifteen nationalities represented. Children were laughing and singing. Testimonies of gratitude were offered. I presented a brief gospel message. Afterward, a sixty-year-old African American man who was visiting said to me, "I've never seen anything quite like this. It feels a bit like heaven." A few weeks later, I baptized his friend, and thirty of his family members attended worship to celebrate the baptism. All glory be to God.

PBC gave far more to me than I gave to it in the eight years we served together. It also presented me with different pastoral challenges than I had ever known. Being a member and leader of a multicultural congregation is hard, and I learned to rejoice in "small victories" and almost weekly serendipities. Many of the metrics by which I had always measured congregational success no longer seemed important, and yet I never experienced more fruitfulness than I did at PBC.

The tenured lay leadership of the church was supportive as tremendous changes were taking place. Eva Traylor, Lamar Savage, Mary Itner, James Hansard, Clyde and Anne Bryant, Agnes Church, Lilly Grimes, Pete and Caroline Combs, George and Bobbye Litchfield, David Jordan, Jim Bracewell, Bill Gordon, Walt and Pam Mott, and others were loving and courageous. New members were added representing significant racial, ethnic, cultural diversity. Zewde Gebre, James Kairuki and Phyllis Mwaura, Cheryl Mitchum, Leticia Castanon and Juan Manuel Henandez, Nelly Mejia and Geoffrey Platta, George Odongo and Skovia Kakai, Karen and Cesar Restrapo, Jimez and Torey Alexandar, Loran Auma, and many others brought their own faith experiences to an emerging church.

As new families were added and the church's ministry expanded, I realized that a full-time pastor was needed. Being a bi-vocational pastor meant that there was never enough time, and I concluded that my season of pastoral leadership was coming to a close. We called Paul Capps as full-time associate pastor, and then, after a year of transition, he became permanent pastor on January 1, 2020. Earlene and I are still members and enjoy watching the church continue to reflect its community and reach out with Christ's love.

My simultaneous experiences of being pastor at PBC, a multicultural church, and teaching at Mercer complemented each other in many ways. My class on leadership was required, so with a racially diverse student body I experienced classroom learning in a multicultural environment and learned more from my students than they did from me. Emmanuel McCall, a respected African American pastor in Atlanta, co-taught a class with me titled "Leadership in Black and White." We taught the class for several semesters, which required me to immerse myself in the literature of racism in America, multicultural churches, and the story of African American denominations (see page 290 for a list of books I found most influential for this study).

Books that Influenced Me

C. Eric Lincoln and Lawrence H. Mamiya, *The Black Church in the African American Experience*

L. H. Whelchel Jr., *The History and Heritage of African American Churches: A Way Out of No Way*

Raphael G. Warnock, *The Divided Mind of the Black Church: Theology, Piety and Public Witness*

Willie James Jennings, *The Christian Imagination: Theology and the Origins of Race*

Brad Christerson, Korie L. Edwards, and Michael O. Emerson, *Against All Odds: The Struggle for Racial Integration in Religious Organizations*

Michael O. Emerson with Rodney M. Woo, *People of the Dream: Multiracial Congregations in the United States*

Allan Aubrey Boesak and Curtiss Paul DeYoung, *Radical Reconciliation: Beyond Political Pietism and Christian Quietism*

Chanequa Walker-Barnes, *Too Heavy a Yoke: Black Women and the Burden of Strength*

Michael O. Emerson and Christian Smith, *Divided by Faith: Evangelical Religion and the Problem of Race in America*

Nancy Isenberg, *White Trash: The 400 Year Untold History of Class in America*

Kate Bowler, *Blessed: A History of the American Prosperity Gospel*

J. Kameron Carter, *Race: A Theological Account*

James H. Cone, *The Cross and the Lynching Tree*

I also learned a great deal from Emmanuel McCall himself, one of the most significant Baptist leaders of my lifetime. His book *When All God's Children Get Together: A Memoir of Race and Baptists* chronicles his fifty-year ministry of racial reconciliation among Baptists in the South. More than any single individual, Emmanuel McCall was responsible for the inclusion of African American Baptist churches in the SBC. When he became part of CBF, his influence was enormous and immediate. His knowledge and experience are exceeded only by his leadership ability and humble spirit. Even though we were teaching together, I became a student in the class as I listened to his lectures and enjoyed hours of conversation.

Again, a deconstruction and reconstruction was taking place within me. While in the middle of a multicultural congregational experience, I was also in a racially diverse classroom experience. I was reading, teaching, and pastoring all at the same time, and I was learning how much I simply didn't know. Both the church and the academy were laboratories that were informing, inspiring, and changing me. If racial reckoning is to take place in America, it will require both personal transformations and systemic transformations. And I believe that those transformations require laboratories of learning where people of different races, cultures, and ethnicities can share authentic community.

Discoveries and Aspirations

Identity

My story is one of discovery, through trial and error, of my vocational identity. That discovery has required me to acknowledge, sometimes painfully and sometimes joyfully, that I am not someone else. I had to learn that I am not my father, the evangelist. I am not the research scholar that I admired in Ray Summers and John Newport, nor am I a rhetorically gifted orator, a politician, or a social prophet. Neither am I a public intellectual, a thought leader, or a monastic.

Rather I am a pastor. Whatever leadership I have offered in various contexts springs from a pastoral perspective. My greatest joys come from offering spiritual guidance and seeing people flourish in their relationships. My richest rewards are those that come quietly, often unseen and unnoticed by others. These are the rewards of seeing spiritual awakening, nourishment, and maturity in others.

Integral to my pastoral identity is proclamation: preaching, teaching, and writing, probably in that order. A sermon is a "word event" through which spoken words compel and confront both the preacher and the hearer. Similar to a speech that can galvanize an audience into action or a poetic reading that can inspire an audience into clarity, a sermon can do both. Martin Luther King Jr.'s "I Have a

Dream" speech continues to be a word event that motivates. Amanda Gorman's poem "The Hill We Climb," delivered at Joe Biden's inauguration, was a word event that inspired millions and will be heard for years to come. A sermon shares those qualities.

The difference with a sermon is that it is offered in the context of a worshiping congregation. It is one liturgical act, among many others, in the corporate worship experience of God. And if the words of the sermon truly proclaim the living Word of God, they must proceed from and be faithful to the written word of God, Holy Scripture. And they must be prepared and delivered in dependence on the Holy Spirit.

The proclaimed word is the "foolishness" by which faith, hope, and love are quickened in the hearts both of believers and unbelievers. Even if the preacher is not eloquent, the preacher is the "earthen vessel" that both contains the "treasure within" and proclaims it for others to hear. The preacher may not be a genius (most preachers aren't), but the preacher can be an instrument of the Word and Spirit. A sermon is a sign and sacrament, a human and divine act that God has chosen to use for the salvation of those who believe.

A person who preaches does so because they have been called to preach, not just because they have rhetorical talent (although it does help to have a bit of it) or because they choose to do so (although one must decide to do it). Preaching is more than a job or career, and it is surely not done for money or fame. Preaching is a vocation, a way of life, and for me it is a great privilege. Because preaching has been so central to my vocational identity, I am including four sermons in this memoir; see page 305).

My vocational identity was also confirmed when Earlene and I married and then, with the passing of time, had children and grandchildren. Marriage, I have discovered, is a vocational laboratory where one learns (or does not learn) the virtues of self-control, patience, and courage. Parenting is not easy but requires perseverance and wisdom that no other vocation requires. Grandparenting has been as rewarding an experience as any I have known. Marriage and family is a vocation, but it is also a joy.

Earlene and Daniel Vestal, 2012

When asked, "What have you done for fun?" my response is that I have discovered life's greatest pleasures within the context of my home. Earlene and I enjoy being together in watching movies, taking walks, having a second cup of coffee in the morning, visiting our children, talking politics, and just being together. Our children and grandchildren are a source of constant delight. My family has given me the greatest of all fulfillment, and I believe my "calling" continues as a husband, father, grandfather.

Beyond my vocational discovery, my story is one of identity discovery. I have learned that my worth is not in what I accomplish, achieve, or accumulate, but in what I have been given. I am human, which means I am fearfully and wonderfully created by God. Even though I am deeply flawed and frail, I am in the image of God. I am redeemed and reconciled by Christ, who is my Savior and Lord. I am inhabited by the Spirit, which means I am a tabernacle or temple of the Holy. I exist on this earth, and will continue to exist in heaven, to love God with all my heart, mind, soul, and strength and to love others even as I love myself. As I approach my eighth decade, I want to "end well," and whenever or however death may come, I want to "die well" and then go to be in the nearer presence of God.

I am an earthen vessel containing a sacred treasure within, and my greatest desire is to reflect the glory of that treasure in my unique humanity and in community with others. The presence of Christ within me is within all who in faith and love receive his presence. Each of us is part of a cosmic plan and a participant in a divine drama. We are each surrounded by a "cloud of witnesses" and a great host of companions.

This memoir has focused a lot on these witnesses and companions, as well as the nature and circumstances of my humanity as an earthen vessel. I have written from and about my cultural context because it is the one I know most about. I would argue that all of us are far more culturally conditioned than we can imagine. We simply can't "jump out of our skin" and see reality objectively. In fact, what we often call reality is itself conditioned by the prejudices and presuppositions of our inherited culture. It's not just that we "see through a glass darkly," but we see through a glass that is the product of our past and wider context.

I have experienced a modest measure of what some would call "trials and tribulations" or what the classic hymn describes as "dangers, toils, and snares." But I have experienced an even greater abundance of blessings. Whatever fruitfulness and fulfillment that has come to me and through me is because of the love and grace of God. This recognition helps me in seeking forgiveness from those whom I have offended and in offering forgiveness to those who have offended me.

Spiritual mentors have guided me in receiving God's love and in offering it to friends and even to enemies. No one has guided me more than Basil Pennington through his book, *Centering Prayer*.

Pennington was a Trappist monk who toward the end of his life became Abbot at the Monastery of the Holy Spirit in Conyers, Georgia, where I took a number of retreats. It was Pennington who introduced me to the words from Bernard of Clairvaux when he was chastising a group of monks who refused to accept his reform efforts: "Beware. All the beauty that you possess as part of your tradition might belong more to me than to you, for it does in fact belong most to the one who loves it most."[30] I continue to love much of the Southern Baptist tradition that nurtured me early in my life, and this has helped me to love those who are still in that tradition with whom I have difference and disagreement.

My aspirations, now more than ever, have to do with nurturing my life in God and encouraging others in their lives of faith, hope, and love. They have to do with celebrating and radiating the presence of Christ in the years that remain. My aspirations have to do more with discernment than doing. The almost constant change in our world, accompanied by deep societal polarization, requires that we, both as individuals and as a Christin community, be sensitive and attentive to the indwelling Spirit more than we have in the past.

Spiritual Discernment

As I look back over my life and anticipate what is left of it, one of my greatest aspirations is for discernment, both spiritual and moral. Spiritual discernment is the word I use to identify an inward listening, learning, and loving in the face of such questions as "How do I view life?" "How do I live each day?" "How do I respond to events, circumstances, people?" Perspective is everything. Vision matters. And the truth is that I have a lot of "blind spots" and a hubris that blurs my vision, deadens my conscience, and dulls my sensitivity to God.

However, the good news we receive from Jesus is that the creator God loves us and desires to commune and communicate with us. We are spiritual beings who can connect with the One who is pure Spirit. Spiritual discernment is credible and possible because of this divine revelation and reality. God is as real as we are real. God is as present as we are present. God is as personal as we are personal. And God is benevolent and beneficent toward us, always seeking us, pursuing us, chasing after us in our waywardness and stubbornness.

Spiritual discernment is about listening for and to God, not just for instruction or guidance (although this is important) but also for the Word and Spirit that sustain life, create courage, generate creativity, and cause faith, hope, and love to blossom. Discernment is deep listening, a mixture of the intellectual and intuitive, a convergence of thought and feeling.

Spiritual discernment is learning of God, not just about God. It is learning God's ways, God's nature, God's mystery. This requires first a lot of unlearning, because so much of what we think we know of God we do not know. We are deceived by our pride and paralyzed by our fears. The knowing that comes from discernment is often preceded by a kind of unknowing because God is other than we are. God is infinite, and we are finite. So our learning will require all eternity. God will never be exhausted in our knowing of God.

Spiritual discernment is about loving God. The goal of discernment is communion with God. Some would even say the goal is union with God. The language of discernment is love language, not scientific or technical but personal, passionate, and poetic. It may even sound foolish and fanciful to many. So much in us is incompatible with loving God, and discernment helps us see it, name it, and seek salvation from it.

Spiritual discernment is both a gift and a quest. Perhaps it is a gift only after the quest. It is similar to wisdom or prudence and given to us only when with all our hearts we ask, seek, and knock for it. Perhaps it is what Jesus referenced in his famous sermon: "The eye is the lamp of the body. If the eyes are healthy, your whole body will be full of light. But if your eyes are unhealthy, your whole body will be full of darkness. If then the light within you is darkness, how great is the darkness" (Matt 6:22-23).

Perhaps it is similar to what the Apostle Paul described as having "the mind of Christ," the internal disposition that is humble, teachable, and obedient to the will of God, regardless of the cost. Such a disposition is keenly attuned to divine purposes and attentive to divine promptings. Having such a mind requires a daily cultivation and tenacious nurturing as well as a fierce faithfulness that is willing to persist and persevere in spite of ambiguity.

The aspiration for spiritual discernment is worthy of my time, energy, and effort required to attain it. Similar to the aspiration for holiness, this pursuit is lifelong. And the reception of it is absolutely dependent on the grace and power of God. We are like the blind beggar, Bartimaeus. When asked by Jesus, "What do you want?" he replied, "Rabbi, I want to see" (Luke 10:51).

I too want to see what only the eyes of faith can reveal. I aspire to be attentive to the Word and Spirit for as long as I live, never to control or predict God, because God is sovereign, free, not to be co-opted to our agenda. But in full assurance that "this treasure within" is also before and after, below and above, I aspire, both for myself and for others, to know even as I am known and to love even as I am loved.

Moral Discernment

I also aspire to moral discernment. I have found that sometimes moral and ethical decision making is easy. The way forward is as clear as a cloudless morning, and I can see the blue sky and everything under it. The exhilaration from such clarity is wonderful. But this is rare. Most of the time, my moral and ethical decision making is tentative and halting. I am either in a fog or desperately in the dark, looking for a ray of light. So often my decisions are not between right or wrong but between the lesser of two evils or between varying shades of gray. I have discovered that life is complex and so many issues are complicated and not as simple as I wish they were.

Applying moral principles to particular circumstances of daily life is difficult. I know that I value the virtues of truthfulness, courage, and generosity, but I frequently do not know what these virtues require of me. I need moral discernment. Complex ethical issues abound, and there is no shortage of perspectives or persuasive arguments defining what the Christian perspective should be. The debates are deafening. The discord between scholars and professional experts, not to speak of popular culture, is enough to drive one to despair. Can anyone really know?

And to make matters even more difficult, moral discernment is not a solitary affair. I do not live as an isolated individual, and I do not discover moral truth all by myself. Moral discernment is personal, but it is not private. We all live in communities where communal decision making is required. In families, churches, denominations, institutions, and society at large, we make moral and ethical decisions that affect and impact everyone in the community.

So where do I begin in moral discernment? I suggest that we begin with grace and "lean into grace." Scripture says that "the law was given through Moses; grace and truth came through Jesus Christ" (John 1:17). If we begin in moral discernment with rules and regulations, no matter how important they are, we will despair. Why? Because none of us (and I do mean none of us) are able to keep the law. If we try to live by rules and regulations, we will soon discover that we will never measure up either to God's expectations or to our own expectations. And neither will anyone else.

I will begin with grace because God begins with grace. I will receive grace, give grace, practice grace. The well-known quip offered by someone who saw another who had an obvious moral failure and said, "There, but for the grace of God, go I" is more than a quip. The grace of God, revealed in Jesus Christ, equalizes all of us and makes our harsh judgments of one another both foolish and impossible.

I have discovered that in our debates about moral issues and moral behavior, it is easy to assume that ours is the moral high ground and that those whose views are different, or whose moral behavior is different, can easily be considered morally inferior. Jesus told the story of the Pharisee who compared himself to the publican and proudly said, "I thank you, God, that I am not like this man." Clearly he didn't understand grace. He did understand the law, and his moral discernment was based on the law and his performance before the law. Argument with him would have been useless because he was convinced of his moral superiority and moral correctness. Yet Jesus condemned his legalistic moral discernment.

Does this mean that grace gives us a license to do whatever we want or to hold whatever moral view we choose? This was the very question that the Apostle Paul asked: "What shall we say, then? Shall we go on sinning so that grace may increase?" (Rom 6:1). Again, he asked, "What then? Should we sin because we're not under law but under grace?" (Rom 6:15). His answer to both questions is an unqualified "No." Grace does not lead to license or irresponsibility. Grace produces life, holiness, righteousness. So in moral discernment I will "lean into grace" because grace is God's way of resolving the human condition of sinfulness. Where sin abounds, grace abounds, and it is grace that saves us, heals us, restores us, reconciles us, and delivers us.

So when it comes to moral discernment, because of my dependence on grace, I will humble myself again and again. I love the apocryphal story told about G. K. Chesterton. When the *London Times* sent an inquiry to famous authors with the question, "What's wrong with the world?" he responded with the following: "Dear Sirs: I am. Yours, G. K. Chesterton." The hard fact is that I am a sinner, and that fact makes moral discernment even more difficult.

I am suspicious of the person who always seems to know the will of God in a matter and is quick to pronounce judgment on the faults of others. Why? Because I know how many times I have been wrong on a moral issue or late in understanding what others saw clearly much earlier than me. I know how many times my moral sensibilities have been dull, my moral compass has been skewed, and my moral fervor has been tepid when it should have been red hot.

I also know how many times my lofty idealism and emotional sentimentality have been shattered by the sober revelation of human meanness. The seven deadly sins are called deadly because they are just that, deadly: anger, greed, sloth, pride, lust, envy, and gluttony define a great deal of human history, and they describe why I so often fail miserably in moral discernment. Proverbs 6:16-19 says, "There are six things which the LORD hates, seven which are an abomination to him: haughty eyes, a lying tongue, hands that shed innocent blood, a heart that devises wicked plans, feet that make haste to run to evil, a false witness who breathes out lies, and the man who sows discord among brothers." Inward humility is the only way to discernment.

Before my mother died in 2018, I visited her often and we would sit in her dining area and talk while I rummaged through my dad's books. Dad did not graduate college or seminary, but he had a very good library. Mother was as close to a saint as anyone I had known, and I listened to her wisdom as often as I could. On one occasion I pulled a small volume from the shelf that was given to Dad when he was in college. He had written the date of its receipt—December 14, 1945—and then affixed his signature as he did on all his books, "Evangelist Dan Vestal." I don't know anybody in the world whose signature includes the title "Evangelist." When I looked at the book, I saw that it was by Douglas Steere, a Quaker philosopher and ecumenist.

Only a few years earlier in 1942, while WWII was ravaging the world, Steere delivered a series of lectures at Harvard University. They were then compiled and published under the title *On Beginning from Within*. Steere argues fiercely that the personal development of the life of God in the individual heart is still the greatest need for the church, the society, and the world. He writes in the introduction,

> These essays, then, affirm again how God works on men and on society through individual, personal instruments in an intensely individual and personal way. They recall that Jesus' word is never general but specific; it is not collective but personal. There is no waiting until the war is over and the peace is won, or until the peace is over and the war has begun, or until brotherhood shall come by state decree, or until society has redeemed itself and removed all environmental obstacles to the frustration of personality. "Come" is the favorite word of Jesus and his followers; "now" is the dimension in time, and "I" is the dimension in human space.[31]

Sainthood is not just for a few. It is the promise and possibility to all who by humble dependence on grace claim and pursue it. Sainthood doesn't make us perfect, but it does impart moral conviction, moral clarity, and moral courage.

Steere begins chapter 2 with the following:

> I believe that what the religious life of the world needs most of all is not a new theology, not a vast new crop of brilliant students as candidates for the ministry, not a union of all sects into one religious body, not a renewed missionary movement, not a revised

program of evangelism. What it needs first and foremost is apostles or saints, men and women prepared to live in the full dispensation of Christian freedom.[32]

Moral discernment is a gift just as sainthood is a gift. I desire those gifts. Since Jesus is the criterion by which all Scripture is interpreted and the model by which discernment is measured, I will listen to his word and Spirit, especially in the Lord's Prayer and Beatitudes, as the framework and foundation to form my character and inform my decision making. I will pray and practice these petitions that Jesus commanded and these virtues that Jesus commended as the way to discernment.

Shalom

In the past fifteen years, no teacher or theologian has influenced me more than the British New Testament scholar N. T. Wright. Both his academic and popular writings have given me a much clearer understanding of Scripture, the life, death, and resurrection of Jesus, the nature of the gospel, and the mission of the church. I had the privilege of meeting N. T. Wright when he lectured at Mercer in 2011. It was a brief encounter but one I will always remember and cherish. After his lecture a luncheon was held in his honor where we were able to have more informal conversation. Toward the end of the event, I asked him how we might pray for him as a brother in Christ. He was transparent in his answer, displaying great humility. Alan Culpepper, dean of the McAfee School of Theology, was so impressed by Wright's response that he called on Gerald Durley, a respected African American pastor in Atlanta, to lead us in a moment of prayer.

My first encounter with N. T. Wright was on October 20, 2006. CBF had granted me a ten-week sabbatical, and I was with one of my grandsons at a pizza restaurant (it was Chuck E. Cheese). While watching him at play, I began reading Wright's *Simply Christian: Why Christianity Makes Sense*. I knew immediately that this New Testament scholar would become a mentor to me. I worked my way through fourteen more of his books in the following years, and his work has profoundly influenced me (see recommended reading included here).

I also watched and listened to a number of interviews and lectures because I wanted to see and hear his presentations as well as read his books. He has both clarified and confirmed so much of the theological deconstruction and reconstruction that was taking place in my life. Increasingly I came to believe that the gospel was not so much about getting people to heaven after they died as it was about the reign and rule of God through Jesus Christ.

The kingdom of God has come. The kingdom of God is coming. The kingdom of God will come. Christ has come. Christ is coming. Christ will come. God's order of reality

Books by N. T. Wright
that influenced me

Surprised by Hope: Rethinking Heaven, the Resurrection, and the Mission of the Church
Jesus and the Victory of God
The New Testament and the People of God
The Resurrection of the Son of God
Evil and the Justice of God
After You Believe
Simply Jesus
Simply Good News
The Challenge of Jesus
Following Jesus
The Day the Revolution Began: Reconsidering the Meaning of Jesus's Crucifixion
Justification: God's Plan and Paul's Vision
Paul: A Biography
History and Eschatology: Jesus and the Promise of Natural Theology

through Christ, past/present/future, is an order of reality that brings reconciliation and renewal. Christ makes all things. I still believe in heaven and hell and do not consider myself a universalist. I still believe that salvation is through Christ alone, but I am simply not willing or able to say who ultimately will be "in" or "out," "first" or "last." That is in the hands of God.

Above all else, my aspirations now are to love, seek, work, and pray for God's *shalom* on earth, believing that it is God alone who gives it but also believing that God uses human agency. We can and should be instruments of divine peace so that, in the words of St. Francis, where there is darkness we can sow light. It is a world of great injustice and inequity, and there can be no *shalom* apart from righteousness and reconciliation.

My aspirations have to do with the message and ministry of reconciliation in Christ and through the Spirit, not partisan politics, or health, wealth, and prosperity, or extending the American way of life, or marketing religious goods and services to a consumer culture, or growing churches or building institutions. I desire a single-minded devotion to Christ's reign and a willingness, like his, to embrace the suffering necessary to see it fully realized. In 2008, I authored *Being the Presence of Christ: A Vision for Transformation*. In it I offered the following:

> The kingdom Jesus incarnated and exhibited is the divine order that has come, is coming, and will come in its future fullness. This order has already dawned within human history. But it awaits consummation. When the kingdom comes in its fullness, there will be justice for all the oppressed. There will be no disparity between rich and poor, no divide between people because of race or social class. It will be no violence and aggression, and there will be peace (shalom). As individuals in whom the presence of Christ dwells, we are to seek and serve this kingdom above all else.[33]

Is not peace what we all desire in our society and in our world? Do we not all yearn for resolution of conflicts and reconciliation between us? Deep within us do we not all long after a wholeness and well-being, not only for ourselves but also for everyone? Then let us, as ones who confess "this treasure within," order our lives and pattern our behavior after the One whose reign brings peace, creates peace, and is peace.

Shalom.

Sermons

A Theology of Cooperation (1978)

1 Corinthians 3:1-9

I preached this sermon for the first time at First Baptist Church, Odessa, Texas, November 5, 1978. It was later published in God's Awesome Challenge: Compelling Messages for Winning the World in this Century *in 1980.*

The chief clerk in a department store was trying to dislodge the crate from a storage room door. He was working hard when an assistant clerk offered to help. For the next couple of minutes on opposite sides of the crate they both worked, lifted, puffed, and wheezed. But the crate wouldn't budge. Finally the assistant clerk said, "I don't believe we will ever get this box out of the storage room." "Get it out?" the chief clerk responded. "I'm trying to get it in."

Cooperation is important in every realm of life. But in the enterprise of extending the kingdom of God, there is no more valuable quality than unity. It is not always easy for individuals or churches to be cooperative, and there are several reasons for it. First, we are highly individualistic. The genius of our American way is to emphasize the right of the individual, and I would not for one moment minimize that constitutional privilege. But the emphasis of Scripture is not so much on individual rights as it is on individual responsibility, primarily the individual responsibility commanded in Scripture to love our neighbor as we ourselves.

Another reason we find it difficult to be cooperative is that we are highly independent. Each of us likes to think of ourselves as self-sufficient, self-made, self-reliant. The popular clichés "Do your own thing" or "I did it my way" convey a philosophy of intense independence. But the truth of the matter is that there is no such thing as a totally independent person. John Donne said, "No man is an island, entire of himself / Everyone is a piece of the continent, a part of the main."

Another reason we find it difficult to be cooperative is that we are highly competitive. All the way from sibling rivalry, to a sports-mad culture, to an economic system based on competition, we are taught to be competitive. We are told again and again to "be number one," that "winning is everything," and that "nobody remembers who comes in second." Yet Jesus Christ, the Son of God, "made himself of no reputation, and took upon him the form of a servant. . . . He humbled himself . . . unto death" (Phil 2:7-8). He was, by the standards of the world, a loser.

As difficult as it is for us to be cooperative, the nature of the gospel demands it. All believers are one in Jesus Christ, and that is the foundation of the church. There is one Lord, one faith, one baptism. The beautiful word "fellowship" means partnership. Jesus prayed the night before he died that all believers would be one so that the world might believe in him. The book of Acts recorded the advance of the early church, part of which was the result of unity in the Spirit. Cooperation is woven into the fabric of God's redemptive plan.

Cooperation does not mean compromise. In order for Christians to cooperate with one another to extend God's kingdom, we need not compromise our convictions or our identity. Nor must churches relinquish their autonomous independence in order to cooperate with other churches. The reason for this is that the basis of our cooperation is the Lordship of Jesus Christ. Because Jesus is our Lord, we each follow him; we each listen to his Spirit; we each obey his word. This means that, in his own beautiful and perfect way, he knits our lives together without violating our individual identities and responsibilities. Cooperation under the Lordship of Christ does not mean compromise. It means unity. It is not a sign of weakness. Rather it is a sign of strength and solidarity.

Of all the churches to which the Apostle Paul wrote letters, none showed more fragmentation and more division than the Corinthian church. In our text he calls them "babes in Christ" and "carnal" because of their envy, strife, and division. Against this background the Apostle said, "We are laborers together with God." Urging the Corinthians to resist a competitive divisiveness, he teaches some very important truths about being coworkers with each other and with God in the extension of God's kingdom.

First, cooperation requires independent responsibility. Each and every person is important to God. Each and every believer is important in God's plan for world redemption. He calls each of us. He equips each of us. He places each of us. There's no such thing as a Christian who doesn't fit into God's strategy. The text asks, "Who is Paul? Who is Apollos?" (v. 5.) Then the answer is given: "We are ministers by whom you believe. I planted, Apollos watered, but God gave the growth" (vv. 5-6.) The clear teaching is that God calls and equips each to a certain task. Each has individual responsibilities, and it is important for each to fulfill those responsibilities.

The first lesson to be learned in teamwork is the crucial necessity of each team member doing their job. In the 1967 football game between Dallas and Green Bay for the NFL championship, there is an interesting story. Green Bay was behind but had the ball on the Dallas 1-foot line with very little time left in the game. In the huddle before the fourth-down play, Bart Starr, the quarterback, said to Jerry Kramer, "You move that man in front of you twelve inches, and you'll make $15,000." There never has been and there never will be a substitute for an individual member of a team doing their job.

In similar fashion, there can be no substitute for individual Christians accepting independently the responsibility God gives to them. There will never be any authentic cooperation until we learn to say what Isaiah said: "Here am I, Lord, send me." Or to say what Paul said: "Lord, what would you have me to do?"

And just as individuals must accept independent responsibility, so must churches. There can be no substitute for churches that seek to fulfill the great commission where they are located. Nothing can take the place of churches that believe God has put them in their community to be like leaven, salt, and light. A local functioning fellowship of believers is still God's strategy for world redemption. When we as churches come to the place where we are willing to do whatever God wants us to do—to pray, to work, to witness—then we've taken the first step in cooperating with God and cooperating with others in extending Christ's kingdom.

But cooperation requires more than individuals and churches accepting their independent responsibility. *Cooperation requires interdependent unity with one another.* The text declares, "Now he who plants and he who waters are one" (v. 8). Using the agricultural analogy again, the text shows how Christians must depend on each other and work together. If no one planted, the watering would be useless. If no one watered, the planting would be useless. Each person fulfilling an independent responsibility must recognize the necessity and importance of others fulfilling their responsibilities. We are linked together; therefore, we must serve together, pray together, and work together.

Interdependent unity means we recognize our need of each other. It means we respect each other's gifts, callings, and commitments. Interdependent unity means we rejoice in each other's victories and weep over each other's defeats. It means we renew our communication with each other and refresh each other with support, encouragement, and prayer.

In praying for each other, we demonstrate our interdependent unity. It's difficult to pray for someone and feel isolated from them. How we pray probably tells how much we feel tied to others in a spirit of cooperation. If all we do is pray for ourselves, our own ministry, our own church, our own needs, probably we haven't realized the importance of interdependent unity. Nothing ties us together as Christians and churches like intercessory prayer.

Also, in financially supporting world missions we demonstrate our interdependent unity. How a church participates in world missions giving tells a great deal about that church's feeling of unity with other churches. How much a church gives to extend Christ's kingdom beyond its own city reveals the extent of that church's vision. If all the church does is build, witness, and work in its own locale, it hasn't realized the importance of interdependent unity with other churches.

When a church makes bold commitment to world missions giving, she is showing her compassion for the whole world. She is declaring her unity in purpose and spirit with other churches. And most importantly, she will accomplish far more in the extension of Christ's kingdom than she could by herself.

There's one more ingredient in a theology of cooperation. *Cooperation requires dependent reliance on God.* Again the text reminds us, "So then neither is he that plants anything; neither he who waters; but God that gives the increase" (v. 7). Again using an agricultural analogy, the text shows how the farmer has the privilege of participating in a very exciting venture. One plants seed. Another waters. But then they must wait, and only God can cause the seed to grow.

We who fulfill our independent responsibility and practice interdependent unity with others are absolutely dependent on the sovereign power of God. Only God can save a soul. Only God can quicken a conscience. Only God can renew a spirit. Only God can redeem a life. And we are totally dependent on God to do it.

The kingdom belongs to God, just as the power and the glory alone belong to God. And God's kingdom will be triumphant with or without us. The day will come when God's glory will cover the earth like waters cover the sea, regardless of what we do. But in God's great grace and love, God has given us the privilege of participating with God in the extension of Christ's kingdom. He has allowed us to cooperate, to participate with one another and with God.

Cooperation is not a regimen. It is a romance. It's not just a doctrine. It's an adventure.

Let's join in it together.

Religious Liberty and Christian Citizenship (1987)

Micah 6:8

I preached this sermon on numerous occasions, but it is reproduced here as it appeared in Southern Baptist Preaching Today, *edited by R. Earl Allen and Joel Gregory (Nashville: Broadman Press, 1987).*

Freedom and responsibility are not mutually exclusive but mutually complementary. Both are biblically true. Since our beginning, Baptists have believed in both freedom and responsibility, particularly as they had to do with our relationship to government and politics. Baptist insistence on religious liberty is rooted in Scripture. At the same time, our insistence on Christian citizenship is rooted in history. We have believed that Christians ought to be "in the world but not of the world."

My purpose is to see how we who have been champions for religious liberty can at the same time be champions of responsible Christian citizenship. The text that forms a partial answer to this dilemma is Micah 6:8: "He has showed you, O man, what is good: and what does the LORD require of you, but to do justly, and to love mercy, and to walk humbly with your God." My method will be to seek understanding of religious liberty and then the practice of Christian citizenship from this prophetic message.

Religious Liberty—A Free Church. Religious liberty means a free church in a free state. A free church means that people enter into

the church freely, i.e., each person must accept Jesus Christ personally. Each person must confess that faith in the waters of baptism for
themselves. That is a free act—done by a person who has reached
the age of accountability. No one can enter the church for you, not
by proxy or infant baptism. The privilege of individual initiative and
salvation must never be put in the hands of parents or sponsors. A
regenerate church membership means that each person chooses to
become regenerate. No one can choose for another.

A free church also means that people of the church are free to
hear and respond to the Holy Spirit for themselves, i.e., no one can
dictate doctrinal convictions or moral behavior to another person.
Each one of us must arrive at convictions of conscience through
prayer, study, and struggle. Each one of us is responsible to God for
the formulations of our convictions.

A free church also means that the people of the church are free
to determine the life and ministry of their church. We have a democratic polity that is born out of conviction of soul freedom and social
competency. Each person in the church has access to God and should
be a part of decision-making. Democratic polity is often cumbersome,
inefficient, tedious, and sometimes borders on being unbearable. But
it is part of the price to be paid for liberty.

A free church also means that we reject the state church. State
churches exist because of the assumption that man without the aid of
the state is incompetent in matters of religion. In contrast to that, we
believe that the individual is competent in himself to relate to God
and doesn't need the state to dictate how that relationship should
be. We believe that under Christ, people have the capacity for self-
government in the church and don't need the state to dictate its life
and ministry.

Finally, a free church means our mission is fulfilled under the
premise of freedom. We do not evangelize with manipulation or
coercion. We cannot be deceptive or devious in any way. We must
maintain integrity of motive and method so as to protect the liberty
of the ones we would evangelize. Even if they refuse our gospel, we
must respect their right of refusal and never seek to evangelize in a
way that would violate their freedom. Our mission is accomplished

as we appeal to people's consciences, not as we coerce them with laws, intimidate them with culture, or combat them with rhetoric. We preach so as to persuade. We pray so as to influence. We live and minister to demonstrate our sincerity and validate our message. We always leave the free choice to the individual.

Religious Liberty—A Free State. We as Baptists believe in a free church, but we also believe in a free state. To say we believe in a free state is to say that we reject the church state. The church state is one in which the government is no longer neutral in matters of faith but becomes an advocate for the church. In the church state, Christ is elevated to rule on Caesar's throne and to use Caesar's power and position to extend the heavenly kingdom. The problem with this is that while on earth Jesus refused Caesar's throne. He didn't want it. The extension of the heavenly kingdom came in other ways—not through political power, coercion, or intimidation.

There have been several noble attempts to make the state the instrument of the church to bring about God's kingdom on earth, but they have all failed. A story is told of the schoolteacher who asked her students, "Why did the Puritans come to this country on the *Mayflower*?" One little boy responded, "To worship in their own way and make other people do the same." The Pilgrims came seeking freedom, but then they practiced the same oppression from which they fled.

The Massachusetts Bay colony was preceded by John Calvin's efforts in Geneva to create a theocracy. This was preceded by the Holy Roman Empire, where the marriage of church and state ended in divorce. If history has taught us anything, it has taught us that when a state ceases to be free and comes under the church's control, it isn't long before the church ceases to be free.

On the other hand, to say we believe in a free state is to say that the state should not discriminate against the church. The state is not to act hostile to the church, to rival the church, or to entangle itself in the church. Some Baptists believe that in recent years the state has moved away from being neutral about religion, has become increasingly hostile to religion, and in its place has endorsed another religion—secularism. Reinhold Niebuhr wrote a letter to Felix

Frankfurter, a Justice of the Supreme Court, before he died: "The prevailing philosophy which is pumped into our schools day after day is itself a religion . . . which preaches the redemption of man by historical development and scientific objectivity. It does not have to worry about the separation of church and state."[34]

A free state is one that recognizes a pluralistic society and seeks to protect that pluralism. Is not an advocate for the church, but neither is it antagonistic to the church. The rights and privileges of all are guaranteed. A free state treats believers and unbelievers alike. One is not to be preferred over the other, nor is one to be discriminated against. The liberty of each is to be guaranteed. The freedom of each is to be protected.

Christian Citizenship. We as Baptists have been champions of a free church in a free state. Liberty is our history and heritage. But there is another value just as precious to us as religious liberty—Christian citizenship. We as Baptists have also championed personal involvement in the affairs of state. We have believed and sought to practice the words of Jesus: "You are the salt of the earth and the light of the world." We have believed that the gospel ought to affect and permeate every area of life, including politics, public policy, and government. We do not believe separation of church and state means separation of God from government, Christ from culture, or faith from life.

But how is the church to influence the state? How can Christians act as responsible citizens in a way that affects the actions of government without manipulation? How do we, who believe in a free church and a free state, act like salt, light, and leaven in a sinful world? How do we guard our freedom and the freedom of those with whom we disagree and at the same time fulfill the mandate of our Lord? How do we recognize the pluralism of our society and the necessary neutrality of the state and at the same time refuse to be neutral about truth as we understand it, injustice as we see it, and the gospel as we believe it? At this point the words of the prophet Micah are important. We must hear, understand, and apply them in our political involvement as Christian citizens.

1. Be careful not to engage in politics with the attitude that the end justifies the means. Our methods of influence and patterns of involvement in politics must always be consistent with the gospel itself. We are to be faithful to our mission and message. Our goal is redemption and reconciliation, not just winning at any price. We are to be prophetic when necessary (which requires courage) and priestly when necessary (which requires mercy), and we are always to be honest in purpose. We are to promote individual and corporate responsibility at all levels of government among our members without any hint of manipulation. I have seen, as you have seen, Christians on different sides of the political/theological spectrum whose personal morality was inconsistent with their public profile, whose rhetoric stretched the truth, whose methods bordered on being deceptive.

In our Christian zeal to influence government, let's be very careful that we don't sacrifice character. Let's do all we can to make sure our motives are pure without judging the motives of others. Let's refrain from rancor or revenge. Let's subject our actions to the standards of justice, decency, and honesty. In other words, let's practice Christian integrity as we practice Christian zeal.

2. Be careful not to reduce or identify Christianity with any particular program. The political agendas of a party or group—however noble—are not identical with the gospel of Jesus Christ. To be sure, certain issues that are political in nature have moral and even biblical implications. But be careful not to equate the social/political causes of the moment with the eternal gospel of the kingdom of God.

In the 1960s, if you didn't protest the Vietnam War, you were considered less than Christian in the eyes of some. In the 1970s, if you believed in gun control or the Panama Canal Treaty, you were considered less than Christian in the eyes of some. In the 1980s, if you didn't subscribe to the political agenda of the Moral Majority, you were considered less than Christian in the eyes of some. The problem with all of these positions is the same—the eternal, unchanging gospel is being too closely identified with current social, political, and moral agendas.

In our zeal to influence government as Christians, let's be very careful in not equating our political convictions with the gospel, and let's be careful that we not label those who disagree with us as non-Christians or nonbiblical. In other words, let's practice Christian charity as we practice Christian zeal.

3. Be careful not to be triumphal in assuming that God is on our side of the issue. Lincoln said in 1862, "The will of God prevails. In great contests each party claims to act in accordance with the will of God. Both *may* be, and one *must* be, wrong. God cannot be for and against the same thing at the same time. In the present civil war it is quite possible that God's purpose is something different from the purpose of either party . . . ."[35]

We must be careful in making God the champion of our cause, of assuming we alone understand his ways, of acting as though we alone have discovered divine providence. This is not to deny a passion for political debate or to apply moral consideration to political decisions. This is not to deny the reality or possibility of knowing and doing the truth, but it is to acknowledge that our understanding of the truth be partial and influenced by our prejudices and presumptions.

In pursuit of right, we need to add the words, as we understand the right. Let's ask God to deliver us from triumphalism and self-righteousness. In other words, let's practice Christian humility as we practice Christian zeal.

The prophet Micah asked the question, "What is good, and what does the Lord require of you?" That question, it seems to me, is not only appropriate for our personal lives but for our public lives and for the practice of politics in particular. He then answers that question: "Do justice, love mercy, and walk humbly with God." Integrity, charity, and humility are the essence of biblical faith. And in this intersection between religious liberty and Christian citizenship, these virtues need to be lovingly embraced, deeply believed, and doggedly practiced.

Of all the verses in Fosdick's hymn, none is more poignant than the last one as we seek to be Christian in the practice of politics: "Set our feet on lofty places / Gird our lives that they may be / Armored with all Christ-like graces / In the fight to set men free / Grant us wisdom. Grant us Courage / That we fail not man nor Thee / That we fail not man nor Thee."

I Will Not Be Afraid (2011)

Luke 12:4-7

I preached this sermon at Peachtree Baptist Church on Sunday morning, August 3, 2011.

Have you heard the story about a New York taxi driver who died and went to heaven? Saint Peter met him at the pearly gate and ushered him into a beautiful mansion. Shortly afterwards, a preacher died and went to heaven and was given a small apartment, whereupon he protested vigorously, "How is it that I have been given such a modest dwelling in comparison to this cabdriver?" Saint Peter responded, "The difference between the two of you is that while you preached people slept, but while the taxi driver drove people prayed."

Fear does motivate people. Some forms of fear can be good, even healthy. We teach our children to use caution in crossing the street because they need to be afraid of approaching traffic. Fear of fire, electricity, or nature is legitimate. It creates caution and care.

Today I don't want to speak about normal or healthy fear but about debilitating and destructive fear. The fact is that we live a great deal of our lives out of fear. We are afraid we won't be happy or successful or that, if we are happy and successful, it won't last. We're afraid we won't have enough money or that we will get sick. We're afraid that something bad might happen to our children or grand-children. We're afraid somebody will not love us or that we won't be able to love in return. Some of us are afraid we will not get married. Others of us are afraid we will get married. Some of us are afraid we will lose our job or won't be able to find a job. We're afraid of the future, of people, of being embarrassed or being a failure.

It is amazing how many things are done in the church because of fear. We're afraid we will not grow as a church, or we're afraid we will grow too much. We're afraid we won't meet the budget or that we might have to change the budget. We're afraid of making wrong decisions. And being driven by fears, churches make bad decisions.

There are many forms of fear. Some of us struggle with dread, an abiding apprehension of something bad that might happen, a deep-seated disposition that creates melancholy especially when it comes to disease and death. Some of us struggle with terror, a stab of fright that paralyzes us mentally and emotionally, perhaps for just a few moments. I remember the first time I flew into New York City, and I had a moment of panic and terror as the plane landed.

And then there is worry, the continuous anxiety that won't go away; the debilitating fretfulness over something in the past, present, or future. Worry can be a heightened anticipation of a possible or even probable development that seems hurtful and harmful. I am reminded of the man who woke up in the middle of the night and realized that a burglar was in the dining room stealing the family silver. He went downstairs and introduced himself to the thief. "Finally, we can meet personally. We've been worrying about your coming for thirty-five years."

And then there's a story about the woman who went to the doctor and was asked, "Do you wake up a worrier every morning?" She answered, "No, I just let him sleep." Worry is a form of fear, and all of us struggle with it.

So what is the cure for fear? The first response is faith; that is, if you have faith, you need not have fear. Where there is faith, fear is absent. This is not a bad answer. On numerous occasions Jesus told his disciples, "Do not be afraid; only believe," or he asked the questions, "Why are you afraid? Have you no faith?"

But there is a deeper solution to the problem of fear. Faith is simply the "means to an end." Faith connects us to the real solution to the problem of fear: God. The ultimate answer to the problem of fear is God, the nature and character of God. And when we discover God's character and discern God's nature, we will not be afraid.

Discerning God's character comes to us as a gift. And it is often received and experienced with great struggle and inner conflict. But once one discovers the character of God and once one discerns the nature of God, one will not be afraid. So what is the character of God, and what is God's nature? These questions lead to the text for this message: Luke 12:4-7. Jesus says,

> I tell you, my friends, do not be afraid of those who kill the body and after that can do no more. But I will show you who you should fear: Fear him who, after the killing of the body, has power to throw you into hell. Yes, I tell you, fear him. Are not five sparrows sold for two pennies? Yet not one of them is forgotten by God. Indeed, the very hairs of your head are all numbered. Do not be afraid; you are of more value than many sparrows.

First, God is sovereign. In the text Jesus does an interesting thing. He tells the disciples not to fear other human beings but to fear God alone. And then he tells them why. He makes it clear that human beings only have limited power, but God has all power. God has power over life and death, heaven and hell, body and soul, time and eternity. God has power to do whatever God wills in this life and in the next. God is sovereign.

On the surface this seems to give little comfort or assurance to the problem of fear, and it even seems like Jesus is being insensitive to his disciples. But the opposite is true. If we discover and discern the character of God as sovereign, there is no need to be afraid of anything. Jesus tells us to fear God, i.e., to reverence and respect God, to humble ourselves in worship and in recognition that God is God. To fear God is to recognize God as the eternal One who has all authority and all power, who knows the end from the beginning and works all things according to the counsel of his will.

To fear God does not mean to live in terror or anxiety before God, but to live humbly and dependently on the One who was, who is, and who is to come. To fear God is to trust in the One who "sits above the circle of the earth, whose inhabitants are like grasshoppers, who stretches out the heavens like a curtain, who brings princes to naught, and reduces the rulers of the earth to nothing" (Isa 40:22-23).

To fear God is to worship the One who is seated on a heavenly throne from whose face the whole of heavens and earth flee away. To fear God is to reverence the One who is high and lifted up, exalted between cherubim and seraphim, and in whose presence the angels cry, "Holy, holy, holy" (Isa 6:3).

Fear this God. Reverence this God. Worship this God. Trust this God, and you will not be afraid of anyone or anything else. God is sovereign.

In my travels to China, I had the experience of having conversations with Chinese Christians who lived during the years of terror when the Communist authorities closed the churches and banned public worship for thirty years. They told me that when churches were finally allowed to reopen, people lined the streets three hours before the doors were unlocked just to get a seat. When they first gathered to worship, the emotions were so intense that it was difficult for them to sing or speak. In one church it was decided that they would recite Scriptures that sustained and strengthened them through the years of persecution. Person after person stood to recite their favored text: Psalm 23, John 14, Isaiah 40, and others. One elder stood to say, "The Scripture that meant the most to me was Matthew 3:8, 'Do not presume to say to yourselves, "We have Abraham as our ancestor," for I tell you that God is able to raise up children of Abraham from these stones.'" The old gentleman then said, "I became convinced that if the Communists killed every Christian in China, God was able to raise up a witness from stones."

If you and I discover and discern that God is sovereign, we will not be afraid.

Second, God is not only sovereign; God is love. In the text, Jesus suddenly shifts the focus of his assurance of God's sovereignty to an assurance of God's personal care and compassion for us. He does this by comparing God's knowledge and care for a sparrow to God's knowledge and care for us as individual human beings. "Are not five sparrows sold for two pennies? Yet not one of them is forgotten by God. . . . Don't be afraid: you are worth more than many sparrows."

God's love for us is not just a general benevolence or universal good-will toward humankind. God's love for us is intensely personal. In fact, Jesus said that "the very hairs of our head are numbered."

If you and I discover and discern that God is not only sovereign but is loving and compassionate to us in the circumstances of our lives, we will not be afraid. Nothing, absolutely nothing, can separate us from the love of God. No pain, no person, no problem is greater than God's passionate and personal love for us.

Not long ago I rode a MARTA train from the Atlanta airport to my neighborhood. It was late at night, and I and one homeless man were the only people on the train. Soon he approached me and began to talk freely when he discovered I was a minister. As we came close to his destination, he looked at me intently and asked, "Reverend, what do you think I should do with my life?" I answered, "I can't answer that question, but I do believe one truth with all my heart. God loves you. God cares for you. You are important to God. You can trust God with your life." As the door opened, he got off the train, and I never saw him again.

A few days afterwards, I was in a church where a prominent Baptist minister was also visiting. After the service of worship, we entered into a long conversation, which ended with his transparent confession. "Daniel," he said, "I am weary and discouraged. At times I wonder if I have made much of a difference. What do you think I should do with my life?" I answered in exactly the same way: "I can't answer that question, but I do believe one truth with all my heart. God loves you. God cares for you. You are important to God. You can trust God with your life."

Later in this text, Jesus speaks to the disciples directly and gives them same command, followed by another assurance: "Do not be afraid, little flock, for your Father has been pleased to give you the kingdom" (Luke 12:32). His message is clear. God is a loving heavenly Father who knows our frailty and weaknesses and desires to give us the kingdom. We do not need to be afraid of anything or anyone.

So please say the words after me: "God is sovereign. God is love. I will not be afraid."

Some of you are thinking, "I have an incurable disease, and I may not live very long." Please say the words after me: "God is sovereign. God is love. I will not be afraid."

Some of you are thinking, "My financial situation is very precarious." Please say the words after me: "God is sovereign. God is love. I will not be afraid."

Some of you are thinking, "We live in a dangerous world and difficult times." Please say the words after me: "God is sovereign. God is love. I will not be afraid."

Some of you are thinking, "I don't know what will happen to my family, my friends, my future." Please say the words after me: "God is sovereign. God is love. I will not be afraid."

Death (2018)

Matthew 17:1-13, Mark 9:2-8, Luke 9:28-38

I preached this sermon at Peachtree Baptist Church on September 16, 2018.

The text and topic of today's message are both difficult to talk about as well as impossible to fully understand. The three texts record the transfiguration of our Lord, each with a slight variation. What is interesting is that this event is recorded with such brevity and few details. For this to be the only recorded event in the New Testament that gives us a brief glimpse of the glorified Christ in his kingdom, Scripture offers us precious little.

The title of today's message is "Death" because I believe the subject of the conversation between Elijah, Moses, and our Lord was death. I also believe that this experience was given to Jesus as a kind of preparation for his coming death. Death comes to all of us, and it is something of a mystery. Scripture defines it both as our enemy and our friend, both as a conclusion and a beginning, both as an arrival and a departure.

What is important for us today is that, unlike anything else, this text and topic can gather us and grow us both as individual Christians and as a church. The crucified, resurrected, glorified Christ draws us to himself and draws us to one another like nothing else. Nothing is as transforming and unifying as Christ, both in his suffering and in his glory. Also, the reality and universality of death has a kind of sobering and leveling impact on us. When we participate in a funeral, everything else stops. All of a sudden, we are all on the same level because we are made conscious and aware of our own mortality.

The event described in today's text is preceded by an event described as "the great confession" at Caesarea Philippi where Peter confesses Jesus as Israel's Messiah and God's Son. After the confession, Jesus explains to the disciples that his cross is coming. He explains the cost for his obedience to his heavenly Father and then explains the cost of obedience for those of us who follow him in discipleship.

Six days after "the great confession," Jesus takes three of his disciples onto a high mountain: Peter, James, and John. And on that mountain he is transfigured before them. His face shines brightly, becoming like light itself. His personal presence shines forth and radiates light. His entire body illuminates a heavenly luminosity. Throughout Scripture the glory of God and the mysterious presence of God is associated with light, brightness, and shining. So before their very eyes, Peter, James, and John behold the essential deity of Jesus as it breaks forth in a radiant and glorious light.

What does all this mean? First, it means that in the humanity of Jesus there is a divinity that is both dazzlingly beautiful and troublingly terrifying. Much of the time this divinity is hidden to the naked eye. Jesus lives as any other human being, eating and sleeping, walking and working. But on occasion it breaks forth for people to see. Here is a miraculous healing; there is an authoritative teaching; and another time there is a flash of beauty and brilliance. It shines through. And now on the mountain of transfiguration, the divinity that exists in the human Jesus breaks forth in a radiant brightness that reveals the glory of God.

But this transfiguration is not only a revelation of what is already present as a reality in Jesus; it is also a prelude and prefiguring of what is yet to come. After his resurrection and ascension, Scripture says Jesus is "seated at the right hand of the Father." This is a symbolic way of saying that the human/divine Christ is now exalted, sharing the glory of God. Christ now reigns in radiance and governs in glory. And there will come a day when, because of that reign, there will be no need on this earth for sun or moon, because the glorified Christ is the light that will shine brighter than the sun.

But before that happens, something else must happen. Before the light of the resurrection, ascension, and glorification of Christ, there is the darkness of crucifixion. Before Christ is forever transfigured, he must experience death. He must taste death just as every human being must taste death. He must drink the cup that every person must drink, the cup of death. He must depart this life as all of us departed this life, by walking through the valley of the shadow of death.

Death is the subject of the conversation between Elijah, Moses, and Jesus. The text says they talked about his "departure" as the fulfillment of Scripture. The word "departure" is the word that means "exodus," which no doubt is a reference to Jesus' death as a personal exodus from this world. But it also is a reference to the exodus of Israel from Egypt. Just as in the Old Testament the exodus of Israel was a departure for God's people from slavery, so Christ's death provides an exodus that will free all of us from the bondage of sin.

It is fascinating to me that Jesus is talking with Moses and Elijah about death. Of all the Old Testament figures, these two men seem to know the least about death. The death of Moses is shrouded in mystery. He died at the age of 120, and God himself buried Moses somewhere in Moab. Elijah seems to have escaped death by being translated into heaven in a chariot of fire and whirlwind. But these two heroes of Israel, Moses who represents the law and Elijah who represents the prophets, are conversation partners with our Lord about his impending death. Their conversation is about how his death fulfills God's plan for the world.

Jesus is anticipating his death. As he and the three disciples descend the mountain, they engage in a conversation about Elijah, and Jesus compares the cruel death of John the Baptist to his own death. With a clear-eyed anticipation of what was ahead of him, is it any wonder that Jesus welcomed the conversation with Moses and Elijah on the mountain of transfiguration? What did they talk about? Perhaps Moses and Elijah offered comfort to Jesus. Perhaps they questioned him. Perhaps they worshiped him. We are not told the content of their conversation. But whatever the content, they demonstrated a solidarity and companionship by their presence and by their conversation.

Then something remarkable happens. The text says that a bright cloud covers them all. Again, here is a reference to light. An audible voice speaks for all to hear: "This is my son, whom I love, with whom I am well pleased. Listen to him." At this point in the narrative, we are standing on holy ground. We are in the midst of great mystery and miracle. The physical body of Jesus is transfigured in a blaze of light, which means that the line between the physical and the spiritual is transcended. Moses and Elijah enter into a conversation with Jesus, which means the line between past and present is transcended. And now God the Father speaks in an audible voice, which means the line between heaven and earth is transcended. In this event the physical, temporal, and earthly are all very real. But also in this event the spiritual, eternal, and heavenly are equally real. And right in the middle of this holy mystery is the reality of death, Christ's death and our death.

The ancient Celtics often spoke of "thin places." These are places where the temporal and the eternal, the earthly and heavenly, the physical and the spiritual converge and intersect with one another. Death is one of those places. Death is an intersection between life in this world and life in the next.

I do not in any way want to suggest that our deaths are as significant as Christ's death. They are not. His death was for the salvation of the world, and our deaths are not. His death fulfilled Scripture and God's plan for the world, and our deaths do not. But the fact is, like Christ, we will all die.

It is important for us, like Christ, to anticipate our death and prepare for it. It is important for us to face our mortality and live in the light of that mortality.

It is important for us, like Christ, to have conversation partners with whom we can talk about our own departure from this world.

It is important for us, like Christ, to hear the voice of our heavenly Father assuring us of his love. That assurance, most likely, will not come to us in an audible voice, but we can hear God's whisper in our spirits telling us that he loves us and abides with us.

It is important for us, like Christ, that as we face death we need not be afraid. Although we may not want to die, any more than Christ wanted to die, we can die with courage and confidence.

It is important for us, like Christ, to see our death, and life, as being in the hands of God.

One never gets too familiar or friendly with death. There is a kind of reverence and respect in the presence of death. But neither should death terrify or paralyze us. We learn from the transfiguration of Jesus that there is a divine presence in this life, and there is a divine glory that awaits us in the next.

We learn from the transfiguration of Jesus that there is a real continuity of friends and faithful conversation partners on both sides of death.

We learn from the transfiguration of Jesus that death cannot separate us from the love and presence of God, our loving heavenly Father.

After these amazing experiences on the mountain were over, the texts record that Jesus told his disciples, "Do not be afraid." Then they tell us that the disciples looked up and did not see anyone but Jesus. Moses and Elijah were gone, but Jesus was there. And when it comes to life and death, that's enough.

I love the African spiritual that says, "When I come to die / Give me Jesus. When I come to die / Give me Jesus. / You can have this whole world / But give me Jesus."

Revivals

1957–1959

Texas: Ashcreek BC, Azle; FBC, Azle; Concord BC, Waco; Grace Temple BC, Dallas; Castle Hills BC, Fort Worth; Moody Hills BC, Ft. Worth; Riverdale Mission, Crosby; Brookhaven BC, Houston; Oak Creek BC, Fort Worth; Second BC, Tomball; Cottage Grove BC, Houston; Southside BC, Olney; North BC, Greenville; East Highway BC, Heidenhymer; Battetown BC, Cameron; Harmony BC, Eastland; Park Street BC, Greenville; Seth Ward BC, Plainview; Good Shepherd Mission, FBC, Dallas; Point View BC, Seagoville; Immanuel Mission, FBC, Dallas; Oakland BC, Canton; Green Hill BC, Snyder; FBC, Stafford; Mont Bellview BC, Mont Bellview; FBC Golden Acres, Houston; Olsen Park BC, Amarillo; Beaumont Place BC, Houston; Port Houston BC, Houston; Northwood BC, Dallas; Acton BC, Acton; Meadow Gardens, FBC, Dallas; Faith Memorial BC, Houston; Morgan's Pont BC, Pasadena; Baptist Temple, Bay City

Oklahoma: FBC, Boswell; Morris Memorial BC, Ada; Golden Hills BC, Tulsa.

1960–1969

Texas: Fairway BC, Wichita Falls; FBC, Boger; FBC, Lela; FBC, Tripp; Woodforest BC, Houston; Mount Houston BC, Houston; Central BC, Austin; Gambrell Street BC, Fort Worth; Second BC, Baytown; Harbor BC, Houston; Tyler Heights BC, Dallas; West Fourteenth BC, Houston; Shiloh BC, Dallas; Polk Street BC, Dallas; Haile BC, Borger; Calvary BC, Monahans; Doverside BC, Houston; Baptist Temple, Texas City; Thomas Avenue BC, Pasadena; Meadowbrook BC, Houston; Grace Temple BC, Terrell; Bethany BC,

Breckenridge; Riverdale BC, Highlands; FBC, Benjamin; FBC, Trenton; FBC, Ben Wheeler; Crescent Valley BC, Victoria; FBC, Wilmer; Area Wide, Dolen; Temple Oaks BC, Houston; Memorial BC, Pasadena; Jefferson Street BC, Wichita Falls; FBC, Saschie; Decatur Avenue BC, Fort Worth; Immanuel BC, Odessa; Northside BC, Odessa; North Dallas BC, Dallas; FBC, Eustace; Southwayside BC, Fort Worth; Tabernacle BC, Fort Worth; Eastwood BC, Houston; Haltom City BC, Haltom City; Field City BC, Dallas; Trinity BC, Boyd; Ridgecrest BC, Fort Worth; Indian Creek BC, Mineral Wells; San Marcos Academy, San Marcos; Young Station BC, Fort Worth; Grove Temple BC, Dallas; North End BC, Port Arthur; MacArthur Heights BC, Orange; West Illinois BC, Dallas; Jefferson Street BC, Wichita Falls; Second Baptist Chapel, Pasadena; Ledbetter Hills BC, Dallas; Associational Youth Rally, Sanger; FBC, Fort O'Conner; Piedmont BC, Dallas; College Avenue BC, McGregor; FBC, North Zulch; Rehoboth BC, Arlington; City Youth for Christ, San Antonio; Dellview BC, San Antonio; Hilltop BC, Irving; FBC, Ponder; Bethel BC, Nocona; Youth Rally, FBC, Oak Cliff, Dallas; Bellaire BC, San Antonio; Adriel BC, Houston; Freeway Forest BC, Houston; Memorial BC, Houston; FBC, Cleburne; Hope BC, Yoakum; FBC, Everman; Ledbetter Hills BC, Dallas; FBC, Crane; Twin Oaks BC, Fort Worth; Otto BC, Otto; Southmore Plaza BC, Pasadena; Northside BC, Weatherford; FBC, Celeste; Westside BC, Corsicana; Park Heights BC, Tyler; FBC, Lipan; Baptist Temple, Big Spring; Youth Rally, FBC, Dawson; FBC, La Feria; West Little York BC, Houston; City Wide Youth Rally, Mexia; FBC, Pearl; Trinity BC, Pleasanton; Southside BC, Grandbury; Live Oak BC, Gatesville; Hilltop Drive BC, Irving; FBC, Los Fresnos; Alamo Heights BC, San Antonio; FBC, Gholson; FBC, Caldwell; FBC, Coleman; FBC, Bosqueville; Meadowbrook BC, Waco; Norhill BC, Houston; FBC, Wortham; FBC, Euless; Western Heights BC, Waco; North Wilmer BC, Wilmer; FBC, Wolfe City.

Other States: FBC, Midwest City, OK; Marlee BC, Denver, CO; Country Estates BC, Midwest City, OK; Southern Baptist Temple, Phoenix, AZ; Western Hills BC, Oklahoma City, OK; FBC, Wade,

OK; Tennessee Avenue BC, Bristol, TN; Joyce City BC, Smackover, AR; FSBC, Durango, CO; FBC, Seminole, OK; Green River BC, Green River, WY; Temple BC, Waldren, AR; FBC, Pawnee, OK; FBC, El Dorado, OK; Walnut Street BC, Evansville, IN; FBC, Cleveland, OK; FBC, Glendale, AZ; Rancho Village BC, Oklahoma City, OK; FBC, Piedmont, OK; FBC, Savanna, OK; FBC, Hinton, OK; Poteat BC, Poteat, OK; FBC, Hydro, OK; Angola State Penitentiary, Angola, LA; Calvary BC, Lilburn, GA; Immanuel BC, Fort Smith, AR; FBC, Woodland Park, CO; Olivet BC, Oklahoma City, OK; Belle Meadow BC, Bristol, VA; Skyway BC, Colorado Springs, CO.

Philippines: Paco BC, Manila; Aurora Hill BC, Baguio; Central BC, Baguio; Matina BC, Davao City; Panabo Extension, Immanuel BC; Mabel-Cotabato area; Immanuel BC, Manila-Batangas; San Fernando BC, Pampanga.

1970 and Following
Texas: FBC, Longview; FBC, Kilgore; Broadway BC, Fort Worth; FBC, Grandbury; Connell Avenue BC, Ft. Worth; FBC, Bedford; FBC, Garland; FBC, Sulphur Springs; FBC, Corsicana; FBC, Monahans; Shiloh Terrace BC, Dallas.

Other Places: FBC, Bristol, VA; FBC, Columbus, GA; FBC, Lawton, OK; FBC, Jefferson City, MO; Lyndon BC, Louisville, KY; FBC, McAllister, OK; FBC, Lake Charles, LA; FBC, Henderson, NC; FBC, Tallahassee, FL; Mountain Brook, Birmingham, AL; FBC, Huntsville, AL; Riverchase BC, Birmingham, AL; Dawson Memorial BC, Birmingham, AL; FBC, Hendersonville, TN; FBC, Murfreesboro, TN; King's Cross, Tullahoma, TN; FBC, Knoxville, TN; FBC, Charleston, SC; FBC, Florence, SC; Baptist Church of Beaufort, Beaufort, SC; FBC, Pensacola, FL; Trinity BC, Oklahoma City, OK; Parma BC, Cleveland, OH; Far Hills BC, Dayton, OH; FBC, Bainbridge, GA; Island View BC, Jacksonville, FL; Peachtree BC, Atlanta, GA; Providence BC, Bucharest, Romania; Rayners Lane BC, London, England; Ruislip BC, London, England; City

Wide Evangelistic Crusade, Taguatinga, Brazil; Zagreb BC, Zagreb, Yugoslavia; New Orleans Baptist Theological Seminary; Midwestern Baptist Theological Seminary; Golden Gate Baptist Theological Seminary; Southwestern Baptist Theological Seminary.

An Address to the Public

INTRODUCTION. Forming something as fragile as the Cooperative Baptist Fellowship is not a move we make lightly. We are obligated to give some explanation for why we are doing what we are doing. Our children will know what we have done; they may not know why we have done what we have done. We have reasons for our actions. They are:

I. OUR REASONS ARE LARGER THAN LOSING. For twelve years the SBC in annual session has voted to sustain the people who lead the fundamentalist wing of the SBC. For twelve years the SBC in annual session has endorsed the arguments and the rationale of the fundamentalists. What is happening is not a quirk or a flash or an accident. It has been done again and again.

If inclined, one could conclude that the losers have tired of losing. But the formation of the fellowship does not spring from petty rivalry. If the old moderate wing of the SBC were represented in making policy and were treated as welcomed representatives of competing ideas in the Baptist mission task, then we would coexist, as we did for years, alongside with fundamentalism and continue to argue our ideas before Southern Baptists.

But this is not the way things are. When fundamentalists won in 1979, they immediately began a policy of exclusion. Non-fundamentalists are not appointed to any denominational positions. Rarely are gentle fundamentalists appointed. Usually only doctrinaire fundamentalists, hostile to the purposes of the very institutions they control, are rewarded for service by appointment. Thus, the boards of SBC agencies are filled by only one kind of Baptist. And this is true whether the vote to elect was 60–40 or 52–48. It has been since 1979 a "winner take all." We have no voice.

In another day Pilgrims and Quakers and Baptists came to America for the same reason. As a minority, they had no way to get a hearing. They found a place where they would not be second-class citizens. All who attended the annual meeting of the SBC in New Orleans in June 1990 will have an enlarged understanding of why our ancestors left their homes and dear ones and all that was familiar. So forming the fellowship is not something we do lightly. Being Baptist should ensure that no one is ever excluded who confesses, "Jesus is Lord."

II. OUR UNDERSTANDINGS ARE DIFFERENT. Occasionally, someone accuses Baptists of being merely a contentious, controversial people. That may be. But the ideas that divide Baptists in the present controversy are the same ideas that have divided Presbyterians, Lutherans, and Episcopalians. These ideas are strong and they are central; these ideas will not be papered over. Here are some of these basic ideas:

1. Bible. Many of our differences come from a different understanding and interpretation of Holy Scripture. But the difference is not at the point of the inspiration or authority of the Bible. We interpret the Bible differently, as will be seen below in our treatment of the biblical understanding of women and pastors. We also, however, have a different understanding of the nature of the Bible. We want to be biblical—especially in our view of the Bible. That means we dare not claim less for the Bible than the Bible claims for itself. The Bible neither claims nor reveals inerrancy as a Christian teaching. Bible claims must be based on the Bible, not on human interpretations of the Bible.

2. Education. What should happen in colleges and seminaries is a major bone of contention between fundamentalists and moderates. Fundamentalists educate by indoctrination. They have the truth and all the truth. As they see it, their job is to pass along the truth they have. They must not change it. They are certain that their understandings of the truth are correct, complete, and to be adopted by others. Moderates, too, are concerned with truth, but we do not claim a monopoly. We seek to enlarge and build upon such truth as

we have. The task of education is to take the past and review it, even criticize it. We work to give our children a larger understanding of spiritual and physical reality. We know we will always live in faith; our understanding will not be complete until we get to heaven and are loosed from the limitations of our mortality and sin.

3. Mission. What ought to be the task of the missionary is another difference between us. We think the mission task is to reach people for faith in Jesus Christ by preaching, teaching, healing, and other ministries of mercy and justice. We believe this to be the model of Jesus in Galilee. That is the way he went about his mission task. Fundamentalists make the mission assignment narrower than Jesus did. They allow their emphasis on direct evangelism to undercut other biblical ministries of mercy and justice. This narrow definition of what a missionary ought to be and do is a contention between us.

4. Pastor. What is the task of the pastor? They argued the pastor should be the ruler of a congregation. This smacks of the bishop's task in the Middle Ages. It also sounds much like the kind of church leadership Baptists revolted against in the 17th century. Our understanding of the role of the pastor is to be a servant/shepherd. Respecting lay leadership is our assignment. Allowing the congregation to make real decisions is the very nature of Baptist congregationalism. And using corporate business models to "get results" is building the church by the rules of the secular world rather than witnessing to the secular world by the way of a servant church.

5. Women. The New Testament gives two signals about the role of women. A literal interpretation of Paul can build a case for making women submissive to men in the church. But another body of Scripture points toward another place for women. In Galatians 3:27-28 Paul wrote, "As many of you as are baptized into Christ Jesus have clothed yourself with Christ. There is no longer Jew or Greek, there is no longer slave or free, there is no longer male and female; for all of you are one in Christ Jesus."

We take Galatians as a clue to the way the church should be ordered. We interpret the reference to women the same way we interpret the reference to slaves. If we have submissive roles for women, we must also have a place for slaves in the church. In Galatians Paul follows the spirit of Jesus, who courageously challenged the conventional wisdom of his day. It was a wisdom with rigid boundaries between men and women in religion and in public life. Jesus deliberately broke those barriers. He called women to follow him; he treated women as equally capable of dealing with sacred issues. Our model for the role of women in matters of faith is the Lord Jesus.

6. Church. An ecumenical and inclusive attitude is basic to our fellowship. The great ideas of theology are the common property of all the church. Baptists are only a part of that great and inclusive church. So we are eager to have fellowship with our brothers and sisters in the faith and to recognize their work for our Savior. We do not try to make them conform to us; we try to include them in our design for mission. Mending the torn fabric of both Baptist and Christian fellowship is important to us. God willing, we will bind together the broken parts into a new company in preview of the great fellowship we shall have with each other in heaven.

It should be apparent that the points of difference are critical. They are the stuff around which a fellowship such as the SBC is made. We are different. It is regrettable, but we are different. And perhaps we are most different at the point of spirit. At no place have we been able to negotiate about these differences. Were our fundamentalist brethren to negotiate, they would compromise. And that would be a sin by their understanding. So we can either come to their position, or we can form a new fellowship.

III. WE ARE CALLED TO DO MORE THAN POLITIC. Some people would have us continue as we have over the last twelve years, and continue to work within the SBC with the point of view to change the SBC. On the face of it this argument sounds reasonable. Acting it out is more difficult. To change the SBC requires a majority vote. To affect a majority in annual session requires massive, expensive, contentious activity. We have done this, and we have done it repeatedly.

But we have never enjoyed doing it. Something is wrong with a religious body that spends such energy on overt political activity. Our time is unwisely invested in beating people or trying to beat people.

We have to define the other side as bad and we are good. There is division. The existence of the Fellowship is a simple confession of that division; it is not the cause of the division.

We can no longer devote our major energies to SBC politics. We would rejoice, however, to see the SBC return to its historic Baptist convictions. Our primary call is to be true to our understanding of the gospel. We are to advance the gospel in our time. When we get to heaven, God is not going to ask us, "Did you win in Atlanta in June 1991?" If we understand the orders we are under, we will be asked larger questions. And to spend our time trying to reclaim a human institution (people made the SBC; it is not a scriptural entity) is to make more of that institution than we ought to make. A denomination is a missions delivery system; it is not to be an idol. When we make more of the SBC than we ought, we risk falling into idolatry. Twelve years is too long to engage in political activity. We are called to higher purposes.

CONCLUSION. That we may have a voice in our Baptist mission, for this is our Baptist birthright . . . That we may work by ideas consistent with our understanding of the gospel rather than fund ideas that are not our gospel . . . That we may give our energies to the advancement of the kingdom of God rather than in divisive, destructive politics . . . For these reasons we form the Cooperative Baptist Fellowship. This does not require that we sever ties with the old SBC. It does give us another mission delivery system, one more like our understanding of what it means to be Baptist and what it means to do gospel. Therefore, we create a new instrument to further the kingdom and enlarge the Body of Christ.

Response to the Membership Committee of the Baptist World Alliance by the Coordinating Council of the Cooperative Baptist Fellowship

As a fellowship of Baptist Christians and churches, we acknowledge the Lordship of Jesus Christ and confess "one Lord, one faith, one baptism" (Eph 4:5). As we make application for membership in the Baptist World Alliance, we sincerely desire understanding and harmony with all member bodies, including the Southern Baptist Convention. We make the following statement "with all humility and gentleness, with patience, bearing with one another in love, making every effort to maintain the unity of the Spirit in the bond of peace" (Eph 4:2-3).

In accordance with the requirements of the Cooperative Baptist Fellowship's (CBF) application for membership in the Baptist World Alliance (BWA), it is necessary that the CBF establish that it is not an integral part of any other BWA member, in this case the Southern

Baptist Convention. Accordingly, we the Coordinating Council, as the governing board of the CBF, in our regular business meeting on October 17–19, 2002, in Atlanta, Georgia, do hereby acknowledge that we have "separated ourselves from the structures and organizations of the SBC, and have a distinctly diverse understanding to the SBC of what it means to be an organized body of Baptist churches and individuals in covenant relationship."

Furthermore, we offer the following twenty indications that we are no longer integral to the SBC:

1. We have repeatedly and publicly stated that we are not a part of the SBC.

2. The SBC has acknowledged that we are a separate entity by refusing to receive funding through the CBF for the past seven years.

3. We have our own publishe000d and widely distributed philosophy, mission statement, core commitments, and key initiatives.

4. We have our own annual assemblies that routinely draw 3,000 to 5,000 of our constituents, in which we elect leadership, pass budgets, and conduct business.

5. Last year we adopted an organization-wide strategic plan setting our direction for the next decade.

6. We have substantial organizational documentation, including a constitution and bylaws, which clearly establishes our unique and separate identity.

7. We have our own organizational structure, including a board of directors, formal annual budgets, and a large group of employed staff and office buildings.

8. We have organized autonomous states and regions with their own boards of directors, formal budgets, employed staffs, and office buildings.

9. We own and operate our own mission sending agency, foundation, and a benefits board with over 300 participants.

10. Our 140 missionaries are in partnership with other autonomous entities worldwide as representatives of the CBF.

11. We share no common agencies or institutions whatsoever with the SBC.

12. We have over 150 partnering churches that have no formal membership in the SBC.

13. We have planted over fifty churches that partner only with CBF at the national and international level.

14. We are recognized as an official endorsing body for chaplains and pastoral counselors by the US Armed Forces board; national pastoral care, counseling, and education organizations; and other viable entities. Since 1998, more than 250 people have been endorsed.

15. We are recognized as a nongovernmental organization (NGO) by the United Nations and have participated as such on the world stage.

16. We have many negotiated partnerships with established entities that recognize us as a separate and distinctive organization.

17. We are listed in the European Baptist Federation directory as a separate entity.

18. Many of our present leaders have never participated in the SBC or considered themselves Southern Baptists.

19. We have applied for membership as a distinctive, autonomous Baptist Association in the Baptist World Alliance.

20. We are recognized by numerous US Baptist state conventions as a legitimate national Baptist body, including Virginia, Texas, and North Carolina, each of which offers a channel for churches to give to CBF through its state budget.

Though fully independent of the SBC or any other union, we do not declare that we are a denomination or convention. Rather, we are Baptist by conviction and we are a partnership of churches and individuals by philosophy. We have chosen instead to define ourselves as a "fellowship," which means that we are "a Baptist association of churches and individuals in partnership for the advancement of God's kingdom."

In keeping with our mission statement, commitments, and initiatives, we uphold the right of autonomous churches to partner (or not) within a global mission agency or congregational entity of their choice. This is consistent with our understanding that the local congregation is the focus of traditional Baptist polity and the centerpiece of any Great Commission, New Testament strategy to transform the world through Christ's love.

Notes

1. "Why I Am a Baptist" by Walter Rauschenbush was published in the *Rochester Baptist Journal*," the first of several articles contending that the personal experience of God's grace revealed in Jesus Christ is what binds Baptists together. See *A Baptist Treasury* (Thomas Crowell: New York, 1958).

2. Keith E. Durso, *Thy Will Be Done: A Biography of George W. Truett* (Macon, GA: Mercer University Press, 2009), 37.

3. Daniel Vestal, *Pulling Together* (Nashville: Broadman Press, 1987), 84.

4. Daniel Vestal, "Quest for Renewal," Cooperative Baptist Fellowship, 2012, 82–83.

5. Daniel Vestal, "The Doctrine of Creation" (Nashville: Convention Press, 1989), 33–34.

6. James Robison, *Living Amazed* (Grand Rapids, MI: Revell, 2017), 135–39.

7. Nancy Ammerman, "Mapping the Future: Southern Baptists in the American Religious Landscape," unpublished address to the Southern Baptist Alliance, March 1991.

8. Peter Steinfels, "Baptist Group Challenges Conservative Leadership," *New York Times*, August 26, 1990, 1:26; Gustav Niebuhr, "Dissident Southern Baptists Act to Form Own Unit and Budget, Skirting a Split," *Wall Street Journal*, August 27, 1990, A12; *Christian Century*, September 9–26, 1990; Mark Silk, "Severing the Baptist ties that bind," *Atlanta Constitution*, August 31, 1990, A14.

9. John Hewett, "Free and Faithful," *CBF at 25: Stories of the Cooperative Baptist Fellowship*, ed. Aaron Weaver (Macon, GA: Nurturing Faith, 2016), 12–13.

10. Aaron Weaver, "Story of a Name," in *CBF at 25*, xi ff., tells the fuller story of how CBF was named.

11. Clarissa Strickland, "And So It Begins," in *CBF at 25*, 4–6.

12. Thomas Merton, *Thoughts in Solitude* (New York: Farrar, Straus and Giroux, 1958), 79.

13. Parker Palmer, *Let Your Life Speak* (San Francisco: Jossey Bass, 2000), 78.

14. Foy Valentine, "Christian Ethics," in *An Approach to Christian Ethics: The Life, Contribution, and Thought of T. B. Maston*, ed. William Pinson (Nashville: Broadman Press, 1979).

15. Oliver Thomas, "A Chihuahua Who Thinks He's a German Shepherd," in *James Dunn: Champion for Religious Liberty*, ed. Brent Walker (Macon, GA: Smyth & Helwys, 1999).

16. Walter Shurden, *The Baptist Identity: Four Fragile Freedoms* (Macon, GA: Smyth & Helwys, 1993).

17. Shurden, *The Baptist Identity*, 14.

18. Shurden, *The Baptist Identity*, 27.

19. Shurden, *The Baptist Identity*, 37.

20. Shurden, *The Baptist Identity*, 52.

21. Shurden, unpublished document.

22. Tom Kennedy, *From Waco to Wall Street: The Story of John Baugh, the Sysco Kid* (San Antonio: Independent Traveler, 2000), 77.

23. Kennedy, "From Waco to Wall Street," 74.

24. Mike Clingenpeel, "Editorial: With Open Arms," *Virginia Herald*, July 17, 2003.

25. Baptist World Alliance, "Covenant on Intra-Baptist Relationships," www.baptistworld.org/intra-baptist-covenant/.

26. Daniel Vestal, "A Prayer for the New Baptist Covenant," in *The National Baptist Voice*, a publication of the National Baptist Convention, USA, Inc., ed. William Epps (Summer 2008): 27.

27. "An Open Letter and Call from Muslim Religious Leaders" can be found at www.islamicity.org/7734/an-open-letter-and-call-from-muslim-religious-leaders-to-christian-religious-leaders/.

28. Elizabeth O' Connor, *The Call to Commitment: The Story of the Church of the Savior in Washington DC* (New York: Harper and Row, 1963), 193ff.

29. Findley Edge, *The Greening of the Church* (Waco, TX: Word Books, 1971), 177–88.

30. Basil Pennington, *Centering Prayer* (New York: Doubleday, 1980), 129.

31. Douglas Steere, *On Beginning from Within* (New York: Harper & Brothers, 1943), xvi.

32. Steere, *On Beginning from Within*, 33.

33. Daniel Vestal, *Being the Presence of Christ* (Nashville: Upper Room, 2008), 14.

34. Richard Fox, *Reinhold Niebuhr, A Biography* (Pantheon, 1985).

35. "Meditation on Divine Will," http://www.abrahamlincolnonline.org/lincoln/speeches/meditat.htm

Made in the USA
Columbia, SC
16 May 2022

60475356R00198